#FIX YOUNG AMERICA

#FIX YOUNG AMERICA

How to Rebuild Our Economy and Put Young Americans Back to Work *(for Good)*

 Edited by the Young Entrepreneur Council

Advantage®

Published by Advantage, Charleston, South Carolina.
Member of Advantage Media Group.

ADVANTAGE is a registered trademark and the Advantage colophon is a trademark of Advantage Media Group, Inc.

Printed in the United States of America.

ISBN: 978-1-59932-325-1
LCCN: 2012936717

This publication is designed to provide accurate and authoritative information in regard to the subject matter covered. It is sold with the understanding that the publisher is not engaged in rendering legal, accounting, or other professional services. If legal advice or other expert assistance is required, the services of a competent professional person should be sought.

Advantage Media Group is proud to be a part of the Tree Neutral® program. Tree Neutral offsets the number of trees consumed in the production and printing of this book by taking proactive steps such as planting trees in direct proportion to the number of trees used to print books. To learn more about Tree Neutral, please visit www.treeneutral.com. To learn more about Advantage's commitment to being a responsible steward of the environment, please visit www.advantagefamily.com/green

Advantage Media Group is a leading publisher of business, motivation, and self-help authors. Do you have a manuscript or book idea that you would like to have considered for publication? Please visit www.amgbook.com or call 1.866.775.1696

Special Thanks

On behalf of the Young Entrepreneur Council (YEC), we'd like to thank all of the individuals and organizations that participated in the #FixYoungAmerica book, including 50 Eggs, Inc., Junior Achievement USA, FBLA-PBL, Inc., Consortium for Entrepreneurship Education, National Association for Community College Entrepreneurship, Babson College, Cogswell Polytechnical College, Network for Teaching Entrepreneurship, Collegiate Entrepreneurs Organization, College Hunks Hauling Junk, Venture for America, Ingrid Vanderveldt, Team Rubicon, Michael Ellsberg, Senator Ron Wyden, Young Invincibles, Congressman Patrick McHenry, Donna Fenn, Brad Hargreaves, Silicon Prairie News, The Idea Village, MassChallenge, Academy for Software Engineering, Codecademy, Indiegogo, MultiFunding, Jessica Jackley, Silver Lining Ltd., The National Society of Collegiate Scholars, MTV, Doostang. com, MAT@USC, and Young & Successful Media. Without their dedication and support, neither this book nor this campaign would have been possible. A special thank you also goes to Lindsey Donner, the book editor behind #FixYoungAmerica. Without her hard work and dedication, it would not have been possible to produce this book in less than three months.

We'd also like to thank the tens of thousands of people and organizations that have already donated to the #FixYoungAmerica crowdfunding campaign or shared the #FixYoungAmerica solutions with their networks. Your actions are directly shaping the dialogue in this country about how to solve the epidemics of youth un- and underemployment—and that's what this campaign is all about. We'd also like to recognize the members of the Young Entrepreneur Council (YEC), who help #FixYoungAmerica every day by providing mentorship, guidance and needed jobs to their young peers.

Finally, we'd like to extend a very special thank you to our generous organizational sponsors, including Dell and LegalZoom. The forward-thinking actions of companies like these are what continue to make America great—and their generosity will pave the way for the young leaders of tomorrow.

CONTENTS

Introduction

Scott Gerber, Founder,
Young Entrepreneur Council

In 2010, a group of successful young founders banded together to form a grassroots movement and mentor aspiring entrepreneurs. The Great Recession was wreaking havoc on young adults, who were twice as likely to be unemployed.[1] The men and women who had started companies like LivingSocial, Mint.com, and HootSuite were suddenly in a unique position: They could offer counsel to their Gen Y peers that no one else could—or would.

What began as a loosely affiliated group of do-gooders is now known as the Young Entrepreneur Council (YEC), an invitation-only nonprofit comprised of nearly 400 of America's top entrepreneurs under thirty-five. We have since mentored tens of thousands of young people around the world, from the United States to Egypt. In doing so, we've seen solutions to the epidemics of youth un- and underemployment firsthand. Now, along with dozens of supporters and partners, we are launching a national campaign to #FixYoungAmerica—for good.

Our urgency is real. The United States government is being strangled by partisan politics. Youth employment is at a sixty-year low—only 54.3 percent of young adults aged eighteen to twenty-

---

1 Jenny Marlar, "Worldwide, Young Adults Twice as Likely to Be Unemployed," Gallup, April 27, 2011, http://www.gallup.com/poll/147281/worldwide-young-adults-twice-likely-unemployed.aspx.

four have a job at all, the lowest percentage since the government started keeping track in 1948.[2] And student loan debt just topped $1 trillion, with default rates rising quickly.

Yet young Americans are far more optimistic and entrepreneurial than the pundits would have you believe. According to a 2011 youth entrepreneurship survey conducted by Buzz Marketing Group and the YEC, 23 percent of America's young people started a business as a result of being unemployed. Fifteen percent started their business in college.[3] And let's not forget our veterans, who are twice as likely as other Americans to own businesses.[4]

So why are so few politicians, pundits and decision makers building on that entrepreneurial energy as a solution to joblessness and economic malaise? From the Arab Spring to the Tea Party, from Occupy Wall Street to the SOPA and PIPA protests, we've seen what like-minded individuals can achieve. And it's high time we funneled that same energy into something positive—namely, rebuilding an entrepreneurial America.

This book is not the end-all, be-all compendium of solutions— far from it. The solutions in this book mark the beginning of an important conversation, one we wanted to play a role in starting. By opening the door and leading with solutions (instead of negativity), we hope to create the momentum needed for long-term change. In that spirit, we will continue to solicit hundreds of new solutions as part of an ongoing national campaign.

---

2   Paul Taylor, et al., Young, Underemployed and Optimistic: Coming of Age, Slowly, in a Tough Economy, Pew Research Center, (Pew Social & Demographic Trends, February 9, 2012), 6, http://www.pewsocialtrends.org/files/2012/02/SDT-Youth-and-Economy.pdf.

3   Data is from YEC and Buzz Marketing Group's annual youth entrepreneurship survey of over 1600 American males and females ages 16-39.

4   Scott Gerber, "Why We Should Help Veterans Start Their Own Businesses," *Time.com*, February 7, 2012, http://business.time.com/2012/02/07/why-we-should-help-veterans-start-their-own-businesses/.

In the pages that follow, leaders who are actually in the trenches making youth entrepreneurship possible share their key findings, best practices, and battle-tested solutions. Our intention is to share these with the decision makers capable of implementing and scaling them across America.

Neither YEC's members nor the authors in this book are willing to allow this generation to flounder—but we need your help to execute our solutions. Here's how.

Integrate Academia and the Real World

In the 2011 YEC/Buzz Marketing Group survey, 88 percent of young people said that entrepreneurship education is vitally important given the new economy—and yet 74 percent of college students had no access to entrepreneurship resources on campus. When resources were available, most students felt they were woefully inadequate.[5]

This is not acceptable—in the twenty-first century, entrepreneurial thinking isn't just for entrepreneurs. Adaptability, creativity and financial literacy are core skills for American employees and intrapreneurs, too. They're also critical assets to our communities. Junior Achievement and the Aspen Institute found that youth-entrepreneurship programs positively impacted dropout rates and community engagement, not to mention the development of success-oriented attitudes of risk-taking and opportunity recognition.[6] But most employers today think high school and college graduates are seriously deficient in entrepreneurial skills like leadership and

---

5   YEC and Buzz Marketing Group survey.

6   *The Aspen Youth Entrepreneurship Strategy Group, Youth Entrepreneurship Education in America: A Policymaker's Action Guide*, (The Aspen Institute, 2008), 5-6, http://www.americaspromise.org/-/media/Files/Resources/NFTE%20-%20policymakers_action_guide_2008.ashx.

innovation,[7] and we face a significant shortfall of science, technology, engineering, and mathematics (STEM) graduates.[8]

If we actually want to change the way Americans work, then our K-12 schools, community colleges and four-year colleges must pair book learning with real-world practicum. Babson, Cogswell Polytechnical College, Junior Achievement, the National Association for Community College Entrepreneurship (NACCE) and the Network for Teaching Entrepreneurship (NFTE), among others, are leading the way.

Eliminate Government Barriers

Even our deadlocked Congress has found bipartisan compromises in entrepreneurship-related legislation, like the recent passage of the JOBS Act. But gridlock is preventing truly decisive action. From adopting self-employment assistance programs in all states to providing federal student loan forgiveness for young entrepreneurs, we need government at all levels to nurture its most valuable resource better.

The Obama administration's Startup America agenda is a step, but we must demand a bolder pro-growth agenda. To start with, let's pass the Youth Entrepreneurship Act, which would defer or forgive student loan debt for young entrepreneurs using the precedent set by the Income-Based Repayment program, signed into law by President George W. Bush and extended by President Obama.[9] And let's pass

---

7   The Conference Board, et al., *Are They Really Ready to Work? Employer's Perspectives on the Basic Knowledge and Applied Skills of New Entrants to the 21st Century U.S. Workforce*, (2006), 9-10, http://www.p21.org/storage/documents/FINAL_REPORT_PDF09-29-06.pdf.

8   Richard Dobbs, James Manyika and Charles Roxburgh, "What business can do to restart growth," McKinsey & Company, September 2011, http://www.mckinsey.com/Features/Growth/What_business_can_do_to_restart_growth.

9   "Income-Based Repayment Plan," Federal Student Aid, U.S. Department of Education, last modified December 7, 2011, http://studentaid.ed.gov/PORTALSWebApp/students/english/IBRPlan.jsp.

legislation like the VET Act of 2011, so our returning vets can use GI benefits to start businesses.[10]

An overwhelming 88 percent of young people feel that the government does not support them.[11] It is our duty to hold our representatives accountable. We can begin by asking them to stop handicapping the youth-owned startups of tomorrow.

Invest in and Mentor Young Entrepreneurs

Initiatives like the Startup America Partnership and Dell's Entrepreneur-in-Residence program are models for the private sector. Business leaders can team up with accelerators, venture funds, campus groups, regional leadership and nonprofits to mentor, finance, and train the next generation of high-growth company leaders.

Or they can help pave the way for the next public software engineering schools, as Union Square Ventures VC Fred Wilson did in New York. Franchisors can extend special financing to youth and veterans—after all, direct economic output in the franchise sector is projected to grow 5 percent in 2012, and employment, 2.1 percent.[12] And we need to openly encourage our young people to start their careers in startups, which generate all net job growth—so those companies keep growing, and young people learn to thrive in the new economy.[13]

Finally, we need to start creating common-sense avenues for financial support. Microloan financiers like Kiva are easing global unemployment throughout the developing world—why can't we do more of the same thing here? Frankly, improving access to capital

---

10   Veterans Entrepreneurial Transition Act of 2011, H.R. 3167, 112th Congress, (2011).

11   YEC and Buzz Marketing Group survey.

12   *2012 Franchise Business Economic Outlook,* prepared by IHS Global Insight for the International Franchise Association, January 2012, 1, http://emarket.franchise.org/EconOutlookFactSheetfinal.pdf.

13   *The Importance of Startups in Job Creation and Destruction,* (Kauffman Foundation, July 2010), 2, http://www.kauffman.org/uploadedfiles/firm_formation_importance_of_startups.pdf.

doesn't necessarily start with banks—having robust mentorship and other non-financial support doubles the likelihood that a young entrepreneur will be approved for a commercial loan.[14]

Teach Tech in and out of the Classroom

The Web has revolutionized the way we do business today, creating a far more level playing field for young entrepreneurs—provided they have the skill set to take advantage of it. Young entrepreneurs who are well-versed in software engineering, design and code have an instant leg up on their peers. One study found that small-to-medium businesses with strong Web presences grew twice as fast as those with only a minimal presence (or none at all), and created twice the number of jobs.[15]

We need to prepare *all* young people for this reality, and arm them with the tools they need to grow businesses (or become valued employees and intrapreneurs). In the classroom, this means we need to teach hands-on computer software engineering, not just computing basics—the Bureau of Labor Statistics is projecting an employment increase for software engineers of 32 percent by 2018.[16] Outside the classroom, companies like Codecademy fill gaps in K-12 and college education by creating peer-to-peer platforms where aspiring coders learn by doing.

---

14   *Global Youth Entrepreneur Survey 2011,* (The Prince's Youth Business International, 2011), 8, http://www.youthbusiness.org/pdf/YouthEntrepreneurshipSurvey2011.pdf.

15   Matthieu Pélissié du Rausas, et al., "Internet matters: The Net's sweeping impact on growth, jobs, and prosperity," McKinsey Global Institute, May 2011, http://www.mckinsey.com/Insights/MGI/Research/Technology_and_Innovation/Internet_matters.

16   Bureau of Labor Statistics, U.S. Department of Labor, *Occupational Outlook Handbook 2010-11 Edition,* "Computer Software Engineers and Computer Programmers," last modified December 17, 2009, http://www.bls.gov/oco/ocos303.htm.

Foster Entrepreneurship at the Regional Level

Not all solutions fit all communities. From a grassroots perspective, one of the most valuable takeaways in this book is that our communities must do a better job of connecting their own thinkers and doers. Cities facing economic decline need to create resource-rich networks that help young entrepreneurs cut through red tape and bureaucracy at the local level, so entrepreneurs don't depart en masse. The Idea Village in New Orleans has helped sustain over one thousand jobs and $83 million in revenue by retaining and supporting the city's entrepreneurs.

Underserved regions must find new ways to develop ecosystems in which idea exchange, growth, and financial support are readily available. From Silicon Prairie to New Orleans, entrepreneurs are bridging gaps between local government, investors, and backyard entrepreneurs. These hyper-local networks provide the momentum Americans need to get new businesses off the ground immediately.

How to #FixYoungAmerica

Let's stop telling our young people they are the future, and give them the resources they need to succeed today. It is our moral, financial and patriotic duty to support new job creation, which is why the YEC and dozens of partners have joined together to #FixYoungAmerica. If we, as a nation, succeed—and succeed we must—we will help restore the American dream to millions of young people. Not every entrepreneur will create a high-growth company, but increasing America's entrepreneur population by as little as 1 to 2 percent would create tens of thousands of needed jobs. This is not about making life easier for Millennials. It's about ensuring that, when they become the thirty-, forty- and fifty-something leaders of tomorrow, they will have the capacity and ability to lead America forward.

In buying this book, you are actively participating in this new national conversation. Your contribution enables us to take our message on the road and influence the decision makers where they are. And as our campaign progresses, we will announce new supporters, media partnerships, book topics, and solutions—including yours, if you share it with us.

What I am asking you for today is this: ten minutes of your time. Yes, I know how big an ask that is—but I also know we're on the brink of real change. So on behalf of the YEC, please help us fix America by sharing our campaign on social media and emailing your friends, colleagues, families, mentors, and elected officials to ask them to join our movement. More importantly, share your proposed solutions with us—so we can execute them together. Visit www.FixYoungAmerica.com now to find out how.

Scott Gerber is the founder of the Young Entrepreneur Council (http://theyec.org) and co-founder of Gen Y Capital Partners. He is also a serial entrepreneur, internationally syndicated columnist, host of the Inc.com web show Ask Gerber and author of the book Never Get a "Real" Job. Scott has been featured in the *New York Times*, the *Wall Street Journal*, the *Washington Post*, *TIME*, CNN, Reuters, Mashable, CBS Evening News, ABC World News Tonight, MSNBC, *US News & World Report*, Fox News, *Inc.* and *Entrepreneur*. Follow him on Twitter @askgerber.

PART I: RETHINKING EDUCATION AND WORK

K-12 EDUCATION

What I Learned from Richard Branson's Mother about Parenting

Mary C. Mazzio, Founder and CEO, 50 Eggs, Inc.

Much has been written about whether entrepreneurs are born or made, with no real consensus. My own opinion, which is anecdotal, is that entrepreneurs can be made—and parents play a central role in making them.

I had a remarkable epiphany while producing *Lemonade Stories,* our documentary film about extraordinary entrepreneurs and their mothers. The film, which features Richard Branson (Virgin), Russell Simmons (Def Jam), Arthur Blank (Home Depot, and owner of the Atlanta Falcons), and Tom Scott (Nantucket Nectars), among others, examines the impact that mothers have on sparking creativity and entrepreneurial spirit in their children.

During her interview, Eve Branson talked extensively about her son's shyness as a boy, which she described as "disabling." That evening, as my crew sat down to dinner, our director of photography and our gaffer started buzzing about Eve's comments. This in itself was unusual. Normally when filming interviews, my team is focused exclusively on their craft (e.g. the operation and movement of the camera, monitoring of sound levels, and positioning of lights) and is not attuned to the actual content of interviews. But I knew we were onto something special when they both described how they might incorporate Eve's advice into how they were raising their own teenaged children.

When Richard Branson was a young boy, he refused to talk to adults and would cling to the back of Eve's skirt. When he turned seven or so, Eve decided that his behavior was no longer tolerable. "Shyness is being introverted and thinking only of yourself," she said. On the way home from a shopping trip to a nearby village, Eve stopped the car about three miles from home and let Richard out. "You will now walk home. You will have to talk to people to find your way home," she told him. By the time Richard arrived some ten hours later, Eve was apoplectic. (She had not accounted for the time he might stop to look at bugs and inspect rocks.) But it worked. Richard started to become more comfortable interacting with adults.

On my flight back to the States from London, I thought about my son, who, too, was shy. When he shrank back from adults, I would often apologize—"I'm sorry, he's so shy." Until my conversation with Eve, it had never occurred to me that being shy was being selfish. When Eve put shyness into that context, I decided that this particular trait would now have a very short shelf life in our household.

I began Project Stick-Out-Your-Hand-and-Look-People-in-the-Eye. And my son, who was seven years old at the time, very quickly learned that there was a significant upside to interacting with adults and making them feel comfortable—like new sunglasses on his birthday from the couple down the street. Now, at the age of fifteen, my son operates like a senator, looking adults in the eye and shaking their hand. It is a lesson that will serve him well as an adult—and one that I wished I had learned early on.

The other lesson that I took away from *Lemonade Stories* and the mothers of these entrepreneurs was about creativity and independence. Today's parents cram their children's schedules with all sorts of adult-supervised activities: organized soccer, baseball drafts, play dates and more. There is very little free time for playing in the woods or daydreaming, and kids have no time to shovel snow or rake leaves to earn money anymore. Layer on top of that an educational learning process geared toward test taking, and it's no surprise that creativity and entrepreneurial thinking is increasingly drummed out of the lives of our children—and with it, innovation, initiative, stick-to-it-iveness, and work ethic.

Because of this landscape, which is bereft of time and imagination, it is imperative that parents create little pockets of time where kids can catch butterflies, elbow a sibling, hop on a bike, or be independent and navigate their surroundings...without us. And without being tethered to an iPod or cell phone. In addition to pockets of time to let the mind wander—a wonderful precursor to innovation—our kids might do better with less parental indulgence. You want a new cell phone? You can earn the money for it. Nothing like that sort of incentive to create initiative in a young person.

Tom Scott's mother, Jane, talked in her interview for *Lemonade Stories* about her response when her kids complained about being bored. Too bad—make up your own games, she'd say. And they did. After wrapping Jane Scott and Tom Scott's interview, I decided that my occasional Toys"R"Us runs when my kids complained about being bored were over. No more working-mother guilt. Not only would they have to make up their own games and amusement, but also the days of subsidized entertainment were over. We still could go to Toys"R"Us, but not on Mommy's nickel. I announced to my children that the Bank of Mama was being shut down and the teller window closing. They would now have to earn their own money.

They went into their room to discuss this unfortunate turn of events. They came out an hour later. My daughter did the talking. "Mama—can we borrow some money for lemonade mix?" I said yes, thinking a modest infusion of angel capital was a positive thing. They disappeared into their room again, arguing about who would reassemble the broken wagon, who would push it, and who would make the signs. When they emerged from their room next, my daughter clutched what appeared to be a list written in crayon. "We're going to sell lemonade at the Boston Marathon," they said excitedly. Their excitement was only marginally damped when I asked them, well, what about the cups? Silence. My daughter suddenly piped up: "Can we borrow another five dollars for cups?" Of course. I then asked them about their pricing strategy. This they had already thought about: a dollar per cup. Really? I asked. Isn't that expensive? They stuck to their guns. "These will be big cups," my son said enthusiastically.

On the morning of the marathon, the kids lugged an enormous cooler of lemonade down to the race, where throngs of people were congregating. It just so happened to be a muggy day, so the lemonade started to go quickly. My son shook the hand of a neighbor who decided to pay the kids $50 for all the lemonade his children could drink. Fast forward to the end of the day: The kids made north of $100 and were ecstatic. (Although they were markedly less ecstatic when informed about their obligation to repay their angel investor for the lemonade mix and the cost of the cups.) With their net proceeds, the kids asked if they could cycle downtown to the toy shop. And as they sailed out the door, it occurred to me that it was not the money that made them so satisfied, so happy. It was independence. No need to ask Mama for five bucks—they could buy what they wanted, when they wanted, with their own money.

Based on what I learned from the mothers in *Lemonade Stories*, it occurs to me that if American parents want to raise children who think entrepreneurially, have initiative, and become innovative and truly independent adults, it might serve us all well if we stepped back and let our sweet darlings make mistakes and fall on their faces from time to time. A story on NPR recounted the effects of helicopter parenting and the extent to which parents are advocating for their children with teachers and college admissions personnel. In the story, one employer recalled a parent who showed up for their child's first job interview—without the child.[17]

Needless to say, the child did not get the job. Helicopter parenting may have made for a closer bond between parent and child, but that bond is sometimes made at the expense of initiative and independence. There's plenty of research showing that parents have a strong impact on their children's achievement. But in the twenty-first century, the applied skills kids really need to achieve, either as entrepreneurs or entrepreneurial thinkers—skills like critical thinking, creativity and innovation, leadership, ethics and professionalism—are skills they're not learning in high school or even college.[18] Why not start teaching them at home, like the mothers interviewed for *Lemonade Stories* did? They uniformly allowed their kids to:

- Make mistakes
- Behave independently, and make their own decisions
- Experiment
- Fail
- And daydream.

---

17 Jennifer Ludden, "Helicopter Parents Hover In The Workplace," NPR, February 6, 2012, http://www.npr.org/2012/02/06/146464665/helicopter-parents-hover-in-the-workplace.

18 The Conference Board, et al., *Are They Really Ready to Work? Employer's Perspectives on the Basic Knowledge and Applied Skills of New Entrants to the 21st Century U.S. Workforce*, (2006), 9-10, http://www.p21.org/storage/documents/FINAL_REPORT_PDF09-29-06.pdf.

They also taught their children to communicate independently (without speaking for them), and instilled in them a strong work ethic. The results speak for themselves.

I feel personally indebted to the Eve Bransons and the Jane Scotts of this world—women who taught their children to be independent and gave them space to experiment, to fail. Russell Simmons' mother gave him a $2,000 loan when no one else would; his business of producing parties hosted by rap artists was losing money and he was questioning his ability and line of work. Russell said in his interview for the film that what was important was not the money his mother gave him, but rather what it represented. Which was the faith that she had in him. After that day, he never had to ask his mother for money again.

Mary Mazzio, an award-winning documentary film director, Olympian, and former law firm partner, is Founder and CEO of 50 Eggs, Inc., an independent film production company. Mary wrote, directed and produced the highly acclaimed award-winning films, *TEN9EIGHT, A Hero for Daisy, Lemonade Stories,* and *Apple Pie,* as well as *we are BlackRock.* She has just completed *The Apple Pushers,* narrated by Edward Norton and funded by the Laurie M. Tisch Illumination Fund. Mazzio is a graduate of Mount Holyoke College and Georgetown University Law Center. For more information, visit www.50eggs.com. For more information about *Lemonade Stories,* visit www.lemonadestories.com.

Closing the Gap: How to Infuse Entrepreneurial Thinking throughout K-12 Education

Jack E. Kosakowski, President and CEO, Junior Achievement USA

Whether examining high school graduation rates, comparative rankings of student performance by country, or the significant skill gap between employers' needs and those possessed by individuals seeking work, it is clear that we must reexamine our approach to education to maintain the United States' stature as an economic superpower. Beyond the economic implications of our failure to reform the education system, the very foundation of our nation is at risk of losing the educated citizenry essential to maintaining our democracy and preserving the personal freedoms we enjoy.

The good news is that the perfect storm created by the current economic, political, and social upheaval has generated a sense of urgency for change. And my personal experience as a student, and later as an observer of successful educators through my work with Junior Achievement, has led me to believe that by infusing an entrepreneurial approach throughout K-12 education, we can improve the system and better prepare young people for the realities of today's global economy.

Though not a trained educator, I am a "trained" student of the traditional education approach, having worked on the fringe of K-12 education for nearly forty years. When I was a student, I was fortunate to attend good public and parochial schools, but it was the strong parental oversight from my father, a Marine Corps drill sergeant, that motivated me to get passing grades.

Despite the good schools and the "wait 'til your father gets home" incentives, it was not until I had an entrepreneurial experience in high school as a member of Junior Achievement (JA) that I connected the dots between the importance of what I was learning in school and my future. Up until then, I believed that life consisted of a series of experiences and stimuli that I would simply react to, not thinking that I could create a future for myself. When I realized that I was in control of my life, education took on a completely new meaning for me, and my learning skills and grades soared.

During my three years of Junior Achievement entrepreneurial experiences, it was not the business teachings that I gained the most from—those were more of a means to an end. Rather, it was the drive to solve problems and meet the needs of others (in this case, customers) that changed my life. By taking action to meet the needs of others, I learned I could change the world. Even the tools that school offered (math, science, reading, etc.) made more sense to me, because I realized the more I knew, the more problems I would be prepared to solve.

After high school, I went to work for Junior Achievement, the same organization that first inspired me to see the possibilities life had to offer. I have since spent my entire career with Junior Achievement, supporting its mission to inspire and prepare young people to succeed in the global economy at both the local and national level.

Making the Case for Entrepreneurial Education at the K-12 level

Nearly forty years with JA has afforded me the opportunity to observe education from multiple perspectives. I've seen many outstanding teachers, and others who were ineffective. The teachers who have the most impact on their students engage them in the real-life application of the subject matter, making it relevant by using an inquisitive or problem-solving approach to learning. In essence, they apply an entrepreneurial approach, without the commerce component we typically think of when using the word entrepreneurial.

Since its founding in 1919, Junior Achievement has led the nation in implementing and promoting entrepreneurship in K-12 education across the United States. JA has conducted many studies that reinforce the importance of providing young people with experiences that give them an understanding of entrepreneurship and the motivation to take this knowledge into the workplace, whether they choose to start their own business or work for someone else.

In April 2009, Junior Achievement hosted a forum in Washington, DC to identify critical factors in preparing the future workforce. To provide a research base for this effort, JA enlisted the help of the Gallup organization to survey more than 1,100 employers and employees about the current state of the American workforce, and what can be done to make it more competitive. The intent of the research was to identify ways to help young people bridge the gap between success in school and success in the workplace.

In the study, the vast majority (96 percent) of employees stated that it is important for the American workforce to become more entrepreneurial to keep America competitive. Forty-six percent of employees and 41 percent of employers expressed the belief that the best place to learn entrepreneurship is in grades K-12, surpassing all other options. This research reinforced what I strongly believed—

applying entrepreneurial principles early opens the doors for young people to envision new possibilities. The research also substantiated the enormous need for entrepreneurial skills and activity in the workforce. Entrepreneurship is the engine that spurs economic growth and societal progress by fueling innovation and social empowerment.[19]

In addition to employers acknowledging the need for entrepreneurship education, youth also see the potential an entrepreneurial approach can have on their future. A 2011 national survey commissioned by Junior Achievement and the National Chamber Foundation asked high school juniors to share their knowledge and perceptions of entrepreneurship, free enterprise and capitalism, and how these factors will influence their future career choices. The results showed that most high school juniors believe entrepreneurs play an important role in job creation and American success, and 64 percent are interested in starting or owning their own business someday.

The survey's results confirm the need for and value in providing entrepreneurship education for high school students, through both classroom-based and co-curricular learning opportunities. At least nine in ten juniors believe it is important to be taught about entrepreneurship, free enterprise, and capitalism, but less than half (45 percent) have been taught about entrepreneurship in school, and only 57 percent have been taught about free enterprise in school.[20]

---

19   JA Worldwide, *The Entrepreneurial Workforce*, (2009), 10-11, http://www.ja.org/files/polls/The_Entrepreneurial_Workforce.pdf.

20   Junior Achievement USA and the National Chamber Foundation, *The Free Enterprise National Survey: Viewpoints from U.S. High School Juniors*, (2011), 1-2, http://www.ja.org/files/polls/2011-Free-Enterprise-Survey-Exec-Summary.pdf. The Free Enterprise National Survey of 2,213 high school juniors was conducted online in July and August 2011 by Harris Interactive on behalf of Junior Achievement USA and the National Chamber Foundation.

How Do We Instill the Entrepreneurial Spirit into Education Practices That Every Young Person in America Can Take Advantage Of?

I believe a starting point is to develop a common path for bringing the experience to scale in our young people. That path should start with curriculum that engages young people in ways that kindle the kind of entrepreneurial spirit that developed in me while I was a student. The following have become "best practices" that have evolved from my work with Junior Achievement:

1. **Make certain the content reflects the latest thinking in entrepreneurship education by engaging actual entrepreneurs in its development.** While entrepreneurship is by no means a new concept, the practices of entrepreneurs change and need to be accurately captured in the curriculum in order to provide young people with a foundation of understanding upon which they can build.

2. **Make the learning experiences real.** Providing young people with an understanding of entrepreneurship upon which they can build is important. Equally important is including activities that reinforce those understandings that are real-life. Young people need to engage in activities where they have to put into practice what they are learning in theory.

3. **Provide successful role models for young people to emulate as they pursue their entrepreneurial endeavors.** The Junior Achievement model includes adults who serve as role models by not only teaching students the concepts behind entrepreneurship, but by sharing their own life stories with young people. In doing so, these adult role models provide young people with a sense of self-efficacy and the desire to take what they are learning and put it into action.

Next Steps for Local Policymakers and School Leaders

Through my work with Junior Achievement, I was part of an entrepreneurship strategy group sponsored by the Aspen Institute. As a result of the group's work, a policymaker's action guide was developed to provide direction to implement entrepreneurship education in America's schools. A strong case was made in support of the link between entrepreneurship education and its impact on the future success of young people.

For example, the study group found that ". . . the experience of a sense of ownership in their lives was four times higher for alumni of youth-entrepreneurship programs than for students who did not take such courses." And the group concluded that entrepreneurship education had a significant impact on ". . . keep[ing] young people in school, learning academic and work skills effectively, [and] motivated to be productive and engaged in their communities and the larger economy, and developing success-oriented attitudes of initiative, intelligent risk-taking, collaboration, and opportunity recognition."[21]

The group made the following recommendations for local policymakers:

- Introduce entrepreneurship training in all schools, with special emphasis on those with large populations of youth from low-income communities.
- Increase funding to support teacher training, curriculum and professional development, and to evaluate program design and outcomes.
- Develop strong partnerships between schools, businesses, and other community organizations, so business leaders

---

21   The Aspen Youth Entrepreneurship Strategy Group, *Youth Entrepreneurship Education in America: A Policymaker's Action Guide,* (The Aspen Institute, 2008), 3-4, http://www.americaspromise.org/~/media/Files/Resources/NFTE%20-%20policymakers_action_guide_2008.ashx.

can serve as mentors, coaches, and provide support to local programs.[22]

School leaders also can turn to the resources of the Consortium for Entrepreneurship Education, a group composed of national, state, and local education agencies and organizations advocating entrepreneurship education for guidance. The Consortium has developed two documents, *National Content Standards for Entrepreneurship Education*[23] and *National Standards of Practice for Entrepreneurship Education*,[24] that provide specific direction for developing and implementing entrepreneurship education programs.

In summary, the evidence is clear. For young people to acquire the knowledge and develop the skills that will instill in them attitudes and behaviors that prepare them for future success, it will take the combined efforts of educators, business, and policymakers to drive the entrepreneurship education agenda. This agenda must include providing entrepreneurship education to K-12 students, introducing them to mentors who show them the real-life applications of the subject matter, and providing them with opportunities to participate in the experiential activities that give them a chance to experiment with solving problems and meeting the needs of others.

---

22 Ibid., 21.

23 *National Content Standards for Entrepreneurship Education*, Consortium for Entrepreneurship Education, 2004, http://www.entre-ed.org/Standards_Toolkit/.

24 *National Standards of Practice for Entrepreneurship Education*, (Columbus, OH: Consortium for Entrepreneurship Education, 2006), http://www.entre-ed.org/_what/stds-prac-brochure.pdf.

Jack E. Kosakowski is the President and CEO of Junior Achievement USA. Junior Achievement (JA) is the world's largest organization dedicated to giving young people the knowledge and skills they need to own their academic success, plan for their future, and make smart academic and economic choices. Today, JA reaches four million students per year in more than 120 markets across the United States, with an additional 6.5 million students served by operations in 117 other countries. Kosakowski has total oversight of JA in the United States. Starting as a student in the JA program in Toledo, Ohio, he attended the University of Toledo on a Junior Achievement scholarship and has since served in a variety of staff positions with increasing levels of responsibility over the past 38 years. He was named President and CEO of Junior Achievement USA in 2007. Kosakowski was appointed by President George W. Bush to serve a two-year term on the President's Advisory Council on Financial Literacy in January 2008. He also serves on the Board of Directors of the Achievement Foundation, is a member of the United States Commission for UNESCO (United Nationals Educational, Scientific and Cultural Organization), and serves on the Council on Competitiveness' Learn to Compete Commission. Kosakowski was recently named a Trustee of America's Promise Alliance.

Education That Works: Three Essential Factors to Build Bridges for Tomorrow's Young Entrepreneurs

Jean M. Buckley, President and CEO, Future Business Leaders of America-Phi Beta Lambda, Inc.

Year after year, I am fortunate to witness the entrepreneurial spirit of America's best and brightest future business leaders at educational conferences, in the classroom, and in the business community at large.

How can we ensure this entrepreneurial drive not only continues to grow, but also becomes an integral part of every student's educational experience? And how can we make sure more students take advantage of entrepreneurial activities, inside and outside the classroom? There are three essential factors that play a role in the formation of successful entrepreneurs: role models, applied business skills, and co-curricular educational programs.

1. Role Models

It's no surprise that young adults are profoundly influenced by the people who surround them. That's why role models are able to play an outsized role in positively shaping the lives of young adults, both personally and professionally.

Within a student's sphere of influence are three groups of people who have the greatest impact on the early formation of entrepreneurs: family members, teachers, and business professionals.

Family members: Family members foster an atmosphere of academic and career exploration. By sharing their career experiences at home, family members are able to remove the "mystery" that surrounds the professional business world.

Do family members need to be entrepreneurs, in the traditional sense? Absolutely not. They merely need to share their experience within the market economy, discussing their careers with their children, and detailing how their daily activities make their companies more effective and successful.

Family members also need to encourage their children to take advantage of extracurricular activities, in particular, involvement with business-oriented groups. These groups allow students to hone their leadership skills, interact with members of the business community, and experience firsthand how their economy functions.

Each year, thousands of parents support FBLA-PBL activities at the local, state, and national level. They are demonstrating, through their actions, that programs that bring people, ideas, and products together in a learning environment are crucial to the long-term development of future business leaders and entrepreneurs. This open spirit of giving back is an important signal to send to aspiring entrepreneurs in their formative years.

Think of these activities as an important component in the evolution of the lemonade stand: Family members nurture the benefits of entrepreneurship at an early age, eventually helping their children become more immersed in the workings of the global economy. First, by interacting locally with customers and suppliers;

then, by experiencing global commerce as consumers, producers, and investors.

Teachers: Teachers provide an intellectual foundation for entrepreneurs. By creating an open environment of learning, inspiring curiosity, and teaching students about the importance of collaboration, teachers are able to make a long-lasting impact on aspiring entrepreneurs.

We all know the importance of effective classroom instruction. FBLA-PBL Advisers use a number of techniques to keep their teaching skills sharp and set the standard for highly qualified instruction in the classroom.

Through FBLA-PBL's extensive national partnerships with learning organizations, we are able to offer FBLA Advisers free Microsoft Office Specialist (MOS) and Microsoft Technology Associate certification exams, as well as free graduate credits through the Insurance Education Institute. In addition, Advisers are eligible to receive Continuing Education Units when they attend workshops at our annual National Leadership Conference.

However, beyond the books, what are other ways teachers can infuse an entrepreneurial component into their classrooms? One effective technique is to build bridges between the classroom and the business world. Successful teachers find ways to immerse their students in the local business environment, bringing in outside guest speakers, arranging community service activities, organizing field trips and business tours, and finding business mentors for students.

Savvy Advisers pair members of the business community with students preparing for competitive events. For example, an Adviser will find a Certified Public Accountant to mentor students who are preparing for the Accounting competitive events.

This type of coaching helps students compete more effectively and it brings them into direct contact with successful business professionals. That way, students learn about the basics of accounting, as well as acquire feedback on how to dress professionally, how to put together a powerful presentation, and how to perfect their speaking skills.

This brings students face-to-face with key stakeholders in their communities, so they can see how local economies function and how their activities can make a positive impact in their neighborhoods. It also requires a dedication and commitment that extends beyond time spent inside the classroom. At FBLA-PBL our advisers spend countless hours outside the classroom, coaching and mentoring their students as they prepare for competitions, hold chapter offices, and organize community service activities. This often means extra time spent during free periods at school, and even during weekends when traveling to competitions or helping students manage school-based enterprises, such as a concession stand at sporting events, a school-based credit union, or school store.

Business professionals: Business professionals offer students the opportunity to interact with successful business leaders and to see the free enterprise system at work. Students also are able to build a supportive network of business contacts and mentors.

Well, if there is one thing students like to see in a classroom, it is someone from *outside* the classroom. Students value a different perspective, and are energized by the interaction with experienced and diverse business representatives. Again, these types of interactions expose students to the world of business, add flavor to a new topic, and provide a different perspective on common business challenges.

2. Applied Business Skills

*"The first company in any industry that significantly improves
its human connectivity skills will take the field."*

Daniel Kahneman, 2002 Nobel Prize for Economics

In order to succeed in the free enterprise system, students need to develop a portfolio of "soft" business skills that include:

Confidence: To instill confidence at an early age, students need exposure to a broad business education that combines rigorous classroom learning with practical, hands-on projects and activities. This exposure helps students adapt to a constantly changing business environment, and to build critical-thinking and analytical skills. Students can develop their self-confidence by competing in business events, holding leadership positions, and fine-tuning their public speaking skills.

Of course, nothing replaces experience, so students need to practice, practice, practice. Nothing builds confidence like mastering a skill. This fact alone will build a student's confidence level and prepare him or her for the challenges that lie ahead.

One way students can "practice" their self-confidence skills is to use business simulation activities to immerse themselves in different business challenges. This will help students apply the skills they learn during these practice sessions to the real-world business situations they will encounter later on.

And don't downplay setbacks. When students are forced to hone and refine their answers due to a deficiency, they will discover new skills sets and enhance existing ones.

Teamwork: The ability to work with others productively is critical in any entrepreneurial activity, whether it's interacting with business partners, funders, employees, or customers. In fact, it's been said that 90 percent of our success in life and business depends on our EQ (emotional intelligence), and only 10 percent on our IQ.

Serving in leadership positions while in school is one way students can build a portfolio of soft skills, in particular teamwork skills. Planning—and launching—a school-based credit union or organizing a March of Dimes fund-raising walk requires group decision making, motivation, and collaboration skills. And there is no better place to find these leadership opportunities than by joining a student club or organization.

How can students strengthen their teamwork skills? During competitive events, students resolve conflicts and delegate work from the planning process all the way through the final presentation. During group presentations, for instance, all students need to present their proposal, meaning everyone is responsible for the success—or failure—of the team.

Adaptability: Students need to quickly recognize and take advantage of business opportunities, especially in today's rapidly changing global economy. By competing and engaging in business simulation programs, students are able to identify emerging opportunities and capitalize on them.

FBLA-PBL's competitive events are designed to simulate the typical challenges a young businessperson will face in the global economy. By competing, students are able to "measure" themselves against their peers, and, most importantly, evaluate how their performance ranks against others. Think of it as securing funding for your startup: You receive a valuation, only instead of a valuation on an idea or product, you're receiving a valuation on your skill sets.

Despite advances in technology, nothing can replicate the face-to-face experiences that a conference provides. Students are able to expand their business-related knowledge during workshops that are run by business professionals, who share time-tested tips and techniques. This type of knowledge transfer is invaluable today.

Conferences also provide students with an opportunity to network with fellow students and established business professionals, hence fostering a cross-pollination of ideas and best business practices. One of the overlooked and unappreciated benefits of conferences is the teachable moment that comes about during face-to-face encounters. What about basic business etiquette in a group setting? How much should you tip hotel staff? How should you dress during a job interview, or when meeting prospective funders?

You won't find these soft skills in a basic business curriculum, but they are infused throughout FBLA-PBL's programs, activities, and conferences.

3. Co-Curricular Educational Programs

What types of educational programs give students a head start on the path to entrepreneurship? The ideal programs provide a bridge between educational curricula and the business community by harnessing classroom learning and applying it to real-world business situations.

Educational programs need to be co-curricular and cover four components:

- **Community service:** Students need to realize they are part of a large, interrelated society and understand how their actions impact their surroundings. Community service activities are one way for students to connect with the communities they will serve as future business owners.

- **Leadership:** Students can distinguish themselves at an early age with high-profile leadership positions that bring them into contact with members of the community, business professionals, government officials, and fellow students. They will be able to fine-tune their interpersonal skills, create a career portfolio, and build a network of contacts that they can access now and in the future.

- **Career exploration:** Entrepreneurs will wear many hats as they build their companies. Therefore, a broad understanding of careers and career functions gained as students will give them an advantage as they grow their businesses and hire top-notch employees for key positions in their growing enterprises.

- **Competition:** Students should take advantage of competitions that allow them to test run their ideas, share best practices, and benchmark their performance against other aspiring entrepreneurs.

One of the best parts of receiving a ranking is the feedback mechanism provided by judges. Students are able to gauge in which areas they need improvement.

Bringing It All Together

What training programs work best? Ideally it's something where students bring a concept from initial stage to launch. When this isn't practical, case studies provide a solid alternative, challenging students to analyze a business situation and come up with solutions. And, hopefully, students will have an opportunity to present their solutions to a group of peers so they can solicit feedback.

To strengthen these programs, we need the support of a broad set of stakeholders: family members, teachers, administrators, legislators, and the entire business community. Funding needs to flow to Career and Technical Education (CTE) programs, so the proper investments can be made in our young students. And student groups need to play a vital role, giving members a hands-on application of business principles.

Naturally, growing membership in these student organizations is vital. The best ways to see increased membership are to continually show members value, create new programs, and encourage all members to continually replenish their ranks.

As the demand for competent business leaders grows, FBLA-PBL has seen a commensurate growth in the demand for its programs, both domestically and internationally. In 2011-12 alone, over 650 new chapters joined FBLA-PBL, including international chapters in South Korea, Canada, Haiti, Puerto Rico, the Virgin Islands, the Cayman Islands, and across Europe. The common bond these chapters share is the desire to produce successful business leaders with the entrepreneurial drive and creativity to propel the global economy forward.

Together with the appropriate role models, a broad and ever-expanding suite of business skills, and co-curricular educational programs that apply business knowledge to everyday situations, our young adults will be positioned to capitalize on the abundant entrepreneurial opportunities that are available today, and in the future. This will ensure that the entrepreneurial spirits I see displayed everyday will continue to thrive.

Jean M. Buckley became president and chief executive officer of Future Business Leaders of America-Phi Beta Lambda, Inc. (FBLA-PBL) in 1997. Under her leadership, the association has grown to become one of the largest career and technical student organizations, involving more than a quarter-million students and teachers across the United States and abroad. During her tenure, she increased the number of business partners, expanded competitive event offerings with a focus on technology, and grew member benefits for all four divisions. Prior to joining FBLA-PBL, Jean had a distinguished 20-year career with Junior Achievement, Inc., where she held several field office and national positions. As the senior vice president of education at the national headquarters, she was responsible for the development and implementation of K-12 business and economics curricula as well as leading the education outreach effort.

Teachers Do Make a Difference: Overcoming Barriers to Teaching Entrepreneurship

Dr. Cathy Ashmore, Executive Director,
Consortium for Entrepreneurship Education

"Entrepreneurs are not 'born'...Rather they 'become'
through the experiences in their lives."

Professor Al Shapero, The Ohio State University

O ver the past thirty years, it has been my passion to pursue the importance of entrepreneurship education and the role educators should have in making it more accessible. My interest began when I was hired as the marketing director for the National Center for Research in Vocational Education at The Ohio State University in 1980. The first challenge was to sell a huge product nationwide (called PACE, or Program for Acquiring Competence in Entrepreneurship) to an audience of career and technical educators. But at that time, few people could even spell "entrepreneur," let alone teach it.

In spite of research that shows students are very interested in being their own boss, we determined that educators have little support for teaching young people about this career option. By 1990, the

Kauffman Foundation had become a major supporter of entrepreneurship education, and produced research that showed that two-thirds of high school students wanted to become entrepreneurs—but more than 80 percent felt they didn't learn anything about it in school.[25] In 2011, the National Chamber Foundation and Junior Achievement found that 45 percent of high school juniors had been taught about entrepreneurship in school,[26] demonstrating that while there has been progress, we still have a long way to go to offer entrepreneurship education everywhere. This essay will expand on the barriers involved in teaching entrepreneurship, and some successful programs educators can leverage to provide powerful entrepreneurial experiences to young people.

Families Are the Incubators

In the 1980s, we encountered data that said that two out of three entrepreneurs had someone in their family who had created a business.[27] My mentor Professor Shapero said it was because people believed, "If dumb old cousin George can do it, I can too." So it occurred to me that living with an entrepreneur, perhaps working for them, and observing the entrepreneurial spirit at home was the central experience that challenged entrepreneurs' sons and daughters to start a business as well.

With this data in mind, we set out to find ways to teach students everywhere (even those who did not grow up in entrepreneurial families) that it was possible for them to be self-reliant and start a

25   William B. Walstad and Marilyn L. Kendall, *Seeds of Success, Entrepreneurship and Youth*, (Dubuque, IA: Kendall/Hunt Publishing Company, 1999).

26   Junior Achievement USA and the National Chamber Foundation, *The Free Enterprise National Survey: Viewpoints from U.S. High School Juniors*, (2011), 2, http://www.ja.org/files/polls/2011-Free-Enterprise-Survey-Exec-Summary.pdf.

27   Albert Shapero and Lisa Sokol, "The social dimensions of entrepreneurship," in *Encyclopedia of Entrepreneurship*, eds. Calvin A. Kent, Donald L. Sexton, and Karl H. Vesper, (Englewood Cliffs, NJ: Prentice-Hall, 1982), 72-88.

business. We thought this would be an easy goal, especially with the support of a policy from the new U.S. Department of Education stipulating that all career and technical programs should teach entrepreneurship. Thirty years later, we have seen some great successes, but it has been far from easy.

Creating the Entrepreneurship Consortium

In 1980, it seemed logical to add entrepreneurship to the career development programs in high schools because, after all, entrepreneurs make their own careers. We saw any career or technical program (in marketing, business, family and consumer science, agriculture, and other trades) as fertile ground for young people to practice innovative thinking and see opportunities for starting a business.

Our strategy for marketing PACE was to form a national Consortium for Entrepreneurship Education, with ten states agreeing to be the initial members (Ohio, Colorado, Minnesota, North Carolina, Nebraska, Missouri, Illinois, Arizona, Oklahoma and Michigan). Their role was to bring entrepreneurship to the career and technical education teachers in their states and to encourage other states to join as well. Interest in entrepreneurship education gradually exploded, and many related organizations came on board, expanding the Consortium's scope to all disciplines and levels of education.

In addition to our own product, we started encouraging teachers to use other resources that were emerging to support entrepreneurship in the early 1980s including Junior Achievement (JA), the Network for Teaching Entrepreneurship (NFTE) and resources from the Small Business Administration. Among the barriers, we found that teachers were not very interested.

Identifying the Barriers Educators Face

We soon discovered why teachers did not embrace opportunities to teach entrepreneurship, including:

- Many had never been entrepreneurs, and most did not even know any business owners.

- Some career and technical teachers were failed entrepreneurs who went to teaching as a more secure career. Their outlook focused on the risk, not opportunity.

- Because many teachers chose this occupation instead of what they perceived as more risky business careers—especially the "failure-prone" choice of starting a business—they avoided encouraging students to become entrepreneurs.

- Teacher training did not include a focus on entrepreneurship in career and technical education, or in any education program.

- It has always been difficult to make changes to curriculum in any discipline, and it is especially hard to do so now because of state and federal requirements.

- Courses were built around a textbook, and few teachers were expected to provide real experiences as part of the curriculum. Teachers who did see the value of providing activities often had to hide their enthusiasm, as the "system"' drew them back to the current norm.

- Business plans became the outcome of entrepreneurship education programs at all levels, from elementary schools through college, and experiential learning was overlooked.

- Social studies classes addressed entrepreneurship as an economic fact, but did not involve students in personal career exploration. Other academic classes did not even recognize entrepreneurship as a potential subject.

- State funding did not recognize entrepreneurship as a fundable program until fairly recently. Those teachers that chose to teach it did so as an extra class activity.
- Colleges of business saw this program as their exclusive territory, although as a major it was far less established or important than management, finance or marketing. The idea that it could be taught in other colleges, or in other departments, was not even considered.

We soon realized that educators at the local and state levels were the major barriers to providing experiences in business creation. Over the course of the next thirty years, we established a vision and mission to help overcome educational barriers to "entrepreneurship education everywhere."

What Is Entrepreneurship Education?

We define entrepreneurship education as not just one course taught out of one textbook. This led us to advocate the importance of the lifelong learning process. Namely, we believe that all kinds of experiences, from elementary levels through college and adult education, are important to encourage an entrepreneurial mindset. Those experiences might even replace the opportunities some entrepreneurs had in growing up around an entrepreneur. Of course, we recognize that all young people will not choose to become entrepreneurs—but a firsthand, practical understanding of how the economic system works can also make them productive and innovative workers.

By mid-1980, we introduced the lifelong learning model[28] to show that there were different purposes for teaching entrepreneurship throughout education. Because the student goals were

---

28   See "A Lifelong Learning Process," http://www.entre-ed.org/Standards_Toolkit/nurturing.htm.

different, there were many different types of experiences and content used.

This "Lifelong Learning Process" became our framework for reaching out to thousands of educators across the country. Although we had been offering teacher training workshops in many states and marketing curriculum resources across the country, we recognized that we could not do the whole job that way. So we turned to innovative educators and organizations to join with the Consortium and expand the field for entrepreneurship through teacher training.

How Do We Teach Entrepreneurship?

The Consortium's lifelong learning message that "no one organization can do it all" encouraged the creation of innovative programs for diverse student groups in all parts of the country. Consortium members and nonmembers alike used their creativity and opportunities to add entrepreneurship education experiences for all kinds of programs. These were both as standalone courses and, more often, infusion in existing courses.

The following models and best practices can serve as guidelines for educators:

Elementary school: At early grade levels, the goal is for all children to understand the components of business, society and government in their hometowns. Experiences in how a business works and practice in creating a business idea that solves a customer problem are often introduced at this level. Designing a product and trying to sell it can teach the laws of supply and demand. Teachers may not know it, but there are entrepreneurs in every neighborhood who will help students. At the same time, these young children can develop life skills and practice basic academic math and communications skills.

Some of the successful examples of this type of program include Marketplace for Kids (ND), Lemonade Day (TX), and TREP$ (NJ).

Middle school: Youth in grades six through eight can begin to think about their own special interests and abilities, and where their passions fit into the career opportunities they are encouraged to explore. Of course, many have not even begun to think about their futures, but experiences with community entrepreneurs as well as moneymaking projects in the schools can open up new possibilities. When focusing on financial literacy, which often begins in the middle grades, these young people can apply money-management skills to their own businesses as well as to consumer needs.

Students are eager to explore career options as they seek ways to fulfill their personal dreams. They need to explore all career clusters that are of interest to them, including the entrepreneurial options in each cluster. Some interesting teaching models for this level include Junior Achievement (nationwide), E-Discovery Challenge (KY), Making a Job (NY), and many summer camps such as those offered by the Delaware Financial Literacy Institute.

High school: Teenagers have the capacity to be innovative and entrepreneurial, but this is rarely tapped while they are in high school. Instead, we see a major dropout problem, often attributed to boredom and lack of engagement in the learning process. A study commissioned by the Bill & Melinda Gates Foundation in 2006 surveyed students who had dropped out of high school and learned that the decision to drop out was linked closely to the lack of challenge and connection to real-life experience faced by students in the public school system.[29] Yet the connections between academic concepts and entrepreneurship allows real-world context for almost every

---

29   John M. Bridgeland, John J. Dilulio, Jr. and Karen Burke Morison, *The Silent Epidemic: Perspectives of High School Dropouts*, (Bill & Melinda Gates Foundation, March 2006).

academic concept currently taught and tested in the United States in core academic subjects.

Career Clusters, which are part of the career education focus on different Career Pathways and component clusters, provide opportunities to help students pursue areas of particular interest. However, most of the skill and knowledge statements in the cluster performance indicators do not include development of entrepreneurial skills, in spite of the fact that every one of the Career Pathways includes opportunities for creating your own business. An emphasis on creating business plans for competition in student organizations such as Distributive Education Clubs of America (DECA), Future Business Leaders of America-Phi Beta Lambda (FBLA-PBL), Family, Career and Community Leaders of America (FCCLA), National FFA Organization, and Skills-USA provides experiences for students that support entrepreneurial skill development.

Emphasizing STEM (science, technology, engineering, and math) encourages specialization that leads to workplace and college preparation, but it has not generally included entrepreneurship or the skills needed to commercialize new ideas generated in the STEM program.

The Partnership for 21st Century Skills has identified entrepreneurship as a content area that was overlooked in the last century, and entrepreneurial literacy is now part of their *Framework for 21st Century Learning*.[30] Most of these skills can best be taught in an entrepreneurial context because of the focus of the skills (including personal responsibility, personal productivity, leadership, ethics, self-direction, critical thinking and problem solving, creativity and innovation, communication and information skills, and collaboration skills).

---

30   Partnership for 21st Century Skills, *Framework for 21st Century Learning*, (Washington, DC), 2, http://www.p21.org/storage/documents/1.__p21_framework_2-pager.pdf.

There is growing interest in supporting entrepreneurship education in the high schools, but little real preparation for the teachers who must implement it. Programs such as REAL Enterprises, NFTE, Generation-E, JA, EntrepreneurShip Investigation (ESI) at the University of Nebraska-Lincoln, and many others offer teacher training as part of providing curriculum for the classroom.

Colleges: Colleges are now recognizing that, in addition to the business department, there are specialties across all departments that greatly benefit from access to entrepreneurship education course options. This is true in both the community and four-year colleges.

There are a wealth of textbooks written by professors to support their courses. Competitions involving writing business plans are also available for college students, within and between campuses. Currently, most US colleges offer some form of entrepreneurship education, nationally encouraged by National Association for Community College Entrepreneurship (NACCE), REAL Enterprises (GA, NC, VT and other state organizations), SBA online courses, the Kauffman Foundation's FASTTRAC Program, and the U.S. Association for Small Business and Entrepreneurship (USASBE).

Adult education: When circumstances leave people unemployed or underemployed, one solution is starting a small business. There are a number of short training programs through community colleges, via U.S. Small Business Administration (SBA) networks and in continuing education programs. If a person is considering this solution, it is first important they determine the areas of training needed. To accomplish this, the Consortium developed and recommends a checklist of what you need to learn using our *National Content Standards for Entrepreneurship Education* and the U.S. Department of Labor's newly released "Entrepreneurship Competency Model."[31] The theory for teaching adults is based on experiential learning, which is also the best way to present entrepreneurial concepts.

Resources for Teachers and Educators

The Consortium's leadership role has provided a wealth of information and activities to share innovative strategies for creating new programs in every state and local community.

- Our website's goal is to share the whole field in an easy-to-access format and an open-to-submissions message.[32]
- *National Content Standards for Entrepreneurship Education* were created with input from early-stage entrepreneurs. The 403 competency statements in 15 standards are freely available to bring unity to the field.[33]
- The Entrepreneurship FORUM is the annual professional development conference focused on every step in the lifelong learning process.[34]
- *Future CEO Stars Magazine* provides stories of personal business ventures written by students in member organizations. These are great resources for teachers to use in any classroom.[35]
- National Entrepreneurship Week, announced by Congress in 2006, honors American entrepreneurs and the education

---

31   *National Content Standards for Entrepreneurship Education*, Consortium for Entrepreneurship Education, 2004, http://www.entre-ed.org/Standards_Toolkit/ and "Entrepreneurship Competency Model," U.S. Department of Labor, Employment and Training Administration, accessed February 18, 2012, http://www.careeronestop.org/competencymodel/pyramid.aspx?ENTRE=Y.

32   See http://www.entre-ed.org.

33   *National Content Standards for Entrepreneurship Education*.

34   See http://www.entre-ed.org/_network/forum.htm.

35   See http://www.fcsmag.com.

programs that are preparing our future entrepreneurial leaders.[36]

- The Youth Entrepreneurship Alliance was formed in 2009 to focus on national priorities to support youth entrepreneurship education.[37]

The Future of Entrepreneurship Education

The significance of entrepreneurship to the American economy can no longer be overlooked, nor can it be assumed that you must be born with the right genes to become a self-reliant business creator. In fact, anyone can start a business, no matter how large or small. Remember, more than 21 million out of 27.5 million businesses have zero employees (just the owner) and report an average income of $46,000 a year.[38]

Believers in the importance of entrepreneurship education are invited to join the Consortium in providing our youth with the knowledge, skills, and mindset to build their own careers and become self-reliant. The Consortium will continue to provide educators at all levels of preparation with the resources and visibility that will encourage and empower them to make major changes in the education of tomorrow's self-reliant adults.

---

36   See http://www.entre-week.org.

37   See http://www.YEAleaders.org

38   "Frequently Asked Questions," U.S. Small Business Administration's Advocacy Small Business Statistics and Research, accessed February 18, 2012, http://web.sba.gov/faqs/faqIndexAll.cfm?areaid=24.

Dr. Cathy Ashmore is Executive Director for the Consortium for Entrepreneurship Education. Created at The Ohio State University, The Consortium is the primary national advocate for the growth of entrepreneurship education nationwide as a lifelong learning process. Serving as executive director of the Consortium since 1980, Dr. Ashmore provided leadership in creating entrepreneurship curriculum and programs, training teachers, developing databases, studying young entrepreneurs, surveying business owners/teachers/students, organizing and managing professional development conferences, and managing the advocacy initiatives of the Consortium nationwide. From 1990-1996 Dr. Ashmore was directly involved with programs that brought entrepreneurship training to the newly developing market economies of Poland, Hungary, Romania, Russia, South Africa and Kyrgyzstan. Dr. Ashmore is a 1990 recipient of the Leavey Award for Excellence in Private Enterprise Education awarded by The Freedoms Foundation of Valley Forge, PA. She is past president of the United States Association for Small Business and Entrepreneurship. In 2006 she received the Lifetime Achievement Award from USASBE in recognition of her contributions in building the field of entrepreneurship education. At a recent Entrepreneurship FORUM the Consortium Board initiated an Award in her name, and awarded it to her as the first recipient.

Consortium for
**Entrepreneurship
Education**

How Our Community Colleges Are Creating New Jobs Nationwide

Heather Van Sickle, Executive Director,
National Association for Community
College Entrepreneurship

Please take advantage of me, and of my ignorance!

It was 2007, and the National Association for Community College Entrepreneurship (NACCE) had just launched our student essay contest, asking students why they thought it was important for their local community college to offer entrepreneurship education.

"I have a BFA in Computer Graphics," the student continued. "I was taught to create, design, inspire, animate but not taught how to price my work, how to negotiate a fair deal, how to manage my finances or be aware of my rights. This ignorance of mine gives my clients and employees the opportunity to take advantage of me. And this knowledge that I'm missing blinds me from recognizing opportunities that I should be taking advantage of."

I knew that feeling! Sitting in my chair, reading this Kingsborough Community College student's essay, I could feel what he felt:

the adrenaline coursing through my body as if I had just averted a car accident.

It is the same feeling that spurs me on every day in my work with NACCE to ensure that community colleges educate their students and the broader community on the powerful impact entrepreneurship has in creating success for individuals and whole regions. NACCE's vision is "creating economic vitality through entrepreneurship." It's all too easy to be intimidated by the notion of running your own business when you have little or no business experience. Our member colleges provide a safe environment to consider what it means to be an entrepreneur or a small business owner; they are a place to try out ideas, ask questions, and get connected to mentors in the community who can help guide the way to a better future.

I have a quiet confidence in my abilities to figure things out, thinking of myself as a "scrapper" with a love of underdog status. However, I have often cried tears of frustration while figuring things out knowing there must be a better way, a little tweak in thinking, like when you can't open a door you've been pushing on and someone yells out "Pull!" Through my work with NACCE's members, I have come to strongly believe that knowledge of how entrepreneurship works should be part of every young person's education.

Education Takes Many Forms

My father owned a mechanics shop specializing in Volkswagen repair. We lived in an old house (built in 1783) that was heated entirely by firewood; the house was located on a sixty-acre piece of property that always needed work done. We learned from a young age that work was just something you did as a contributing family member. The older kids worked in the garage with my dad and the younger ones, including me, stacked wood in the fall, put hay up in the summer, and did whatever else needed doing. I remember envying my friends because they had simple chores, like feeding the cat or dog.

As a result, I never saw a distinction between working for someone else or creating your own business. The idea that you are selling yourself and your abilities, whether it is to one person (your employer) or many people (your customers), was something that wasn't overtly taught, but understood. I learned early on that if you are willing to do what most people won't, you will always have work.

When my husband mentioned that he wanted to start his own business soon after we were married, I immediately had something along the lines of the opening sentence of that student's essay flash through my thoughts. Although I was raised with a strong work ethic, hard work alone can only take you so far. In his book *Be A Sales Superstar*, Brian Tracy writes, "You cannot get more or better results by simply working harder using your present abilities. If you want to earn more in the future, you must learn and apply new methods and techniques."[39]

Where could I find "new methods and techniques?" I had a copy of the local community college course catalog that had been mailed to my house, and I noticed that they were offering courses in entrepreneurship. I signed up. All I needed were some suggestions, tips, and new ways to look at things so I could be more confident.

How to Support Entrepreneurship in Community Colleges Nationwide

Learning is a lifelong process and can be very enjoyable; however, the structured educational system is at times at odds with cultivating the very interests it hopes to leverage in young students. Entrepreneurship is a mindset that needs to be inculcated throughout the

---

39   Brian Tracy, *Be a Sales Superstar: 21 Great Ways to Sell More, Faster, Easier in Tough Markets*, (San Francisco: Berrett-Koehler Publishers, Inc., 2003), Google e-book, chap. 6.

educational system and, indeed, throughout entire communities. In our free market economy, we are all participants, producers, and consumers of goods and services, so it makes sense to infuse those concepts and experiences throughout the educational process, both amongst disciplines and along the continuum of education.

A Kauffman Foundation report entitled *Entrepreneurship in American Higher Education* observes, "Entrepreneurship naturally and authentically draws together subjects usually taught and studied separately."[40] If subject areas such as the arts or STEM (science, technology, engineering and math) are taught through the lens of entrepreneurship, those subjects come alive. Students are not just creating art for art's sake, or inventing products that will never work in the market; rather, they are taught to provide solutions to problems in their communities. When students are taught to actively seek out challenges and to view them as opportunities to create a solution, education becomes extremely relevant.

Until they are graded and "tracked" according to artificial success measures, kids aren't afraid to fail and try new things. Catering to the natural inquisitiveness of children and shaping them as they explore the world through outcomes-based learning allows youth to understand how what they are learning fits into their real lives. And entrepreneurship is the perfect vehicle for practical application.

Across the country, NACCE member colleges are actively building pathways to entrepreneurship that often begin in grade school, continue through high school, and then move into the community colleges. North Iowa Area Community College (NIACC) in Mason City, Iowa, teaches fifth graders the difference between being an employee and being an entrepreneur. Their hope is to create more entrepreneurs in their rural community. During the first day

---

40 *Entrepreneurship in American Higher Education*, (Kauffman Foundation, 2006), 10, http://www.kauffman.org/uploadedfiles/entrep_high_ed_report.pdf.

of this two-session program, NIACC trained facilitators visit the students' classroom and introduce terms and concepts about entrepreneurship. On the second day, students visit the NIACC campus where they choose a product, borrow money from a "bank," buy resources they will need, make the product, and then sell the product and determine if they've made a profit. The visit ends with a tour of NIACC that offers students a sense of campus life and validates college for these students, many of whom will be the first in their families to attend college.

At the high-school level, Cayuga Community College in Auburn, NY, shares its infusion model of entrepreneurship with area high schools, and helped establish an annual Business Plan Competition through which students could test their new skills. In the program's first two years, 160 teens learned about entrepreneurship in their English classes and in specific career and trade programs. They develop a business plan for a product that they will sell to their peers and then, in the annual Business Plan Competition, they make ten-minute presentations and vie for cash awards. In short, the students learn to parlay practical expertise into innovation plans for small businesses that will ultimately benefit the community. Competition winners thus far have included business plans for a dog obedience training school, a cloud hardware sharing company, a traveling spa and salon, and a graphic design firm.

I imagine if all K-12 students went through exercises like this, they wouldn't feel like I did, sitting through my algebra classes in high school and wondering what the information had to do with anything I might ever use. If I had the opportunity to apply that knowledge to something that had a practical outcome—a use in the marketplace I engaged in everyday outside the school walls—a sense of accomplishment would have reinforced my learning, encouraging continued curiosity and an interest in learning more. It would have created a momentum of learning.

The challenge, then, is how to make sure this momentum and the enthusiasm for entrepreneurship behind it carries through to college. In California's Central Valley, a project called the Entrepreneur Pathway is underway to address this challenge. Led by the Lyles Center for Innovation and Entrepreneurship at California State University, Fresno and funded by the Coleman Foundation, the program provides common training to the high school and community college faculty to ensure that students receive an understanding of entrepreneurship that builds at each level. The educational material is not simply handed down from the university. Rather it is worked and reworked at all levels based on experiences and situations.

A second critical feature is articulation. The university is currently in the process of achieving articulation with eleven community colleges and nineteen high schools in their region. Students taking entrepreneurship at a high school can carry the credit to the community college and/or Fresno State. A third critical feature is monthly gatherings of faculty, who collaborate and share ideas for improvement in the delivery of entrepreneurship education.

The State of Entrepreneurship Efforts Today

The breadth of the entrepreneurship efforts at community colleges has expanded tremendously over the ten years since NACCE's formation in 2002. This increased interest and dedication to entrepreneurship education is highlighted by the fact that, since it became a membership organization in 2006, NACCE has attracted over three hundred community colleges as members. Our annual conference attracts over 450 administrators and faculty members, all of whom are seeking information on how their institutions can better serve their region's entrepreneurs. And our *Presidents for Entrepreneurship Forum*, launched in late 2011, has already prompted nearly 150 community college presidents, both NACCE members and nonmembers, to sign on to five commitments designed to spur entrepreneurship in their communities.

On campuses across the country, you'll find everything from degree programs in entrepreneurship to curriculum-infusion initiatives that bring entrepreneurship learning into all programs, so that no matter what profession young people are preparing themselves for, they are exposed to the concepts they'll need to launch their own businesses. Community colleges host entrepreneurship centers and incubators, both physical and virtual—and in some cases, they're even helping entrepreneurs gain access to funding.

These entrepreneurship education and support programs work because of the unique role community colleges play in the regions they serve. In many communities, the community college is now the nexus for economic development through entrepreneurship, moving far beyond the institution's traditional role in workforce development. This has occurred because of the unique assets community colleges have that make them such an appropriate setting for entrepreneurship education. These assets include:

- Partnerships in place with businesses and with economic development organizations that can help inform their development of educational and support programs for entrepreneurs and small business owners.
- Flexibility in addressing the economic development needs of their communities. This flexibility shows through in their scheduling of workshops, networking events and other resources for entrepreneurs so that they are accessible to ultra-busy small business owners and entrepreneurs.

- A welcoming atmosphere that makes all the difference to students of all ages and backgrounds who desire to learn about entrepreneurship. From high school students who want to get a jump start on learning about entrepreneurship, or mid-life individuals who have decided it is finally time to make their entrepreneurial dreams come true, community colleges know how to make these people feel at home and at ease.
- Affordability. These colleges are accustomed to doing a lot with a little and are adept at figuring out ways to make their offerings affordable.

These assets set community colleges apart and make them the perfect setting for making entrepreneurship education and support available to everyone. In doing so, they are democratizing entrepreneurship, taking it out of the realm of the MBA program and making it accessible to all.

Here are two examples of how community colleges directly spur entrepreneurial activity in a community, creating new jobs and products:

- Wisconsin mom Kristin Benson Ellsworth's business idea derived from solving a problem for her child. Her daughter loved to play dress up but refused to wear eyeglasses that were prescribed for her at the age of three. Kristin's solution was to develop Peeps Eyewear, an innovative company that combines kid-friendly glasses with motivational storybooks and dress-up accessories for preschool children. Kristin turned to her local community college, Fox Valley Technical College, for help and there she found a broad spectrum of resources at her disposal through the college's E-Seed Program. Perhaps most pivotal was the college's

Fab Lab, a fabrication facility where she was able to design a virtual 3D model of her product. Peeps Eyewear placed first in the Wisconsin Governor's Business Plan Contest in 2010 in the business services category. Kristin used her prize winnings to help fund Peeps. Now, her eyewear is being sold through five retailers and is available in ninety-five stores.

- In December 2010, entrepreneur Chris Angel opened Sparians Midtown Bowling Boutique, a 30,000 square-foot, $3.6 million complex in Raleigh, NC, that blends bowling, dining and family entertainment. Chris had been earning a six-figure salary in software marketing and sales yet still yearned to be an entrepreneur. He decided to enroll in "Planning the Entrepreneurial Venture," a Kauffman Foundation-developed course that is offered at Wake Technical Community College. The course prepared him to write what his instructor, a successful entrepreneur himself, said was the best business plan he's ever seen, a plan that enabled Chris to attract the venture capital he needed to open Sparians. The company employs about one hundred people, and Chris hopes to franchise the concept to other cities.

It's Never Too Early or Too Late

So, it comes down to this. What do we (as a collective) value, and what do we want to promote? How can we structure our educational systems to promote that which we value? If we acknowledge the role that entrepreneurs play in building our economy, and in creating jobs and security in our communities, then why aren't we demanding correlation between what is being taught in the classroom and the role those entrepreneurs play? It is time to stop having our children sit through hours of irrelevant classes with marginal benefit. It is time to prepare our youth for the real world. And our community colleges provide a practical, affordable and democratic place to start.

We know it's never too early or too late to be an entrepreneur, which is why NACCE works with community colleges, and emphasizes the critical role they play as the access point for opportunity in communities. Community colleges are often the connectors between the K-12 system and the universities, and of educating the adult population—including displaced workers and immigrants, and those requiring remedial education. They are an integral network of organizations throughout the country that provide access to opportunity and possibilities. And they educate students like Eduardo Minera, the student I quoted at the outset, who closed his essay by saying, "Thanks to Kingsborough Community College and its Entrepreneurial Program, now I can say, I'm no longer ignorant, and I dare you to take advantage of me!"

 *Heather Van Sickle* is executive director of the National Association for Community College Entrepreneurship (NACCE), an association representing educators, entrepreneurs, and distinguished business development professionals providing quality programs and services in entrepreneurship education at the community college level. Founded in 2002, NACCE is at the heart of the "entrepreneurship movement." Heather is personally influenced by a history of family entrepreneurs and inspired by the mindset of Frances Perkins, who famously said: "I came to Washington to work for…the millions of forgotten, plain common workingmen," and tirelessly

works to ensure entrepreneurship is accessible to any who choose to take it on. Through her work at NACCE, Heather and her team connect community colleges nation-wide through stories in their quarterly journal, *Community College Entrepreneurship*, face-to-face networking at their Annual Conference, and best practice models in printed form and on www.nacce.com. NACCE is a founding member of the White House-led Startup America Partnership. Heather lives in Western Massachusetts with her husband, Brett, and two kids, Madison and Jacob.

Learning Entrepreneurship Means Living Entrepreneurially:
An Action-Based Approach to Teaching Entrepreneurship at Colleges and Universities

Leonard A. Schlesinger, President, Babson College

When I became president of Babson College in July 2008, I was taking the helm at a school that was consistently ranked number one in entrepreneurship for its undergraduate and graduate programs. My own experience with entrepreneurship education was limited at best, and I had no detailed understanding of entrepreneurship as an academic discipline. I also had no idea that I would soon see a straight line between the work I was embarking on and the potential for changing the world through entrepreneurship.

Fast forward three and a half years, and entrepreneurship is more central than ever to Babson's strategy. Our faculty has developed a teaching method, Entrepreneurial Thought & Action® (ET&A), which applies the entrepreneurial mindset and behaviors to every aspect of academic and co-curricular life. ET&A is focused on action-based experiential learning and a pedagogy of practice—and this method can be learned and adapted to virtually any context.[41]

---

41 Research that led to ET&A's development includes Saras D. Sarasvathy, *Effectuation: Elements of Entrepreneurial Expertise* (2008); Peter Drucker, *Innovation and Entrepreneurship* (1985); and Danna Greenberg, Kate McKone-Sweet, and H. James Wilson, *The New Entrepreneurial Leader* (2011).

None of this was obvious to me in the fall of 2008, when the Great Recession was wreaking havoc on global financial markets and the economy. Understandably, many colleges and universities considered it a less than ideal time to embark on a growth strategy, but I believed that any institution that teaches entrepreneurship should also model it.

So we seized the moment, and Babson began a community-wide conversation about how we would cement and extend our position in entrepreneurship. This could not have been timelier because, with rapidly deteriorating conditions in the global economy, long-held assumptions about economic growth and the nature of entrepreneurship were being called into question.

Seizing the moment meant making entrepreneurship more pervasive than the discipline and connecting it to each department, division and person on campus. Throughout the fall of 2008, I met with every faculty and staff member in small group sessions on what entrepreneurship meant to them, what curriculum innovation would mean around a broader definition of entrepreneurship, and how we could develop our capacity to live entrepreneurship rather than just teach it. I also met individually with our trustees.

From these conversations, task forces were formed that brought together faculty from all disciplines. Their work set into motion a process leading to curriculum review and renewal in our undergraduate and graduate programs by embedding key concepts, such as ET&A and sustainability, into the curriculum.

The conversations also led to a staff and faculty Living Entrepreneurship Working Group to build a new framework for student engagement as an entrepreneurial learning experience that occurs inside and outside the classroom. Familiarity with what the faculty is teaching and how they are teaching it has enabled staff to reinforce those principles in all parts of the student experience.

What Is Distinctive about Our Framing of Entrepreneurship Education—and How Do We Execute on It?

ET&A is based on research showing that entrepreneurial leaders think and behave differently. Entrepreneurs start with an opportunity and the resources they have. They commit in advance to what they are willing to lose, so they can better assess what they want to do next. They look for "good enough" solutions, not necessarily what is optimal. Entrepreneurs also negotiate with stakeholders who are willing to make commitments to the venture and are ready to change goals based on who comes on board.

Taking a first step enables an entrepreneur to reflect on that action and learn from it. Taking another step provides new data for making entrepreneurial decisions and taking further action. Our entire college revolves around this orientation to taking action. This approach is broad, in-depth, and connects all academic disciplines, including arts and humanities. Also, ET&A as a way of describing our entrepreneurial teaching method and culture has proven to be important because language is critical in building strategy and aligning the community around entrepreneurship.

For undergraduate students this begins in their first days as freshmen with action-based learning in the required year-long Foundations of Management and Entrepreneurship (FME) course. With $3,000 in startup funds from the College, students work in teams to create, develop, launch, manage, and harvest a business—donating the profits of their enterprises to nonprofit groups. While other colleges teach venture creation in the junior or senior years, FME begins at the outset of the undergraduate experience. Putting this course up front in the educational program underscores how the teaching/learning model is going to be strikingly different throughout the undergraduate career. The curriculum enables students to recognize opportunities; work effectively in teams; learn marketing, accounting, and other disciplines related to running a business; think holistically; and develop a leadership style.

The Coaching for Leadership and Teamwork Program (CLTP) provides undergraduate students (first as freshmen and again as juniors or seniors) with developmental coaching on their leadership, communication, and interpersonal skills—all are essential for entrepreneurs. Coaches are generally alumni and current advanced MBA students who first go through a day of intensive training in coaching. At coaching sessions, student teams discuss cases dealing with ethics and problems that businesses encounter, and junior and seniors also do an "elevator pitch." Afterwards, coaches meet to discuss student performance; then students meet one on one with their coaches to receive confidential feedback and mentoring.

In an entrepreneurial culture, what we do and how we do it is always evolving. In 2009 I set out a challenge to the leaders at our Arthur M. Blank Center for Entrepreneurship to make our co-curricular programs for student entrepreneurs as innovative as our entrepreneurship curriculum. I wanted our team to rethink the new venture creation process to replicate the method we were advocating in ET&A. This resulted in the launch of our Venture Accelerator—a tiered program of workshops, advising, space, and mentoring for undergraduate and graduate students. Resources become more individualized as students move their ventures forward.

Most incubators or hatcheries deal only with ventures at the launch and grow level. We work with student entrepreneurs at three levels—explore, pursue, and launch-and-grow—and there is work space available at each level. Resources become more sophisticated as the venture develops. At the explore level, there is group mentoring and peer mentoring; at the launch-and-grow level, mentoring is individualized. Faculty advisers are available at each level. The results after the first year: Instead of working with twelve teams in a hatchery, we worked last year with over two hundred students and 190 venture ideas.

Not only do we teach students entrepreneurship, we teach them to live entrepreneurially. Students are in class for only about fourteen hours a week, spending most of their time—154 hours—elsewhere. We empower students to play an increasingly high-profile role in their own learning outside of class, thereby augmenting faculty-centered teaching with student-centered learning. Students experience leadership through their own actions rather than learning about leadership from others. This model allows students to be deeply involved not just in coming up with ideas, but in implementing those ideas.

Our students live entrepreneurship in myriad ways, including clubs, groups, out-of-the-classroom faculty interactions, business startups and shutdowns. It's not just about what they start but how they start it, and each generation of students makes its own Babson experience.

A case in point is our special-interest housing. Students with a shared interest—such as entrepreneurship, healthy living, and sustainability—can request space in a residence hall. Each community of students lines up a faculty adviser, runs its own programming, works with the facilities and residence life staff, organizes activities to be a resource to the rest of campus, and holds its members accountable for the way the community operates.

Last spring a student from one of our special interest residence halls invited Daymond John, CEO of FUBU and host of ABC's *Shark*

Tank TV show, to come to campus. The student found out that he needed to raise funds to bring him to campus and, after succeeding, worked with the Administration to invite him to become Babson's first African American entrepreneur-in-residence. Daymond John is working with two graduate Management Consulting Field Experience teams to vet and bring to market product opportunities that were featured on his show, and is engaged with students on campus in many more ways. It all began with one tenacious student.

Of course, not every student-led initiative or program is successful. Living and learning entrepreneurially provides one of the most powerful frameworks to get students to appreciate the need to take calculated risks—figure out when a risk is worth taking—and learn from failures. Providing opportunities for students to think and act entrepreneurially gets them to be aware of, and accept, the role of failure in the entrepreneurial experience.

Entrepreneurship encompasses leadership in enterprises of all sizes, in all stages of growth, and in any setting. We believe in educating entrepreneurial leaders—some may choose to start new businesses, others may participate in family businesses, some may create new products and processes within existing organizations, and still others may engage in new social ventures, services, or movements. This is not the case at most schools, where entrepreneurship is defined narrowly as new venture creation. Also, social entrepreneurship is typically seen as separate from entrepreneurship. We maintain that there is one kind of entrepreneurship—and it's about creating economic and social value...everywhere.

Partnering with like-minded institutions multiplies new kinds of entrepreneurial opportunities. Babson is partnering globally and locally with other institutions in ways we could never have imagined a few years ago.

In 2009, Babson joined a three-college consortium with the F.W. Olin College of Engineering and Wellesley College. The idea was to enable students, faculty, and staff to reshape undergraduate education in ways that leverage the capacities that exist on three very different campuses. It would probably have been a nonstarter if the three college presidents decided how to engage their communities. Instead, we opted for a "bottoms up" approach, enabling our communities to find and create opportunities...and they have. For example, the faculty initiated a three-college sustainability certificate that was launched last fall that integrates business, engineering, and liberal arts and sciences; and students are leading a biweekly ideas discussion series.

How Can Other Schools Build an Environment for Living and Learning Entrepreneurship?

Here are some thoughts for other college presidents:

1. **Define what entrepreneurship means for your institution; involve faculty, staff, students, and governance in the process; and make sure it fits with your culture.** Take small steps to test out how new ideas and pilot projects might work. Align all your communications on and off campus to reinforce the way you are framing entrepreneurship education.

2. **For entrepreneurship to be taught it must be unleashed.** Unleash the capacity of faculty, staff, and students by giving them the space to come up with new ideas and encourage them to try something different. The key is to create incentives for a culture around allowing people to pursue

their passion—as long as there's the potential for engaging the community.

One way I do this is through the strategic use of the President's discretionary budget—pockets of small amounts of money that are seeded broadly around the campus. Each of these expenditures should be on message with the way you have framed entrepreneurship. An advantage of this approach is that it is not costly to the institution. High energy is the resource that matters the most at this stage.

On the student side, create an environment where there are plenty of leadership opportunities—for example, to run conferences, reach out to alumni and others for resources, arrange for other institutions as co-sponsors, and draw in professionals from the area. The message is clear: If you want to have a forum or start a program, it's up to you.

3. **Convene a multidisciplinary faculty group around broadening entrepreneurship.** In the case of our faculty task force that focused on ET&A in the curriculum, the co-chairs were not from the entrepreneurship division. One outcome of the task force could be the design of a course that builds your own brand around entrepreneurship. FME is our signature undergraduate course, and many students are attracted to Babson because of it.

4. **Facilitate a set of cross-campus conversations that look beyond the classroom experience.** Most of these conversations should include students. We have listened to how students describe what it means to live entrepreneurially and the challenges from their perspective—and these do not necessarily match what faculty and staff have assumed.

5. **Build a culture of entrepreneurial leadership among alumni and celebrate them.** Every school has alumni who are successful entrepreneurs, so find and engage them. Use alumni as a central part of the living and learning experience rather than only as an extended part of the institutional network. Whether they become adjuncts, entrepreneurs-in-residence, coaches in a program similar to Babson's CLTP, or keynoters at student-run forums, alumni entrepreneurs can have an enormous impact on students.

6. **As you broaden your school's definition to embrace living as well as learning entrepreneurship, hire faculty and staff who are going to fit well into the culture.** New hires should be able to work collaboratively with their colleagues across disciplines and departments and commit to your framing of entrepreneurship education.

7. **Multiply the possibilities for action-based learning by partnering with institutions in ways that lead to entrepreneurial opportunities.** For Babson this includes a network of colleges and universities across the world that are committed to entrepreneurship education—enabling each school to benefit from the most innovative approaches and latest advances in faculty and curriculum development around entrepreneurship.

One final thought: Spend as much time with people outside your institution as with those who are on campus. I have found that chance encounters with individuals who are doing interesting work have led to some rewarding relationships for the school that have strengthened our entrepreneurial activities. These encounters also give me more opportunities to talk about why Babson exists, what we are trying to do, and why it matters.

Three and a half years ago, I did not consider myself an entrepreneur. Today, I know that college presidents can be especially effective as entrepreneurs—and I'm doing whatever I can to "spread the gospel" about what is the most powerful force in the world for economic and social value creation.

Leonard A. Schlesinger became President of Babson College in 2008 after serving as Vice Chairman and COO of Limited Brands. He also spent over 20 years teaching at Harvard Business School, where he led MBA and executive education programs and was architect and chair of Harvard Business School's MBA Essential Skills and Foundations programs. He is author or co-author of eleven books, including *Just Start: Take action, Embrace uncertainty, Create the future* (Harvard Business Review Press, 2012). At Babson he has led a strategy of broadening the method for teaching entrepreneurship—Entrepreneurial Thought & Action®—extending the context through Entrepreneurship of All Kinds®, and taking Babson's pedagogy to the world. In 2011, the Historically Black Colleges and Universities named him the Most Entrepreneurial University President in the U.S.

How to Graduate More High-Growth Entrepreneurs

Doug Mellinger, Trustee, Cogswell Polytechnical College

The United States of America was founded by a group of entrepreneurs. The success of this country is built on the backs of great entrepreneurs during the agrarian age, industrial age, and now the information age. And our future is going to be stronger because of the innovation, employment, and wealth created by tomorrow's entrepreneurs and the companies they lead.

Yet this has happened largely in spite of the education system. Too much of the real-world education that entrepreneurs need to succeed happens after their formal education, in the "school of hard knocks." In a Zogby poll of 2,141 Americans commissioned by Cogswell Polytechnical College, 93 percent of the eighteen- to twenty-four-year-olds surveyed stated that entrepreneurship is "very important" to the future competitiveness of the US economy—and 62 percent said the most effective way to teach someone to become an entrepreneur was by creating a small business or interning in a startup. Only 2 percent said it was through class work or lectures. Another 57 percent said that launching companies in college would make them more successful in creating companies and jobs.[42]

---

42   "College Students Aren't Getting Entrepreneurial Skills; Schools Need to Focus on Giving Start-Up Experience, According to New National Poll," Reuters (press release), May 13, 2011, http://www.reuters.com/article/2011/05/13/idUS151878+13-May-2011+PRN20110513.

Our education system can and should play a more critical role in developing tomorrow's rapid-growth entrepreneurs by providing the inspiration, academic framework, and experiential activities they need. The education system can also form a critical part of the ecosystem that supports the infrastructure needed to accelerate entrepreneurial ventures. Great athletes, artists, and business people all practice their skills over and over before they become second nature. We need the same approach to our country's most valuable natural resource: our entrepreneurs.

Planting the Seeds for a Culture of US Entrepreneurship

Growing up, I experimented with various business ventures without ever hearing the word "entrepreneur." At Syracuse University, I pursued a degree in computer science. One day in the spring of my freshman year, as I was walking through the business school, I saw a poster with the word "entrepreneur" on it. I was fascinated with the word and what it meant; I felt for the first time that there was a word to describe who I was.

I approached the dean about studying to be an entrepreneur and getting a degree in entrepreneurship. After he stopped laughing, he told me there was no such thing. I was appalled by this answer. The year was 1983, and there was virtually no entrepreneurship education happening in the United States or the rest of the world.

A group of students and I started an organization for collegiate entrepreneurs at Syracuse University, and then we found other students at schools such as Wichita State University, MIT, Harvard, Babson and Boston University, beginning a movement and an organization called the Association of Collegiate Entrepreneurs (ACE).

ACE grew dramatically throughout the 1980s to eventually include over ten thousand students, professors and young entrepreneurs. There were only about five schools with entrepreneurship classes in the early '80s; by the end of decade, there were over six hundred schools.

The Evolution of Modern Entrepreneurship in the 1980s and 1990s

Personally, I was fortunate to have a wonderful man named Barry Wells, who was then the dean of academic affairs at Syracuse, work with me to create my own major in entrepreneurial science. I am proud to be the first graduate at Syracuse University to have an entrepreneurial degree, and one of the first in the world to have such a degree.

In the early '80s, the United States did not have a culture that celebrated youth entrepreneurship. You were still expected to join a big company and stay there your whole career. As such, the group of students who started ACE all believed that we had three missions: one, to create a network of young entrepreneurs to support each other; two, to create educational programs to educate entrepreneurs both in the classroom and outside the classroom; and three, to create credibility for the movement.

In 1986, we created the ACE 100 list of the top young entrepreneurs under the age of thirty, based on revenue. We wanted the media to stop calling us "whiz kids" and instead write about the great companies we were creating and the economic impact we were having in our communities and on the lives of the people we employed.

That very first list included people who today are household personalities, people who led world-changing companies—including Steve Jobs of Apple Computer, Michael Dell of Dell Computer, Julie Brice of I Can't Believe It's Yogurt, Mitch Kapor of Lotus Software, and Neil Balter of California Closets—and many more who would go on to change the world, but who were all very young when they started. The list even included names like Mark Cuban, who had a very small company back then, but who went on to become a billionaire.

These entrepreneurs, along with the educational programs that were started in the 1980s, provided the inspiration for an entrepreneurial revolution in the 1990s. If you look back at most of the great companies, you will find that they were started by young entrepreneurs. Great entrepreneurs start young, when they have very little to lose—or in the words of the late Steve Jobs, "He did not know he could not do it." The naiveté of youth is critical for an entrepreneur's success.

Unfortunately, the entrepreneurial education ecosystem did not integrate the non-academic experiential activities of organizations like ACE into the academic program then. Many of the early professors who were entrepreneurs themselves were pushed out by the "publish or peril" mindset of most colleges. By the end of the 1990s, theory reigned, and the majority of professors teaching entrepreneurship had never had to make payroll in their lives.

Why Youth Entrepreneurship Education Matters

We rely on entrepreneurs to create new companies that take advantage of emerging technologies and fill gaps in the marketplace. While entrepreneurs are the ones who lead countries out of recessions, it is hard to find examples of highly successful entrepreneurs who become known for their first business. Most entrepreneurs will start two, three or more companies before they find the successful formula. Additionally, most entrepreneurs' careers start very young. They experiment in their teens with companies like lemonade stands, painting companies, and lawn-care companies.

In other words, entrepreneurship is a career—and entrepreneurs need practice and experience to become great leaders.

This is natural and logical. Entrepreneurs are no different than large corporate employees. Large corporations do not hire college graduates to be their CEOs. Employees enter a company at the bottom, and work their way up the ladder as they learn the critical knowledge, skills and develop their networks. Why would this be any different for successful entrepreneurs?

To improve young entrepreneurs' chance of success, the education system should begin teaching entrepreneurship in elementary school and gradually add more sophistication and experiential learning. In addition to the more theoretical subjects taught in the classroom, it is important to give students real work experiences so they can learn by doing.

What can happen as a result of learning entrepreneurship early is stunning. In the 1980s, I met a group of fifth and sixth graders from an elementary school in Hunt, TX who blew me away. They came with their teacher, Tracy Gilbreth, to the ACE conference. The moment I met these young entrepreneurs, I realized that there was something special about them.

In 1973, the Hunt 5th & 6th Grade Class, Inc. was formed to provide a laboratory for the students to learn and grow. The business ran the school store, manufactured products, and put on mock trials and gave speeches throughout the United States on the free enterprise system. At the end of each year, the sixth-grade class took a school trip funded by the profits of the business, and then donated a gift to the school. Tracy worked to incorporate all of the classes into the business in some way. For example, the math class would use the financial statements as a way to learn their math lessons, and they met with bankers on a regular basis. In science class, they studied weather, earthquakes and geology, leading to the development of a weather rock that they sold in Sharper Image. (One of the weather rocks was even in the Oval Office during the Reagan Administration.) These kids all loved school, because they were able to take academic, theoretical knowledge and apply it to the real world.

Today, there are programs like Junior Achievement, which I belonged to in high school. It was clearly part of my entrepreneurial journey—which started around the age of ten, when I started my first quasi-business mowing lawns and then getting some kids to do lawn work and tar driveways for me. But why aren't schools—and specifically, colleges—doing more?

One Solution: Designing More Integrated Entrepreneurship Colleges

This country needs entrepreneurs who are going to build the next generation of high-impact Fortune 500 companies—and add hundreds, thousands, and even tens of thousands of jobs. But to do so, we need to reduce the amount of time to success and the total number of failures that entrepreneurs make. We need an ecosystem of financiers, suppliers, customers, accountants, lawyers and others to start interfacing with the students while they are still in school.

One way to do this is to have a large number of schools completely integrate the academic and practical experiences of entrepreneurship into one cohesive program. We also need this program offered to science and arts students, because those are the fields where most entrepreneurs actually come from. Business students often lack the expertise in an industry to start a company or have that next killer technology idea—most entrepreneurs I know studied computer science, engineering, art, math or some other subject, and then hired business students to do their marketing, sell their products and be their CFOs. Yet most entrepreneurship programs today are embedded in the business school, and have set up hurdles and land mines for nonbusiness students to get into the courses. It just does not make sense.

During the last year, I have been involved with Cogswell Polytechnical College, which is a design, engineering and digital-media college based in Silicon Valley. Together we have launched an entrepreneurship program that is completely integrated with the rest of the school. Its initial design was based on my twenty-nine years of hands-on experience with young entrepreneurs through my involvement with ACE and Entrepreneurs' Organization (EO), as well as my experience starting and growing companies.

The idea was to design a program that graduated growth-oriented entrepreneurs by combining Cogswell's emphasis on digital media and engineering with real-world business experience starting and interning in high-growth, entrepreneurial companies. Why should entrepreneurship degrees not be the same as law, architecture, computer science, medical, performing arts or any other specialized degree offered at universities today? Medical students do not sit in class and talk about dissecting a frog—they do it. Computer science students do not just talk about writing software—they do it. Performing arts majors do not just sit in class talking about putting on a musical—they do it. And this is exactly what all entrepreneurship majors should do: They should work in an entrepreneurial business while still in school.

The goal of Cogswell's program today is twofold:

- **Impact.** Our focus is on working with people who want to accelerate or launch high-growth companies, which have a greater impact on new job creation.

- **Scalability.** We want to graduate young, high-growth entrepreneurs—or students who are prepared to perform well in an entrepreneurial environment—in the thousands, not a few dozen or even one hundred, as other similar programs have done.

To refine it, we hired a team, including Chuck House (Cogswell's current chancellor), who came to us from Stanford's renowned Media X@ program, and then the team worked directly with the engineering and digital-media departments already in place. We want the students studying gaming or 3D animation, who often have a dream of building the next great Facebook, XBox or Apple App Store game, to learn everything they need to graduate as an entrepreneur.

And that means that we want students to understand what company offices look like, what each function actually does, what types of employees work in each functional area and what tools they use to do their jobs. We want them to understand the nuts and bolts too, like why they would want to start their company as an LLC vs. a C corporation vs. an S corporation. They need to understand global markets and global sourcing.

More importantly, they will work in an entrepreneurial business while in school and tie the experiential learning back to their classes. Entrepreneurship students should build their own ecosystem and their own network of fellow entrepreneurs. This is not just about writing a business plan—it is about going all the way through the launch, with all the successes and failures that go along with it. Initiatives like Cogswell's E-Tours, which take students through dozens of entrepreneurial companies and conduct exploratory meetings with founding teams, must go hand-in-hand with required internships and entrepreneurial forums for peer learning. Hopefully, students will launch or prepare to launch their own businesses during their senior year.

The growing demand for Cogswell's unique program is extraordinary. We doubled the school in 2011, and are anticipating doubling it again in 2012. When we started, the school had a little over one hundred students; we anticipate having approximately five hundred by the end of 2012.

The idea of an integrated program of entrepreneurship with vertical degrees is not rocket science. Many schools could implement this idea if they become committed to being a part of the economic recovery and long-term growth of the United States. The first step is to align the programs and activities of the college with the end game: graduate entrepreneurs, or accelerate businesses. If you put the students first, then the solution becomes easier to architect and execute. The strategy that is being implemented at Cogswell along with other programs such as Acton and Babson can and should provide the model for others to replicate.

One of the barriers often cited at universities is the accreditation demand. We need to work with the accreditors to design programs that both support the stringent academic program while also providing the needed knowledge, skills and experiences to be prepared to launch their own business, if that is their goal. I am certain this can be accomplished if we begin with the end game in mind when the program is being designed.

This country needs tens of thousands of new entrepreneurs who build growth companies, because growth-oriented wealth creators are the ones who will create the most new jobs. The educational system can play a critical role in this starting in elementary school and proceeding through college. The United States has a strategic advantage over much of the world, because we celebrate entrepreneurship today and look at failure as a badge of honor. A business or venture can fail, but an entrepreneur never fails.

 **_Doug Mellinger_** is a Managing Director at Palm Ventures and focuses on investments in the education, business services, technology, financial services and health and wellness sectors. Mr. Mellinger is on the boards of Cogswell College, Palm Publishing, Acrossworld, Producteev, Ascentis, IEC and until recently was the Chairman of Sequest Technologies which was sold to Netsmart Technologies. Mr. Mellinger was the founder and Vice-Chairman of Foundation Source, the nation's leading provider of outsourced services for private foundations, serving over 1000 of the wealthiest families in the US from 2000 until his retirement in 2011. Previously, he was a Partner at Interactive Capital Partners where he founded six companies, including Foundation Source. Before Interactive Capital Partners, he was CEO of Enherent (formerly PRT Group), a global software development and services company which he founded in 1989 and ran until 1999. He was named Entrepreneur of the Year for New England, CEO of an Inc 500 company twice and created one of the top 100 software companies. Mr. Mellinger is a founder of the Young Entrepreneurs Organization and was the International Director for the Association of Collegiate Entrepreneurs after graduating from Syracuse University with one of the first degrees in Entrepreneurship in the world. He has been active in the philanthropic and civic sectors through volunteer and board service with organizations such as the Young Presidents' Organization, Norwalk Maritime Aquarium, Stepping Stones Museum for Children, Clark University, University of New Mexico, SUNY Stony Brook and London Business School's Centers for Entrepreneurship, Kauffman Foundation Center for Entrepreneurial Leadership, National Commission on Entrepreneurship, Small Business Administration, US Patent and Trademark Office and many others during his career.

Reinventing Career Exploration and Counseling

Jennifer Kushell, Founder, Young & Successful Media

O ver the past twenty years, I've built my career around helping young people discover their career paths and find success. With The Young Entrepreneurs Network in 1993, we created the first online community to connect aspiring, emerging and successful entrepreneurs and prove that owning a business at a young age was a viable option.

After the dot-com crash, we shifted our energies to Young & Successful Media—to explore how young people in any field could accomplish incredible things by taking a more entrepreneurial approach to building their careers. Though YSN, our online network, we've armed tens of thousands of ambitious young people in 160 countries with the insights and tools to pursue their potential. Essentially, we've studied the global workforce as up close and personally as it gets.

After one million miles of travel, and many deep dives with major corporations, educators, government leaders, youth organizations and the media on youth empowerment, employment, entrepreneurship initiatives, there's one issue that continues to baffle me: the universal inadequacy of career exploration, counseling and training. Today, there are three billion young people under the age of thirty, one billion of whom are entering the global workforce.[43] And the *2011 United Nations World Youth Report* found many of them questioning the quality of education and whether or not it is relevant to available jobs as one of their biggest employment concerns.[44]

When it comes to workforce development, there is little question that our global competitiveness is at stake. But a more systemic problem is lurking beneath the surface: In an increasingly complex world where "traditional" work is disappearing, we're not teaching one of the most important skills of all—opportunity recognition, and the ability to execute on it.

Changing the Tone

Young people transitioning from school to work are anxious about venturing into a world where unemployment, employee dissatisfaction and financial security seem so ominous. Even for those better educated and connected than the norm, 85 percent of college graduates are boomerang kids who return home after college, according to survey data from Twentysomething Inc.[45] For those who venture out of the nest, the Quarterlife Crisis (the heavily documented, new mid-mid-life crisis) hits those in their mid to late twenties who become distraught when their lives are not what they expected. Many end up relying on family, or even continuing to live at home, well into their thirties. In impoverished communities, the outlook is even more bleak—day-to-day financial pressures and the perceived irrelevance of school results in one million high school

---

43 Christopher Altchek, "Hillary Clinton Outlines Global Youth Engagement Plan to Tunisian Millennials," *Policymic*, February 25, 2012, http://www.policymic.com/articles/4651/hillary-clinton-speaks-about-global-youth-engagement-to-tunisian-millennials/latest_articles.

44 "The Situation of Youth Employment: Trends and Young People's Views," in *United Nations World Youth Report*, United Nations, (December 29, 2011), http://unworldyouthreport.org.

45 Erica Ho, "Survey: 85% of New College Grads Move Back in with Mom and Dad," *Time.com*, May 10, 2011, http://newsfeed.time.com/2011/05/10/survey-85-of-new-college-grads-moving-back-in-with-mom-and-dad/.

students a year dropping out, subsequently forfeiting $260,000 of prospective income.[46] When higher education isn't even a conversation in their homes, work becomes something they must do to survive, assuming less legitimate pathways don't entice them to veer off track in search of a different kind of success.

The conversation with young people about their futures needs to dramatically change—in substance and tone—from one of despair to one of possibilities.

Relieving the Pressure

The unemployment problem is a pressure cooker. There is intense demand on our political leaders and corporations to create jobs; there is mounting pressure on millions to find them. An August 2011 Gallup survey found "30 percent of workers worried about being laid off in the near future, an all time high."[47]

As graduation looms for three million college students each year, and 1.3 million who drop out of high school also venture into the workforce, young people are routinely pushed into work situations for money.[48] A February 2012 Pew research report revealed that nearly half (49 percent) of eighteen to thirty-four-year-olds have taken a job that they didn't want just to pay the bills.[49]

In Human Resources speak, the net cost of a bad hire (someone who doesn't work out after lead generation, recruiting and training) is on average fifteen times base salary. That's a huge loss for a company

---

46   *FactSheet: High School Dropouts in America*, Alliance for Excellent Education, (September 2010), 4, http://www.all4ed.org/files/GraduationRates_FactSheet.pdf.

47   Lymari Morales, "More U.S. Workers Unhappy With Health Benefits, Promotions," Gallup, September 5, 2011, http://www.gallup.com/poll/149324/workers-unhappy-health-benefits-promotions.aspx.

48   *FactSheet: High School Dropouts*, 1.

49   Paul Taylor, et al., *Young, Underemployed and Optimistic: Coming of Age, Slowly, in a Tough Economy*, Pew Research Center, (Pew Social & Demographic Trends: February 9, 2012), 1, http://www.pewsocial-trends.org/files/2012/02/SDT-Youth-and-Economy.pdf.

to absorb, especially when young workers tend to change jobs every few years. This kind of rampant turnover wreaks havoc on corporate operations and morale, and companies also suffer the consequences from significantly diminished discretionary effort—the amount of energy an employee chooses to put into their job. BlessingWhite said, that only 31 percent of employees are actively engaged.[50]   Gallup reports over 70 percent are unhappy with on-the-job stress.[51]

Bottom line? Pressuring people into jobs they don't want actually hurts the economy.

Teaching Opportunity Recognition

We know that not everyone is cut out for traditional work—or a full-blown entrepreneurial venture. What if we shifted our focus from jobs, to opportunities? What if we employed more entrepreneurial *approaches* to finding work? There really is an exciting array of choices. They are just hard to see given the limiting paradigms guiding current career planning approaches in our colleges, high schools, homes and workplaces.

Think about it this way. You can go online or pick up newspapers and search endlessly through job listings, or you can walk outside your front door and think about what's not working right, who needs help, and what's lacking—and then figure out what to do about it.

This totally unorthodox but highly practical approach brings up an interesting solution to rampant youth unemployment that is often completely misunderstood, and far too easily dismissed.

Opportunity recognition, as part of entrepreneurship education, is a fundamental life skill. The idea behind teaching entrepreneurship

---

50   "Employee Engagement Report 2011," BlessingWhite, January 2011, http://www.blessingwhite. com/eee__report.asp.

51   Morales, "More U.S. Workers Unhappy."

is not to turn everyone into a business owner, but instead to have young people understand how opportunities are created, organizations are born, ideas are brought to life, and value is created and monetized. Yes, the potential for new venture creation is there, but it's not the goal. It provides new understanding of what drives organizations, teaches business and financial literacy, and literally transforms ordinary workers into better employees and even management. At the very least, entrepreneurship training teaches us not to wait for opportunities to be offered, but to find and create them. But if students aren't getting that education, what can we do from a counseling perspective?

There's another approach to traditional career counseling, one we've tested over many years with young leaders around the world, Ivy League students, middle-class teens, and the most disadvantaged of youth just struggling to make it through trade school. We've deployed it through books, through curriculum, even fancy corporate marketing campaigns. We even called our book *Secrets of the Young & Successful: How to Get Everything You Want Without Waiting a Lifetime.* In essence, it's simply teaching opportunity recognition, with tangible, actionable steps and strategies to leverage those opportunities.

The Opportunity Spectrum

On day one in any economics class, you learn about the law of supply and demand. Consider all the needs and demands that this economic crisis has created and the new forms of work emerging. Why are we still teaching young people that there are only two career choices: a job, or a business?

That very line of thinking is what inspired me to develop the Complete Opportunity Spectrum™, part of a tool that looks at all the ways you can build a successful career. We've found that the most successful teens and twenty-somethings have amassed a lot of these different experiences quickly, rather than putting all their time and energy into a handful of more traditional jobs.

When the jobs aren't there, using opportunity recognition can fill the gaps—through experience, employment, entrepreneurship or any combination thereof. Here are the three main components of the spectrum, which can be broadly leveraged in many contexts:

1. Education:

- **Exchange, immersion:** Getting into an environment for the purpose of learning, developing understanding, gaining hands-on experience through schools and youth organizations and occasionally, programs sponsored by governments and corporations. Anyone can coordinate his or her own unique experience.

- **Apprenticeship:** Working with a craftsman or expert directly in their environment creates unparalleled access and exposure, not to mention training in their specific area of expertise.

- **Internship:** Short-term positions in organizations of all sizes for the purpose of learning, exploring, resume building. When brokered between schools and the firms, the protocols can be carefully structured or not. Small businesses can also offer internships. The experience amassed inside is often far richer too, because small business interns deal with more senior people, have broader access, and get a lot more raw practical experience as to what it's really like to deliver goods and services to clients.

- **Volunteerism:** Donating time to a charity or special cause isn't just a good thing to do; it can also be a smart career move. Volunteering time strategically offers raw work experience, exposure to specific industries, events, great projects, and amazing contacts. Often it leads to paid positions, the potential to provide ongoing goods or services as vendor, or even consulting opportunities.

2. Employment:

- **Full-time employment:** Working for a firm full-time is an ideal scenario for most people because of the structure, training, stability, compensation and benefits. Millennials entering the workforce have caused many companies to change their expectations when hiring young people too. Namely, they no longer expect to retain them for more than two or three years—so smart HR departments are starting to lay out possible career paths with milestones and benchmarks up front, to incentivize employees to stay longer.

- **Part-time employment:** Part-time employment is about getting a solid foot in the door, and can offer many of the same benefits of full-time work. At the same time, part-time employment also allows people to more easily continue their education, take care of family, take on other projects, or even build businesses on the side.

3. Entrepreneurship:

- **Freelancing, independent contracting, consulting:** Projects, gigs, assignments—from little activities like tutoring to long-term consulting assignments, this is where the options are unlimited. Millions of people support themselves like this; contracting can fill in free time, plug gaps when someone is underemployed, offer a range of experiences quickly, build a client list or lay the foundation for a robust career or small business.

- **Licensing:** There are tons of business systems, products and programs that can be licensed for a fee. Often there's an ongoing royalty attached too. Essentially, a company with a solid name and proven process will train, offer materials and systems and even sometimes prospects to those who become their licensees.

- **Franchising:** Becoming a franchisee is a popular route for millions because it gets you into business for yourself without being in business *by yourself.* One of the fastest-growing segments of multi-unit owners is young people, so franchisors are starting to focus more attention on attracting younger prospects. Franchising can offer an ideal career path for people looking for training, mentoring, a proven model and systems, support, and the freedom to build and run an operation on their own.

- **Partnerships:** New ventures are often easier to start with partners. It's also possible to join an existing small business as a partner without having to start from scratch. While group dynamics can be tricky, balancing the workload and benefiting from different opinions and talents offers that extra level of comfort that many need to dive into the entrepreneurial waters with a new venture.

- **Business startup/ownership:** Starting or taking over a business can be a casual endeavor or a major life commitment. Recently, the cost and process of starting something from scratch has become more manageable. Personal computers have enough power to run serious operations. Smartphones keep entrepreneurs connected from anywhere. Businesses can be registered online. Working from home is perfectly acceptable. Entrepreneurs can easily hire interns, contractors, part- or full-time people to grow. This is why entrepreneurs are celebrated as powerful drivers of the economy: because we are. Most entrepreneurs say they'd never go back to working for others once they cross over.

We must teach young people to see work as a spectrum of opportunity, not an either/or proposition—and that they can apply just about any passion or skill to any industry.

In the career counseling world, the concept of function and industry is critical. Function is your core skill or competency at work in a role—like writer. Industry is the field you work in, like sports. Writers can write in any field: medicine, science, gaming, hospitality, the arts, etc. And if you are drawn to a field or industry, like sports, you don't have to be an athlete—you can be a coach, trainer, broadcaster, publicist, physical therapist, financial planner, ticket broker, vendor of paraphernalia, or owner.

Want to see people start buzzing about their futures? Teach them this. This is exactly how we've found people can discover bliss in their work, in any economy: by reveling in the possibilities.

Strategies for Key Stakeholders

Career planning should be an exciting time. The people who have the greatest impact on the decision making of young people—families, peers, educators, employers, career counselors, and media—can make all the difference in how young people perceive the world and opportunities around them.

We must make a paradigm shift and teach, formally or informally, five concepts:

1. **Opportunity recognition:** Encourage young people to ideate solutions as to what's possible or lacking.

2. **Opportunity spectrum:** Explain the different options to engage in work, amass experience, and build competency and expertise.

3. **Function and industry:** Hone in on what young people are naturally gravitating to—whether it's a skill or ability or an industry—and get them exploring all of the things they can do with or in it specifically.

4. **Exploration:** Starting work does not have to involve lifetime decisions. Sampling different opportunities and fields can happen in a few hours, days or a summer internship.

5. **Industries:** Many young people aren't even aware of most industries, let alone that they have their own little ecosystems, but instead rely on parents, teachers and environment to guide them.

Young people forming personal identities are easily excited about the possibilities for them as individuals; that energy needs to be unleashed. If you've ever seen the spark suddenly appear in the eyes of someone recognizing the possibilities in their life for the first time, you know this is an epiphany we need to replicate systematically. I have witnessed it firsthand many times over and can say with certainty that that's where ambition to achieve truly kicks in.

As a nation, we need to show young people that they do in fact have the chance to affect their world, sculpt their own environments and manifest the experiences they crave. As parents, educators, counselors and mentors, we can show them how. Let's commit ourselves to shifting the public discourse about unemployment by relieving some of the pressure to find jobs and instead encouraging young people to reimagine work—to look at this as a world of possibility through the spectrum of opportunity, leveraging more entrepreneurial thinking and truly supporting innovation at every level.

Jennifer Kushell is the Founder of Young & Successful Media and YSN.com ("Your Success Network"), a leading destination for career exploration, professional development, tools and resources serving young professionals and entrepreneurs from over 160 countries. Author of the NY Times Bestseller, *Secrets of the Young & Successful* and The Young Entrepreneur's Edge, Kushell has been a relentless advocate for the Generation X and Y, impacting the lives and futures of millions over the past two decades. A recognized thought leader on the emerging global workforce, Kushell works with a wide range of leading corporations, industry associations, youth organizations and universities as a speaker and strategic consultant building campaigns and content to inspire young people into action. Most recently, she has had the opportunity to work with the Aspen Institute and US State Department's Global Entrepreneurship Program in supporting the growth of entrepreneurial ecosystems throughout North Africa. Called "The Career Doctor" by *Cosmopolitan* and a "guru" of her generation's entrepreneurial movement by *US News & World Report*, Kushell has appeared in front of over 300 million people via major media such as CNN, CNBC, BBC, NPR, *Reuters, The Wall Street Journal, USA Today, Entrepreneur* and *Business Week*. Find her on Twitter at @ysnjen, Facebook.com/jennifer.kushell or learn more at www.jenniferkushell.com.

The Glorious End of Higher Education's Monopoly on Credibility

Michael Ellsberg, Author, The Education of Millionaires: It's Not What You Think and It's Not Too Late

A few months ago, I happened to observe a sales conversation between a twenty-something Internet whiz kid, Neil Patel (founder of CrazyEgg and KISSmetrics analytics companies), and a fifty-something founder and owner of a business that had been around longer than the kid had been alive.

The fifty-something was considering whether to buy an expensive marketing consulting package provided by the twenty-something.

Neil has a BA, but other than that, zero formal credentials in business or marketing. He has no MBA, no impressive list of Madison Avenue advertising agencies or Wall Street investment banks as past employers: in the formal credential department, no nothin'.

And yet, the older gentleman was listening attentively to what Neil had to say, and eventually did go on to sign a contract with Neil worth six figures.

Could you imagine a similar scenario playing out in, say, 1955? A twenty-something with no employment history in corporate America, no fancy educational institutions certifying his knowledge in marketing, receiving a fair and enthusiastic hearing from a business owner nearly twice his age?

The times they are a changin', and in this essay, I'd like to suggest they are changing in a very specific way: sources of credibility are becoming democratized, decentralized, and diversified.

In the example above, Neil did not bring a lot of *traditional, formal* credibility to the table, in the form of graduate degrees or other formal credentials to ply his trade. And yet, think of all the other forms of credibility Neil brought to the table:

- A track record of two successful multimillion-dollar businesses in the field.
- A highly regarded industry blog with well-written, lively, detailed posts on his area of expertise, which receives dozens of comments and hundreds of Tweets, likes and shares per post.
- A Google PageRank on his blog coming in at a solid five, with a fantastic Alexa traffic ranking <10K.
- An impressive about page on that site, which narrates in detail his rags-to-riches story of rising from first-generation immigrant to serial entrepreneur with multiple successful businesses under his belt (with many ups and downs along the way.)
- 11,700 Twitter followers (while he follows less than half as many) and 17,000 Facebook subscribers—he's clearly a celebrity in social media.
- 500-plus LinkedIn connections, including six glowing recommendations from clients.
- A large swath of the New York and San Francisco entrepreneurial community are his friends on Facebook— he's clearly not a loner, but rather, is embedded in a vibrant, relevant network of friends and connections.
- Perhaps more important than all of the above, Neil had come to the client via a powerful referral from a colleague whom the client trusted. In other words, in this case,

Neil was the recipient of most powerful (and also most informal) type of credibility on the planet: word of mouth.

Clearly, any discussion of higher education needs to distinguish between two basic and distinct concepts: *learning*, on the one hand, versus *credibility about having learned*.

Learning is and always has been available all around us, at every age and life stage, often inexpensively or even for free.

My wife Jena, whom I write about in my recent book about self-education, dropped out of college her junior year to travel around India as a spiritual seeker, subsisting on $6,000 she earned herself while teaching English in Martinique.

She regards this experience as the greatest sustained educational experience of her youth: You learn a lot about self-reliance, independence, communication, cross-cultural understanding, and how to make your way in the real world, traveling around a foreign country on a self-earned shoestring—a lot more than I was learning on the same topics, at the same time (though we didn't know each other then) during each of my $45,000 years at Brown University.

Learning is available at the library for free; under a tree with a dog-eared paperback; at a job with a boss who gives you responsibility and mentorship; while traveling; while leading a cause, movement, or charity; while writing a novel or composing a poem or crafting a song; while interning, apprenticing, or volunteering; while playing a sport or immersing yourself in a language; while starting a business; and now, while watching a TED talk or taking a Khan Academy class, or via a zillion other ways on the Internet.

And yet, while learning has always been available around us, inexpensively, free (or even paid on the job), until recently, sources of *credibility* have been highly centralized, and highly expensive. There was basically only one source: higher education. The more elite, the better.

The Internet, however, is "changing everything," as news stories tell us each day. One way it's changing everything revolves around the concept of credibility.

Simply put—and much to the consternation of college administrators everywhere—the Internet is taking away higher education's centuries-old monopoly on granting credibility.

True, in the most traditional of professions—law, medicine, engineering—traditional credibility systems are still strongly in place, and probably will be for the foreseeable future. I, for one, am happy my surgeon has a medical diploma on his wall.

Outside of traditional professions, however, these days you simply don't need a stodgy old professor or some crapulent college dean in a ridiculous faux-medieval gown to tell you—and the world—that you're credible in your field of study.

Rather, as Neil did, you can go out build a business that demonstrates your credibility. You can put up a bunch of great blog posts or videos that demonstrate your credibility. You can build a following that demonstrates your credibility. You can get referrals from within a trusted social network attesting to your credibility.

To use a beloved buzzword of the Internet era, in most fields beyond traditional professions, credibility has become "disintermediated." The gatekeepers and middlemen and cattle-herders of credibility (i.e., college admissions officers, professors, and bureaucrats) are finding some stiff competition from cheap, on-the-fly, decentralized solutions: via WordPress, YouTube, Facebook, Twitter, LinkedIn, and Limited Liability Company forms (i.e., the ability of nearly anyone, anywhere, to start their own business).

"But you learn so much else in college!" I can hear the shepherds of credibility within higher education yelling—while herding their sheep-students towards their expensive sheepskin diplomas.

Yes. But in that case, we're talking about *learning*, not credibility. This whole essay is devoted to distinguishing between the two. True, you can learn a lot in college. You can also learn a lot reading $1 paperback books from a used bookstore, and participating in online discussions.

With grade inflation, diminishing study hours, and binge drinking endemic across campuses, don't tell me that the $100 textbooks taught in stadium auditoriums are automatically a superior form of learning than the $1 paperbacks available at your local used bookstore, consumed in a vibrant cafe.

"But the results speak for themselves," the skeptics will say. "Those with more formal credibility earn more."

There's a rather obvious problem with this retort. Badges of formal credibility, being formal and centralized, are easy to measure. Either you have a degree or you don't.

The newly enabled informal credibility arising within business, however, is decentralized, diffuse, and difficult to define—so it's almost impossible to measure in any systematic, widespread way who has it and who doesn't. Thus, those (such as Neil and my wife) who have devoted their attention to seeking out informal markers of credibility don't show up in the statistics.

"But employers demand formal credibility," I can hear skeptics saying. True, and they also used to demand white skin and male private parts. It's all changing. In addition to the valiant efforts of civil rights and women's movement pioneers of the past, at a certain point, simple business logic also began (and continues) to prevail: Any firm that continues to insist on hiring only white males is missing out on oodles of non-white and female talent, and thus, is putting itself at a distinct disadvantage against its more open competitors.

In a like manner, as more and more bright, talented young people explore various forms of self-education outside of formal institutions (due in large part to the increasingly ridiculous amounts of student debt and tuition associated with those institutions), the employers who continue to insist on stale paper credentials are increasingly missing out on some of the most dynamic, innovative minds of today's youth.

Furthermore, a lot of these brilliant young minds aren't seeking employers anyways. They're seeking to *become* employers right away, bypassing the whole corporate ladder out of the gate.

In the midst of a massive jobs crisis, I can only view this as a good thing. America needs jobs, which means America needs to groom the next generation of job creators. One way we adults (including educators, parents, business leaders, and politicians) could aid in that process is by promoting the idea that creating a business is a worthy sphere of learning—as worthy as a classroom or a college curriculum.

We could also stop promoting the idea that college is a necessary credential for starting a business. It just isn't—certainly not any longer. Nor is it clear that college is even that helpful in that endeavor—compared to other ways a young person could learn about starting a business (such as, for example, starting one).

Let's cut the BS about needing to learn everything important you're ever going to learn in life between the ages of eighteen and twenty-two while enrolled in college. And while we're at it, let's cut the BS about how a BA certifying these four years is the only form of credibility.

Life is long these days—you can learn throughout, with or without college. And you can seek out credibility in a multitude of ways, many of which don't involve oppressive mountains of student debt or regurgitated facts in lecture-hall quizzes.

In the meantime, you can start creating jobs *now*, for yourself and for others. America can't wait, so get to it.

 *Michael Ellsberg* is the author of *The Education of Millionaires: It's Not What You Think and It's Not Too Late* (Penguin/Portfolio). He spent two years interviewing the nation's most successful people who didn't graduate college, and who instead majored in street smarts. Connect with Michael on the web at www.ellsberg.com.

NONPROFIT PROGRAMS

Owner-Entrepreneurship Education Can Close the Wealth Gap and Revitalize America

Steve Mariotti, Founder,
Network for Teaching Entrepreneurship

Whether you consider yourself conservative, libertarian, liberal or moderate, there's no denying that the wealth gap in this country is widening. A June 2010 report from the Center on Budget and Policy Priorities suggested that the gap between rich and poor in the United States has reached levels not seen since 1929.[52] Currently, the United States ranks fourth in the world in income inequality after Chile, Mexico and Turkey.[53] Income disparity is more severe in the United States than almost anywhere else in the developed world.

Historically, high levels of income disparity have led to civil unrest, riots and even revolution. In his third State of the Union address in January 2012, President Obama called income inequality "the defining issue of our time."

The question is: What can the young Americans inheriting this situation do about it?

---

52 Available at http://www.cbpp.org/files/6-25-10inc.pdf.

53 "Country Note: United States," in *Divided We Stand: Why Inequality Keeps Rising*, OECD, (December 5, 2011), 1, http://www.oecd.org/dataoecd/40/23/49170253.pdf.

Closing the Wealth Gap

As the founder of the Network for Teaching Entrepreneurship (NFTE) and an educator of at-risk youth for over thirty years, I can tell you that I've seen only one thing consistently create new members of our middle class: owner-entrepreneurship education. Teach a young person living in poverty to start and operate a small business, and you've given him or her every tool necessary to move into the middle class. Each young person who successfully navigates that journey narrows the wealth gap a little bit.

I've personally witnessed thousands of young people born and raised in poverty discover their potential through our owner-entrepreneurship courses. I've seen apathetic, at-risk kids whose families have been on welfare for generations get excited about their futures and take a renewed interest in school, simply by learning to start their own small businesses.

These kids discover that for entrepreneurs, being street-smart is an advantage; being comfortable with risk and ambiguity is an advantage; having nothing to lose is an advantage; and having unique knowledge of your community is an advantage. I've watched with pride as many of our 400,000-plus alumni have successfully moved into the middle class—either as lifetime entrepreneurs or as educated, productive members of the workforce.

At NFTE, we call our programs *owner*-entrepreneurship education because we want to stress the power of ownership to create wealth. Other organizations providing entrepreneurship education include Junior Achievement, Students in Free Enterprise (SIFE) and Distributive Education Clubs of America (DECA). Babson College is also at the forefront of this movement—constantly working with corporate, university, government, and foundation partners to advance entrepreneurship education worldwide.

At NFTE, we teach not only entrepreneurial skills like record keeping, sales, finance, negotiation, opportunity recognition, and marketing, but also ownership skills. Our students learn how to properly value and sell a business, and how to build wealth utilizing franchising, licensing and other advantages of ownership.

Disadvantaged youth are seldom let in on the connection between ownership and wealth creation. I once asked a leading venture capitalist and philanthropist, who has donated millions to helping low-income children attend private schools, "What about teaching kids the ownership skills that made you your fortune, so they can become financially independent?"

He responded, only half-jokingly, "But then who would do the work?"

His comment illuminates a core issue in our society: If only the wealthiest people own the increased profits resulting from better educating our low-income youth, how much has really been accomplished in helping more of our citizens achieve the American dream?

Teaching business skills without also teaching the power of ownership potentially creates wealth for an owner down the line, not necessarily for the entrepreneur who created a business. Even well educated entrepreneurs can find themselves at a disadvantage when dealing with professional owners who are experts in valuation and procuring a high rate of return in exchange for investing in a business.

Fighting High Youth Unemployment and Dropout Rates

It's been really tough for young people to find jobs since the financial crisis. The youth unemployment rate has hovered between 16 and 25 percent. Professor Andrew Hahn of Brandeis University points out the social consequences this can have for a generation. He says,

"Research shows the scarring effects of early unemployment. The lack of work experience among minority teens contributes to a host of more serious challenges in their early twenties." According to Hahn, "Studies demonstrate that NFTE's owner-entrepreneurship programs create jobs and are among the few strategies that work during these periods of massive youth joblessness."

Ongoing research commissioned by NFTE and conducted by Brandeis University and the David H. Koch Charitable Foundation confirms this. For example:

- Entrepreneurship knowledge increased 61.9 percent among NFTE alumni (versus 3.2 percent of the control group)
- 83 percent of NFTE alumni wanted to start their own businesses (compared to 57 percent of the control group)[54]
- 36 percent have actually started businesses (compared to 9 percent of the control group)
- 76 percent believe starting and owning a business is a realistic way out of poverty (versus 46 percent of control group)
- 95 percent report that NFTE improved business skills and knowledge.[55]

I've seen firsthand that entrepreneurship education gets disaffected teens excited about school again, and about their futures. It teaches them that they can participate in our economy and make money. They quickly realize that to do so, they must to learn to read, write and do math. I've also seen how owning even the simplest small business fills a teen with pride.

Owner-entrepreneurship education is a great way to teach basic subjects to children who are failing to learn through tradi-

---

54   *Brandeis University Research,* Network for Teaching Entrepreneurship, (1993-1998), http://www.nfte.com/sites/default/files/brandeis_university_research_0.pdf.

55   *David H. Koch Charitable Foundation Evaluation Results: New York City,* Network for Teaching Entrepreneurship, (1998), http://www.nfte.com/sites/default/files/research_koch_ny_0.pdf.

tional academic approaches, because it provides concrete incentives. Owner-entrepreneurship education teaches young people that they can create jobs for themselves and that they do not have to be victims of an economic downturn, but can rather view it as an opportunity to start a business. It also makes them more employable in the long term, because by running their own small businesses, they learn how business works and what makes an employee valuable. This shift in viewpoint can immeasurably benefit the psyche of an unemployed teenager, and also benefits companies that hire them.

Teach Owner-Entrepreneurship Education in Schools

Currently, our national strategy to combat poverty among low-income youth is built around improving K-12 education. That's a good choice, and yet we're not teaching entrepreneurship—even though most Americans would probably agree with President Obama that small business is the driving engine of our economy.

I believe we need both statewide and national discussions about the role owner-entrepreneurship education can play in fixing America. I would focus this discussion on four goals:

1. **Engage young people in school** by teaching math, reading, writing and communication within the motivating context of starting and operating a small business.

2. **Teach young people about the market economy** and how ownership leads to wealth creation.

3. **Encourage an entrepreneurial mindset** so young people can succeed whether they pursue higher education, enter the workforce or become entrepreneurs.

4. **Make young people financially literate** so they are able to save and invest to achieve their goals.

Owner-entrepreneurship education empowers young people to make well-informed decisions about their future, whether they choose to become entrepreneurs or not. They become aware of five assets that every individual has: time, talent, attitude, energy and unique knowledge of their communities. And they learn to use these assets strategically as they move along in their careers—which may include creating businesses and jobs, and building wealth in their communities.

A Hip-Hop Success Story

Let me share with you the story of two at-risk youth who traveled from extreme poverty into the middle class through the power of owner-entrepreneurship education. Jabious and Anthony Williams were living crammed in with their mom and eight other family members in their aunt's two-bedroom apartment in Anacostia, a violent Southeast Washington, DC neighborhood. Every day the boys walked miles to the nearest Exxon station to pump gas for tips. "Typically, we would earn about thirty to fifty dollars a day to help support my mom," says Jabious Williams.

Luckily, the Williams brothers met Mena Lofland, a caring NFTE-certified business teacher at Suitland High School in Maryland. She got the boys into a NFTE entrepreneurship class. NFTE currently reaches over 60,000 students a year in the United States and twelve other countries. There are 400,000 NFTE graduates globally.

Like many of our low-income students, Jabious and Anthony experienced tough childhoods that encouraged independence, toughness, salesmanship and hard-won street smarts, and as a result, both showed great aptitude for entrepreneurship. I've observed repeatedly that our-risk youth are uniquely equipped to handle the risk and uncertainty inherent in entrepreneurship.

They also have valuable insights into their local markets. The Williams brothers started their own hip-hop clothing line, for example, with support from Lofland, and two local mentors—Phil McNeil, managing partner of Farragut Capital Partners, and Patty Alper, a dedicated volunteer, philanthropist and former entrepreneur.

Now twenty-four years old, Jabious is a scholarship graduate student at Southeastern University and operates Jabious Bam Williams Art & Photography Company. Anthony heads a youth-mentorship program. They recently gave their mom $5,000 as down payment on a house. "If it weren't for the NFTE classes and the support of our teachers and mentors, we would have likely dropped out of school," Jabious says.

New Initiatives to Support Entrepreneurship Education

The story of the Williams brothers is just one of countless examples from NFTE's files that beg the question: If entrepreneurship education can create jobs, prevent students from dropping out, and provide economic rescue for people in our low-income communities, what's it going to take to make owner-entrepreneurship education standard in every high school in America? Here are my suggestions:

1. **Pass the Learn to Earn Act.** For starters, we can work to pass the "Learn to Earn" Act, sponsored by Congressman Dave Loebsack of Iowa, which seeks to create incentives for states and local school districts to implement high-quality entrepreneurship programs in communities all across the country.[56]

   According to NFTE president and CEO Amy Rosen, "This bill will help spark even greater interest around the US in arming our young people with the basic skills, the motivation and the aspiration to seize hold of their futures,

---

56   Learn to Earn Act of 2011, H.R. 3445, 112th Congress (2011).

stay in school and plan for successful futures. When young people learn to see opportunity in the face of obstacles and are equipped with the mindset of an entrepreneur, they are better prepared for the workforce, for higher education and to be the job creators of the future."

At NFTE, we've determined that, to succeed, an owner-entrepreneurship education program needs three things: one, quality curriculum that ties entrepreneurship to reading, writing and math; two, teacher training that creates certified entrepreneurship teachers who truly understand the subject and how to teach it; and three, alumni services to continue to help students network and succeed even after they complete the program.

2. **Enlist our seniors in owner-entrepreneurship education.** I'd also like to see a program developed that would tap into one of our nation's great underused resources—retired Americans. Many would love to work part-time; let's teach them to become entrepreneurship educators, and use their experience and wisdom to mentor our youth.

3. **Reform the tax code to spur small business.** Let's continue to pressure Congress to reform the tax code and reduce government regulations to make it easier for small businesses to operate successfully in our economy.

Owner-entrepreneurship education's track record reveals that anyone can start a business and use it to create wealth. This awareness can be a matter of life or death for at-risk young people like the Williams brothers. Through owner-entrepreneurship education, they discovered the value of their assets and created a business out of a comparative advantage—in this case, their unique knowledge of hip-hop culture and what kind of clothes would appeal to other kids in their community. As a result, they became motivated to stay in high school, went on to college and helped their mother become a homeowner.

And as the Williams brothers learned, owner-entrepreneurship education can also help solve the youth unemployment crisis, rescue our low-income communities by increasing home ownership and employment, and even bring about a fairer distribution of wealth.

We need a national debate on owner-entrepreneurship education, particularly for low-income youth. We must raise the consciousness of those who have been left out of our economic system, so that they comprehend the joys and responsibilities of ownership.

As Jabious Williams says, "Because I own my business, I know I have a future."

Steve Mariotti, Founder of the Network for Teaching Entrepreneurship (NFTE), is an expert in education for at-risk youth. For more than 20 years, he has been helping young people develop marketable skills by learning about entrepreneurship. Steve founded NFTE in 1987. NFTE's mission is to provide entrepreneurship education programs to young people from low-income communities. Since 1987, NFTE has reached more than 450,000 young people, and currently has programs in 21 states, 11 cities and 10 countries outside the U.S. NFTE has more than 1,500 active Certified Entrepreneurship Teachers, and is continually improving its innovative entrepreneurship curriculum.

Creating an Entrepreneurial Culture on Campus: Collaboration of Private Enterprise and Collegiate Institutions

Katie Sowa and Dr. Gerald Hills,
Collegiate Entrepreneurs' Organization

A t colleges and universities across the United States and around the world, entrepreneurship has become a leading area of study at both the undergraduate and graduate level—at least two-thirds (or more than 2,000) colleges and universities now offer at least one course in entrepreneurship.[57] Students and educational advisors are realizing the importance of giving young adults an opportunity to pursue their dreams and create their own careers. In order to enable this entrepreneurial path, students and academic institutions must recognize and encourage opportunities for networking not only at the peer level, but also with fellow entrepreneurs as mentors.

We at the Collegiate Entrepreneurs' Organization (CEO), which originally began as a regional Midwest conference in 1983 and evolved into a national membership organization that is now on over 240 university campuses, along with leaders of other entrepreneur-

---

57 Judith Cone, "Teaching Entrepreneurship in Colleges and Universities: How (and Why) a New Academic Field Is Being Built," Kauffman Foundation, accessed February 17, 2012, http://www.kauffman.org/entrepreneurship/teaching-entrepreneurship-in-colleges.aspx.

ial support organizations, are helping colleges and universities foster the entrepreneurial spirit beyond the classroom. Our belief is that private enterprise and nonprofits can work together with institutions to create platforms for developing successful student entrepreneurs.

How Can Nonprofits and Private Enterprise Work with Colleges and Universities to Create an Entrepreneurial Culture?

"Culture is one of the most precious things a company has, so you must work harder on it than anything else," said Herb Kelleher, founder of Southwest Airlines and former inductee into the Collegiate Entrepreneurs' Organization (CEO) Hall of Fame. Culture is vital when it comes to setting a mindset that leads to success. Entrepreneurs and aspiring entrepreneurs also need to create and maintain an entrepreneurial culture, which helps set the tone to attract and retain the right team members, partners, mentors, employees, and even investors. The entrepreneurial spirit drives passion, motivation, and goals into new venture creation, turning an entrepreneurial dream into a viable business. And this spirit helps sustain entrepreneurial culture by directing the success of the business—and creating the overarching passion that ultimately influences everyone involved.

Nonprofits and private enterprise can help academic institutions create a lasting entrepreneurial culture in several ways. It starts with seamless and integrated understanding across industries that entrepreneurial and creative thinking are important, not only for entrepreneurship, but for intrapreneurship as well; and that entrepreneurial thinking can drive new venture creation within an existing company as well as grow and change a business internally. Companies offering internships, shadowing opportunities, and even mentoring for young professionals can showcase and reinforce an entrepreneurial culture, setting expectations for future business leaders.

Academic institutions teach business fundamentals, and entre-preneurship students are expected to know and understand all key elements of business. Private enterprise can collaborate with universities by setting up programs to give hands-on experiences to supplement those studies through consulting projects, mentorships, and competitions, transforming classroom information into practice and cementing the concepts and lessons learned. To work with universities, organizations and businesses must be flexible. Many universities offer resources for aspiring entrepreneurs, so you must be interested in supplementing the goals and needs of the faculty and students at a particular campus.

Why Is It Vital to Supplement the University Curriculum with Programs outside the Classroom?

Education is more than just information presented in lectures or learned from case studies. Extra-curricular activities engage students beyond the classroom, providing the hands-on activities and real-world experiences that make ideas taught in the classroom come to life. The demand for entrepreneurial extracurricular activities is growing—the number of CEO Chapters on university campuses increased 20 percent from 2010 to 2011. Experiential learning creates:

Passion: Students are excited to get involved with things they are passionate about. With entrepreneurship, students no longer have to find a job to pay the bills; they can love what they do and truly own their futures. Many students see it as an opportunity to make a difference and impact the world in a positive way. Student clubs such as the Collegiate Entrepreneurs' Organization (CEO) bring together students who share a common interest—entrepreneurship—while helping them follow their individual passions.

Beyond emotional and peer support, such organizations also provide access to outlets and resources matching their passions and can even expose students to unrealized interests. Whether through matching of industry-specific mentors, shadowing opportunities, virtual chats and webinars, or access to conferences and networking events, entrepreneurship support organizations help students engage on a deeper level with opportunities that they might otherwise be unaware of.

Exposure: Exposure to new resources enhances the understanding of what entrepreneurship actually encompasses. Whereas groups like CEO support entrepreneurship as a whole, other support organizations expose students to special interest topics, such as Self-Employment in the Arts (SEA) for arts entrepreneurship, Net Impact for social entrepreneurship, or the National Collegiate Inventors and Innovators Alliance (NCIIA) for technology entrepreneurship. A key benefit is that these organizations impart to students how entrepreneurship can have a larger impact, one that expands beyond the campus bubble and affects the global community. Organizations can team up with campuses, either by cohosting or sponsoring events, or by supporting a cause as a means to success.

For example, the entrepreneurial students of the CEO Chapters at Illinois State University and the University of Houston participated in the 2011 National Lemonade Day, a day dedicated to teaching young children how to start their own lemonade stand while donating some of the proceeds to charity. Lemonade Day is part of a national program organized by Prepared 4 Life, started by entrepreneur Michael Holthouse. Entrepreneurship also led students at Brigham Young University (BYU) to give back through their Rock Paper Scissors Contest. In 2008, BYU attracted a world record number of participants with 826 competitors (pending certification from Guinness), raising money for Enterprise Mentors International, an organization that provides mentoring, microfinance, business training, and other services to entrepreneurs in developing nations.

Likewise, competitions give college students an added push on their entrepreneurial journey. Competitions exist at all levels, including global events such as the Global Student Entrepreneur Awards (GSEA), national competitions like the CEO National Elevator Pitch Competition, and even local or campus-based elevator pitch, business plan, and idea competitions. Competitions that give aspiring entrepreneurs recognition and prizes to invest in their idea are most successful.

For example, Nick Chmura, a student at the University of Tampa, pitched his business idea in the CEO National Elevator Pitch Competition at the 2010 National CEO Conference. Since then, he has acquired angel funding and launched his company BetterBoo.com as an affiliate of Amazon. And Adam Blake, a former CEO member and Texas Christian University alum, received support as a student entrepreneur, having won the Global Student Entrepreneur Award (GSEA) in 2005. Today, Adam is a serial entrepreneur with companies including Atlas Properties and Silicon Solar Housing Solutions, which created the first solar-powered real-estate sign light and a line of solar water-heating products now known as SunMaxx.

Here are some best practices for creating a successful competition:

- **Maintain a clear goal and vision.** Whether you intend on hosting a business plan, sustainability, idea, or pitch competition, have a clear focus going into the planning process. Determine what the reach of the competition will be and who will be allowed to participate: your campus, the local community—or will it be regional, national, international? Make sure that everyone involved is on the same page. Decide at the onset the end goal of the competition.

- **Be realistic.** Make sure that the requirements of the competition set realistic expectations for the participants. Consider the university's schedule; know what the semester timeline involves, such as major campus events like homecoming, holiday breaks, and finals week. Finally, realize it will take time and resources to plan and manage, plan a competition you and your managing partners can handle.

- **Create excitement.** The nature of a competition alone creates excitement and anticipation, so use it to your advantage. Engage everyone involved, from students who may be participating, to faculty who may be encouraging participation or acting as mentors, to local private enterprises that maybe have an interest in being involved. Use campus and local community media outlets to create excitement leading up to and following the success of the competition.

- **Engage quality partners.** A competition presents the opportunity to engage your local community and to involve local organizations to help host or sponsor the event. You can even use your community to find judges. Be sure that you select partners that fit with your competition's mission and purpose.

- **Give students a reason to compete.** If the prize isn't worth it, then students won't compete. Put together a prize package that is not only relevant to the goal of the competition, but is enticing enough to garner participants. Seek out involvement from your partnering organization or other private enterprises to donate services that may be of interest to aspiring entrepreneurs, such as legal services, marketing assistance, or rental space. Give winners exposure. And don't forget cash prizes; as entrepreneurs say, cash is king!

Leadership: Whether it involves running a business on campus, hosting a charity fundraiser, or running a group meeting, students who participate in leadership activities outside the university classroom gain firsthand experience leading a team. Student clubs and professional organizations provide invaluable leadership opportunities, which help students gain leadership experience that will play a vital role in their professional careers.

For example, the students in the CEO Chapter at Genesee Community College started a business selling their own Scholars Apple Cider Syrup and Cram & Crunk Snack Mix. With the profits, the students gave back to their school by donating money to be used for student scholarships.

Or there's Matt Wilson who, as a student at Bryant University, started and ran their campus CEO Chapter. Now, Matt runs Under-30CEO.com, a website he founded to drive young entrepreneurs to build profitable businesses, lead people and solve problems. Derek Henze also started his university's entrepreneurship club as a student at the University of Wisconsin-Whitewater. Today, Derek is an entrepreneur and franchisee owner of Topper's Pizza.

Connecting Private Enterprise, Nonprofits and Collegiate Institutions

If we want to foster entrepreneurial thinking, we need to teach our students to be proactive. Carl Kirpes, a student at Iowa State University who attended the 2011 National CEO Conference was inspired by the attitude of the conference speakers. He said, "I saw the same 'I just do it' attitude displayed in all the keynote speakers and breakout sessions I attended. I have begun to apply that philosophy not only as an entrepreneur but also in other aspects of my life such as athletics, academics, and community service. I am already starting to see the positive effects of doing what I know is right even if at the time I do not feel like doing it."

1. **Encourage risk taking in classrooms and workplaces.** Encouraging young adults to have an entrepreneurial mindset and take more risks should be reinforced in our society, both in and out of the classroom. Companies should inspire entrepreneurship and entrepreneurial thinking internally, instead of being afraid to recruit and hire entrepreneurs. Trial and error within the classroom and workplace will help establish an entrepreneurial culture in our nation. Enable entrepreneurially minded individuals to explore new market opportunities, create new projects, play with social media, employ new trends, and engage in open-door policies all to help empower them to make out of the box decisions with the responsibility of keeping the organization's best interest at the forefront. As Vivek Wadhwa remarked during a panel about the success of Silicon Valley as a pool for entrepreneurial success, "What makes the Valley tick? It's a giant social network, we're not afraid of failure, we share ideas openly. People don't shoot you down—they tell you how to make it better."[58] If we encourage interns, employees, and students to be entrepreneurial, we can help future generations realize the potential for contributing to the greater good.

   Tasty Catering of Elk Grove Village, IL consistently maintains an entrepreneurial mentality. After twenty years in business, this company continues to encourage its employees to be entrepreneurial, resulting in the creation of several new and successful companies from the ideas of their employees.

---

58 Angie Chang, "Mentorship and Networking Especially Important for Women Entrepreneurs (Stories of Leadership)," Women 2.0, November 7, 2011, http://www.women2.org/mentorship-and-networking-especially-important-for-women-entrepreneurs-stories-of-leadership/.

These startups have led to increased growth for the company as a whole, which has expanded into new market segments and lines of business, all while creating an award-winning culture and work environment. To stay on top of innovation and technology, the company follows the direction of younger employees who understand market change and are able to act on it. The founders also routinely mentor and invite students to their facility to experience entrepreneurship in action.

2. **Professionals and entrepreneurs can mentor students or companies.** Entrepreneurship is a journey with many trials and tribulations along the way. Students look to successful entrepreneurs for guidance as role models and mentors. In and out of the workplace, business leaders, seasoned professionals and successful entrepreneurs should volunteer as mentors to students and startup companies, or as speakers to help share their wisdom and experience. Future mentors can reach out to the business department or entrepreneurship program on college campuses or to student organizations and express interest in getting involved. Be willing to work with upcoming events the university or student group may have planned in a one-on-one setting to mentor and share insight, or even invite a group of students to events for other professional networks.

For example, Jennifer Prosek, founder of CJP Communications, not only donates her time to speak to students, but she also ran a contest in conjunction with the 2011 National CEO Conference in which a student won the chance to visit her in New York to shadow her life as a global entrepreneur. Not only was the winning student thrilled to have the opportunity to learn directly from a true role model, he was also inspired; after boosting the student's self-esteem, the experience made him realize what kind of company he would like to work at and one day own.

3. **Businesses and consumers can support young entrepreneurs by giving them business.** For real change to occur, current businesses and consumers must also respect and actually do business with young entrepreneurs. If the support of entrepreneurship in colleges and universities can be extended into the workplace throughout all industries, the way business is done will change and future generations will view innovation and creativity as a standard, leading America with a true entrepreneurial spirit.

Collaboration among nonprofits, private enterprise and collegiate institutions is necessary to positively impact the future of America. Encouraging entrepreneurship and small business creation as real options for students graduating and entering the workforce will help reshape and revitalize America's economy. Entrepreneurship gives young people the opportunity to start a business and have a say in their future—and in the future of our nation.

Katie Sowa is the Assistant Director for the Collegiate Entrepreneurs' Organization (CEO), which is the premier entrepreneurship network with chapters on university campuses across North America. Prior to joining CEO, Katie helped found DePaul University's Graduate Entrepreneurs' Organization, the university's first graduate-level student entrepreneurship organization. Katie has also worked in and with many startups and small businesses, including her role as a financial and HR manager for a $6M online electronic refurbishing startup and as a consultant and research assistant for a technology commercialization incubation center. Katie received her MBA from DePaul University and her Bachelor's degree in Entrepreneurship from Bradley University.

Dr. Gerald Hills is a pioneer in the development of the entrepreneurship discipline. As the Executive Director and Co-Founder of the Collegiate Entrepreneurs' Organization (CEO), he helped take CEO from its start as a regional Midwest conference in 1983 into a national membership organization in 1997, which is now at over 240 universities. Dr. Hills currently holds the endowed Turner Chair in Entrepreneurship and is Professor of Entrepreneurship at Bradley University. Prior to coming to Bradley, he led the development of an entrepreneurship program at University of Illinois at Chicago that was consistently ranked in the top 10 nationally. He has written and edited more than 100 entrepreneurship articles and 25 books. Besides helping launch CEO, he was the co-founder and first president of the U.S. Association for Small Business and Entrepreneurship and president of the International Council for Small Business. He chaired an advisory board of the U.S. Small Business Administration under President Reagan, and advanced entrepreneurship in Poland through a congressional commission project. Dr. Hills earned his bachelor's degree from Rochester Institute of Technology, his master's and doctorate from Indiana University.

PRIVATE ENTERPRISE

Franchising the Future:
How We Can Help Young People Own a Small Business Instead of a Piece of Paper

Nick Friedman and Omar Soliman,
Co-Founders, College Hunks Hauling Junk

A quiet revolution is taking place on college campuses across America, as those students about to be denied entry to the workforce ditch useless résumés for entrepreneurial basics. From dorm rooms to garages, young people are realizing that there is no better time than right now to start a business.

We were blown away during the Collegiate Entrepreneurs' Organization's annual conference in Chicago recently, where dozens of well-known entrepreneurs addressed 1,500 bright-eyed college kids, all eager to start out on their own. The message delivered over and over? *Go for it.* If you try and fail, you will gain experience no MBA or college degree can give you. If and when you do succeed, you never need to worry about that résumé again.

Five years ago, we ditched our own résumés and founded College Hunks Hauling Junk instead. The salaries we gave up by quitting our day jobs were our largest single cost, far eclipsing what we spent on phone lines, office supplies or an old beat-up truck. It was a risk. It didn't make our parents happy. But it was a whole lot of fun—and ultimately, it worked.

Establishing a startup is risky, but right now, starting out the traditional way is equally risky. In the midst of the recession, the unemployment rate for sixteen- to twenty-four-year-olds hit a staggering 48 percent in July of 2011.[59] July, typically the month with the highest youth employment rate due to summer vacation from school, offers a glimpse of what the competition may be like when this next batch of students graduates. With current rates of job creation barely enough to keep up with labor force growth, there are few signs that things will radically improve any time soon.

One overlooked way to mitigate the risks of failure (at either finding a job, or starting a new business) is to consider a strategic third alternative: franchise ownership.

Franchising as a Viable Alternative to Costly Four-Year Degrees and MBAs

Franchises offer an excellent opportunity for first-time entrepreneurs to build experience while benefiting from the infrastructure and expertise of an established company. Young people do not necessarily need to strive to become the next founders of Google or Facebook; instead, they can take a simple business concept, service, or product, and differentiate it enough to make it better or more popular.

At College Hunks Hauling Junk, we've witnessed an explosion in interest among young people under thirty in our franchise program. Generally, they're either fresh out of school and can't find a job, or have forgone the formal college experience altogether but don't know how to start a company from scratch. Unlike entrepreneurs going it alone, franchisees benefit from an intense, in-depth education that would have cost them $100,000 or more in business school (and no MBA comes with a guaranteed job on the other end).

---

59 "Employment and Unemployment Among Youth Summary," Bureau of Labor Statistics, U.S. Department of Labor, August 24, 2011, http://bls.gov/news.release/youth.nr0.htm.

Perhaps the hardest minds to change when it comes to encouraging our youth to franchise are those of their parents, who cling nostalgically to what they were told by their own folks for so many years about going to college. Our advice to parents is to wipe the slate clean and encourage your kids to think about creating their own jobs by becoming small business owners.

You might surprise your children—and who knows? One day soon, those same children might be offering you a job and a regular paycheck as they rev up the economic entrepreneurial engine that will help put the world back to work.

For those who fear facing oppressive student loans without a guaranteed job opportunity following graduation, franchising can provide an alternative to attending college in the first place. Paying for a degree is just as risky as franchising, but franchising offers a solution to graduates who cannot find a job at all.

Imagine a struggling college student working for eight dollars an hour before or even after graduation, with limited or no growth potential. Now imagine that same college student earning equity in a franchise business instead of a degree. If successful, the business would provide both the financial and professional security sought from a degree. It would also provide more valuable lessons in life and add much more value to the economy.

Furthermore, franchisors like us jump at the opportunity to interview motivated and goal-oriented youth who have a sincere interest in learning how to run a business and a willingness to work toward owning a franchise. Motivation can carry an entrepreneur a long way, despite a lack of experience. We stand as proof of that, having been in our early twenties when we started our business. For that reason, we're plenty willing to offer opportunities to any youth in whom we see that same spark of genuine determination. After all, methods, practices, and business models can be taught, but the hunger for success needs to come from within the individual.

Dave Hughes of Little Rock, for example, bought a College Hunks Hauling Junk franchise two years ago for his son, Nolen, who was then twenty-two and graduating from college.

Dave had to cash in a retirement account, and Nolen moved back home with his dad to conserve money. But Nolen has worked hard, often rising before dawn to drive his big trash-hauling truck around the city during rush hour for marketing purposes. The business is running in the black, and Nolen is well on his way to becoming financially independent.

For all intents and purposes, *why* Nolen works so hard is of secondary concern to the fact *that* he works so hard. Whether it's to ensure his dad doesn't lose his retirement money or for some other reason that we will never know, what we do know is that he had that same spark of determination that we had so many years ago and maintain to this day. His father saw it and decided to back him financially. We saw it and offered him a chance to purchase a franchise.

While the risk was steep, especially for Dave, it wasn't any steeper than financing tuition and hoping to one day pay it off through a near-minimum-wage job in a field otherwise unrelated to the degree itself.

Franchises Provide Needed Structure—and the Promise of Near-Term Growth

Many young entrepreneurs choose franchises because they offer marketing, branding and management support. While job growth overall remains sluggish, direct franchise employment is expected to increase by 2.1 percent in 2012, and economic output is expected to grow by 5 percent—from $745 to $782 billion.[60] And from 2001 to 2005, the franchising sector grew at a faster pace than many other sectors of the US economy, expanding by more than 18 percent.[61]

Startup costs, including leases for space and equipment, range from roughly $5,000 to $10,000 for low-cost operations like cleaning franchises, to $1 million or more for popular fast-food restaurants. While entrepreneurs run a risk of losing their investment, the dollar amount is often comparable to a college or graduate degree, and the lessons learned can be much more valuable to someone who may wish to re-enter the workplace.

For many, the potential rewards are worth the risk. The best investment you can ever make is to set yourself up to be happy, successful, and equipped to make a living. Just like a college degree, you should not expect any short-term return on your investment. Starting any kind of business is a long-term investment in your financial and professional future.

How to Make Franchise Ownership More Accessible to Young People

Today, franchising is a nearly $500 billion industry that will directly employ more than eight million people in 2012—and it's projected to grow into the foreseeable future.[62] Increasing franchise ownership is a direct stimulus to the US economy as a whole. Unfortunately, the smallest demographic of franchise owners is people under thirty.

Some parents may be able to help set a child up in business, but for franchise ownership to become a more commonly viable alterna-

---

60   *2012 Franchise Business Economic Outlook,* prepared by IHS Global Insight for the International Franchise Association, (January 2012), 1, http://emarket.franchise.org/EconOutlookFactSheetfinal.pdf.

61   *The Economic Impact of Franchised Businesses, Volume 2,* prepared by PricewaterhouseCoopers for the International Franchise Association Educational Foundation, (January 31, 2008), 12, http://www.franchise.org/uploadedFiles/Franchisors/Other_Content/economic_impact_documents/EconomicImpactVolIIpart1.pdf.

62   *2012 Franchise Business Economic Outlook,* 1.

tive to either a degree or a brand-new business, franchisors and banks need to establish programs that give young people an economic shot at franchise ownership.

Here are six paths that the government, banks and franchisors alike can take toward establishing that viability:

1. **Offer franchise discounts** for recent college or high school graduates.

2. **Offer lower interest rates** (or no interest at all) on loans to recent high school graduates who opt to skip college, at least until such time as the loan is repaid in full.

3. **Lobby to create legislation for benefactor programs** that partially subsidize loans specifically for this demographic in order to aid long-term economic recovery

4. **Create a government program that specializes in capital for franchises.** We already know the enormous positive impact that the franchise industry has on the economy, so why don't we drive this with an actual initiative that gives people under thirty access to capital? The Small Business Administration's loan program is not enough; there needs to be a government organization that specializes in capital for franchises.

5. **Put our veterans at the top of the list.** There are an overwhelming number of military veterans returning home from service (one million by 2016).[63] Not only have these people made tremendous sacrifices for our country, but they also make tremendous franchise owners. Running a successful franchise is all about capitalizing on a winning system, and our men and women of the U.S. Armed Forces are trained to

---

63 *Report to the President: Empowering Veterans Through Entrepreneurship*, U.S. Small Business Administration, (Interagency Task Force on Veterans Small Business Development, November 1, 2011), 1, http://www.sba.gov/sites/default/files/FY2012-Final%20Veterans%20TF%20Report%20to%20President.pdf.

do just this. The VetFran program through the International Franchise Association is a great organization. But to expand opportunities for young vets, we also need to pass legislation like the AGREE Act, which contains provisions of the Help Veterans Own Franchises Act and establishes a tax credit to help offset 25 percent of veterans' franchise fees.[64]

6. **Increase franchise-related education at the college level.** Let's add specialized courses at the undergraduate level that focus on the macro and micro of the franchise industry. One way to do this is through partnerships and scholarships like those offered by Distributive Education Clubs of America (DECA) in conjunction with the International Franchise Association.[65] It's hard to get young people excited about something they know very little about. Furthermore, if universities put together these courses, they would soon have local franchises knocking on their doors wanting to get involved. This could include case studies on specific franchises, strategic analysis, and incubator programs that would benefit the students, the franchise and the university.

Regardless of what steps are taken to help our youth get started, nothing is guaranteed: small-business failure is common, and franchise owners do risk losing their entire investment, their life savings, or more. But this economic climate has shown us that nothing is certain post-graduation, either. We see business ownership as a better bet for young people's futures than a degree. And in this era of renewed interest in entrepreneurship, franchise ownership is a

---

64   American Growth, Recovery, Empowerment and Entrepreneurship Act, S. 1866, 112th Congress, (2011).

65   DECA, in partnership with IFA, offers an Introduction to Franchising Manual, scholarships for high school and college students, and a Collegiate DECA Entrepreneurship Academy & Challenge, to name a few initiatives. See http://www.deca.org/partners/ifafoundation/.

way for our youth to recapture a stake in the American dream—that is, to control their own destiny and have a chance at growing wealth.

Omar Soliman is Co-Founder & CEO of College Hunks Hauling Junk. Omar is a published author, entrepreneur and TV personality. During his senior year at The University of Miami he submitted a business plan for College Hunks Hauling Junk to the Leigh Rothschild Entrepreneurship competition. Omar won first place and $10,000 in the competition for his business concept which included junk removal, moving services and an online junk exchange. Today, College Hunks Hauling Junk is a national franchise and is listed in the Inc. 500 for fastest growing companies in the nation. He is co-author of the bestselling book *Effortless Entrepreneur: Work Smart, Play Hard, Make Millions* (Random House, 2010).

Nick Friedman is President and Co-Founder of College Hunks Hauling Junk, the largest and fastest growing US-based junk removal and moving franchise opportunity. He was recently named Top 30 Entrepreneurs in America Under 30 by *Inc. Magazine*, was named on the same list as Mark Zuckerberg, founder of Facebook as the 30 Most Influential CEO's Under 30 by Under30CEO.com, he was named Top 35 Entrepreneurs Under 35 by Bisnow.com, and is an Ernst and Young Entrepreneur of the Year Award Finalist. Nick was also recently featured in a *Newsweek* story entitled "College Kid to Millionaire," along with the founders of FedEx, Dell Computers, Facebook, Google, and Microsoft. Nick's company was recently named #156 on the Inc. 500 List of Fastest Growing US Companies, and has also been profiled numerous times on CNN, MSNBC, CBS, NBC, FOX News, and Oprah. Nick has appeared as a guest on national television shows such as CNBC's *The BIG Idea* with Donny Deutsche, Fox Business News, and ABC's reality based show about entrepreneurs entitled Shark Tank. He has been interviewed by *Entrepreneur* and *Fortune* Magazine as well as the *Wall Street Journal* for his expertise on franchising, branding, and young entrepreneurship. Nick recently co-authored his first book along with his business partner Omar Soliman, entitled *Effortless Entrepreneur: Work Smart, Play Hard, Make Millions* (Random House, 2010).

Providing a Path to Entrepreneurship for Our College Graduates

Andrew Yang, Founder and President,
Venture for America

L eadership matters. We have to show our young people what we want them to be and support their training and development in those directions. We have to make it as easy and obvious to be an employee at an early-stage growth company, or an entrepreneur, or a math or science teacher, or a research scientist, as it presently is to become a lawyer, banker, or consultant.

I've been working in startups for twelve years now. But I didn't start out that way.

When I graduated from college, I had little clear idea of what I wanted to do. I had a general desire for stature and training, so, like no small number of my aimless peers, I took the LSAT and went to law school.

Three years at Columbia didn't clarify much. I wound up practicing law in the mergers and acquisitions department of a big firm in New York. It didn't take me long to realize that I was in the wrong place. It was 1999, and there were people building companies right and left in the first dot-com boom. The last place I wanted to be was in an office sorting through others' paperwork, and I left the firm after just five months to cofound an Internet startup of my own. Eight months later, with some difficulty, we managed to raise money and launch a website.

Our timing left something to be desired, as the tech boom was quickly followed by a bust in 2001 that washed away my little company along with just about every other startup in New York. I'd gone to glitzy launch parties hosted by companies that were reduced to selling off their furniture just months afterwards. I saw office after office empty out. It was as if a giant hand swept through the urban canyons of lower Manhattan, or what had been deemed Silicon Alley at the time.

We ran out of money and couldn't raise more. But I had been bitten by the bug—I couldn't unlearn what I'd learned. I wanted to know more and get better. Through contacts I'd made while running the company, I became the lieutenant to a more experienced entrepreneur. The CEO was very talented, and I took in as much as I could. I spent five years learning, hustling, and developing as VP-of-something-or-other before becoming the CEO at another early-stage company, which was acquired by a large public company five years later. I then founded Venture for America to make it easier for our best and brightest to become the business builders and job creators we need to revitalize our economy.

What Path Do You Take After College?

If you are a smart college student and you want to become a lawyer and go to law school, it's pretty easy. You go to a good school, get good grades and take the LSAT. There is little anxiety in terms of divining the requirements, which are clearly spelled out and well known to most college students. The path-location costs are low.

The same is true if you want to become a doctor. You have to complete a battery of life science college courses, study for the

MCAT, and spend a summer or even a year caddying for a researcher or in a medical setting. For finance and consulting, it's even easier. If you attend a national university, legions of suit-wearing representatives from all of the big-name investment banks and consulting firms will show up at your campus and conduct interviews to fill their ranks each year, even in a bad year.

These structured paths are the default options for students with access to them—and were pursued by approximately 50 percent of Harvard grads in 2011 (65 percent if you include med school).[66] Perhaps this is somewhat surprising—wouldn't top college students be well positioned to blaze their own trails and pursue less conventional routes?

The truth is, few college students arrive their freshman year dreaming about becoming investment bankers or management consultants or corporate lawyers. Yet the institutional messages they receive throughout their college careers are that these are the "prestige" paths to follow. These are the firms, industries, and schools that have the resources to recruit you and train you, and thus they become the direct and obvious paths of a literal majority.

In contrast, if you want to start your own business or work at a small-growth company, you're on your own. You'll have to hustle or network your way to an opportunity of uncertain merit. You won't have a group of peers around. There are no guarantees of training, advancement or success. Your parents might prefer that you go to law school, medical school or a name-brand firm. And your peers won't recognize or value the path that you're taking.

---

66   Data from "Next Steps for Harvard Seniors: 2011," Harvard University Office of Career Services, May 2011, http://www.ocs.fas.harvard.edu/students/jobs/seniorsurvey.htm; *Top 240 ABA Applicant Feeder Schools for: Fall Applicants,* (2005-2010), http://www.lsac.org/LSACResources/Data/PDFs/top-240-feeder-schools.pdf; and "Table 2-7. Undergraduate Institutions Supplying 100 or More White Applicants to U.S. Medical Schools, 2011," AAMC, 2011, https://www.aamc.org/download/161116/data/table2-7.pdf.

It's no wonder that so few of our top graduates decide to head down this road—it's more than contrarian, it's borderline irrational. Yet if we want to build the next generation of business job creators, this is exactly what we need them to do.

It's Time to Build a New Path

I have spoken with hundreds of college seniors in the past year during my visits to college campuses, and many of them are frustrated by the limited range of options presented to them. They want to do something they believe in, in an environment where they can achieve an impact. They recognize that there is a universe of different industries and opportunities out there, but they don't have the resources, network, time or experience to effectively access them.

It's the same situation on the growth-company side. V-Charge is a renewable energy company in Providence, Rhode Island, led by Jessica Millar, a PhD in math from MIT who is working to make our energy grid more efficient. V-Charge is a new enterprise and doesn't have the personnel, money, or time to go on campus and recruit alongside the large established firms. Many other exciting young companies around the country are in the same position. There is a disconnect here that we must address.

Teach For America illustrates how successful an organization can be that sets up a concrete and clearly defined recruitment and application process. In 2011, 48,000 college seniors applied for 5,200 spots in Teach For America, including 12 percent of Ivy League seniors.[67] There's clearly a massive desire among our young people to both contribute and develop their skills in less traditional areas

---

67   "Teach For America Announces the Schools Contributing the Most Graduates to its 2011 Teaching Corps," Teach For America (press release), August 2, 2011, http://www.teachforamerica.org/press-room/press-releases/2011/teach-america-announces-schools-contributing-most-graduates-its-201-0.

of impact. Yet there are few paths for them to take beyond those provided by high-resource industries and institutions.

We need more organizations like Teach For America to create real choices for our young people. We need to present them with a more complete set of alternatives, so they can advance and grow in ways that both they and we as a society would like to see.

Imagine a country where the same proportion of talent that currently goes to finance, law, and consulting went instead to early-stage growth companies around the country, which generate all net new job growth each year on average.[68] That would help address our unemployment issues as a country within a generation or two. Our young people want the same things—they see the problems our country is facing, and they want to do something about it.

This goal is one we can readily achieve, but the issue is one of resources. Goldman Sachs, McKinsey & Company, Boston Consulting Group (BCG) and their peer firms each spend millions of dollars a year on recruiting the best and brightest. Their brand equity is high. Teach For America, to its credit, has developed a similarly robust recruitment infrastructure and brand. There's a war for talent, but only certain sides are fighting.

For the growth companies like V-Charge that represent our next level of innovation and job creation, there is little way to compete. The same is true for companies engaged in scientific research. For example, I met a woman who was completing her PhD in biology from Harvard who said that exactly two firms recruited her and her program mates: not drug companies or biotechs, but McKinsey and BCG.

We need to recognize as a society that the market for our most important resource—our talented young people—requires active

---

68   *The Importance of Startups in Job Creation and Destruction,* (Kauffman Foundation, July 2010), 2, http://www.kauffman.org/uploadedfiles/firm_formation_importance_of_startups.pdf.

participation and leadership. Asking them to ignore the enormous institutional forces brought to bear, or ignoring them ourselves, is unrealistic and destructive. We have to build the paths we want them to walk and enable them to make genuine choices that will benefit both them and our country as a whole.

This is not something that any one institution can address alone. But there are concrete steps that would have a significant impact:

1. **Make growth companies a distinct category for university career services.** University career services offices should invest in identifying diverse opportunities with growth companies around the country. Each career services office should have a "growth company liaison" to reach out to small and mid-sized growth companies and determine their hiring needs. Career services offices should be evaluated based on the breadth and nature of opportunities that are promoted to students. Ideally, national universities would pool resources to invest in an agency that would act as a clearinghouse and ensure that a level playing field exists between firms large and small. Our national universities are publicly funded and supported (at a minimum, they receive tax-exempt status saving them hundreds of millions of dollars); what their graduates do should be regarded as a public policy concern.

2. **Present entrepreneurs as role models.** Universities should promote as role models entrepreneurs who have started successful companies and invite them to tell their stories every year. Leaders such as Miles Lasater of Higher One in New Haven, Charlie Kroll of Andera in Providence, Brian Balasia of Digerati in Detroit, and Jen Medbery of Drop the Chalk in New Orleans are all inspirational figures who have created dozens of jobs around the country. Every university should

have an "Entrepreneurship Hour," as does the University of Michigan, when an experienced entrepreneur comes and speaks to hundreds of students. Campus newspapers should regularly profile appropriate alumni and ask them how they got where they are. Role models and narratives are important.

3. **Improve entrepreneurship education.** Entrepreneurship education should become action-oriented and real-world driven. One student at Columbia said to me, "All we see around here are successful entrepreneurs who have made it and have happy endings. What about the others?" At present, the study of entrepreneurship is analytical and often ends upon graduation, when it's time to get a real job. Entrepreneurship coursework should consist of actions undertaken for real organizations (i.e. raise money for a local nonprofit, conduct market research for a local startup, optimize a website for search engines for a local business, etc.). Most business building is not a clever idea, but high-level execution.

4. **Enlist entrepreneurs as mentors.** Universities, business schools, and even law schools should develop a roster of alumni entrepreneurs who are willing to take on paid apprentices. Interested applicants should compete via a fellowship application process in order to qualify, followed by individual interviews to determine fit (i.e. create "The Yale Entrepreneurship Fellowship"). Many veteran entrepreneurs would enjoy having an ambitious young person from their school around, and most entrepreneurs believe that the best training is to work alongside a more experienced veteran.

5. **Make accelerators and incubators more accessible.** It's difficult to devise a business plan and develop a company that is accepted by an accelerator that then goes on to raise additional funding. The bar is way too high for most recent graduates. To make opportunities more accessible, each accelerator and incubator should maintain a selective database of students and recent graduates who are willing to act as volunteer unpaid labor or interns for their companies. Startups would select workers from the talent bench. Over time, graduates would get some experience and wind up connected to any emerging startups.

6. **Form and expand regional innovation hubs.** Public-private partnerships such as Cincytech in Cincinnati, RI-CIE in Providence, and TechTown in Detroit have each served as an invaluable launch pad for a host of businesses. Each also serves as the physical center of a startup community, offering inexpensive real estate and a natural place to network. Government officials and leaders, community foundations, economic development corporations, universities, Chambers of Commerce, and local enterprises should support existing innovation hubs, or create new ones to attract and create young companies.

7. **Provide scholarships and loan forgiveness for graduates heading to growth companies.** Universities and MBA programs ought to fund post-graduate scholarships for and forgive the loans of any honors graduate who starts or joins a qualifying early-stage business upon graduation. We should do whatever we can to encourage not just starting a company, but joining a recently founded one. Early startup hires often become the next generation of executives and founders, and

most any entrepreneur will tell you that a strong early team is a crucial element to getting a business off the ground. Companies and regional entities could assist in funding these scholarships to benefit local enterprises (e.g. Procter and Gamble could offer a scholarship to pay back loans for honors students who join a Cincinnati-based startup).

8. **Entrepreneurs should reach back.** Successful entrepreneurs often are very focused on their current venture or latest interest—it's one of their defining traits. Their early career quickly recedes into the rear-view mirror, and it's tempting to let others address the concerns of recent graduates. Yet the entrepreneurs themselves remain the best equipped to supply the insight, perspective and resources to enable others to follow in their footsteps. Many could do more to share their stories and make sure that others understand the process from the view of the trenches. Tony Hsieh of Zappos is an example of an entrepreneur who has done an outstanding job reaching back to inspire others; Tony has funded and mentored many other entrepreneurs, in addition to founding Delivering Happiness and the Downtown Project.

9. **Provide a path to entrepreneurship.** We need to provide a direct and concrete path for motivated graduates to learn and develop what it takes to build a business. Entrepreneurship is like most things—you tend to get better at it over time. The toughest part is getting started. We have to make it easier to get started as an entrepreneur. For example, Venture for America offers a competitive two-year fellowship program that sends top graduates to work in startups in low-cost US cities (e.g. Detroit, New Orleans, etc.). Fellows first attend a five-week training camp and then complete a group curriculum

throughout. And $100,000 in seed investment is awarded to the best performers at the end of the two-year period. Our goal is to help create jobs by providing growth companies the talent they need to expand and training our best and brightest to themselves become job creators and business builders. Recent or impending graduates can apply today.

Our young people desperately want the chance to participate in and lead our nation's economic and cultural revival. It only remains for us to present the opportunity.

Andrew Yang is the Founder and President of Venture for America, a fellowship program that places top college graduates in start-ups for 2 years in low-cost U.S. cities to generate job growth and train the next generation of entrepreneurs. Andrew has worked in start-ups and early stage growth companies as a founder or executive for more than twelve years. He was the CEO and President of Manhattan GMAT, a test preparation company that was acquired by the Washington Post/Kaplan in 2009. He has also served as the co-founder of an Internet company and an executive at a health care software start-up. He has appeared on CNBC, Fox News, Forbes, TechCrunch, the *Wall St. Journal*, Reuters, and many other media outlets. Andrew was named a Champion of Change by the White House in 2011 for his work with Venture for America. He is a graduate of Columbia Law and Brown University.

The Power of Intrapreneurship and the Opportunities It Creates for Youth and Women

Ingrid Vanderveldt, Entrepreneur-in-Residence, Dell

O ur nation is at a juncture that often makes me think back to John F. Kennedy's famous quote, "It's not what your country can do for you, but what you can do for your country," especially when considering the current generation. Today's youth are very much in line with the larger economic, social, and political challenges that we face in the United States and globally. We must encourage and enable our young people to dream big and embrace a sense of personal responsibility and community. One way for business owners to do that is by creating a culture of intra-preneurship, where employees behave like entrepreneurs within a larger company that actively fosters their new ideas and innovative solutions.

This new era of young and emerging workers in our country, known as the Millennials, represented fifty million people at the start of the twenty-first century.[69] They identify themselves as unique and distinctive, and they personify the tech-savvy, innovative culture that every business is seeking now. According to a Harris Interactive

---

69   "The Millennials: Confident. Connected. Open to Change," Pew Research Center, February 24, 2010, http://pewresearch.org/pubs/1501/millennials-new-survey-generational-personality-upbeat-open-new-ideas-technology-bound.

survey, 37 percent of eight- to twenty-one-year-olds want to invent something if given the opportunity, and 59 percent know someone who has started his or her own business.[70] These statistics not only motivate me, but also make me realize there are so many untapped workers and resources that can be connected today. What better way to develop Millennials and their ideas than to embed these young workers inside our own companies? Intrapreneurship offers a mutual benefit to companies seeking innovation, and entrepreneurs seeking an opportunity to build their skills with some level of stability.

To illustrate how this concept works in the current business world, let's examine Dell, whose entrepreneur-in-residence program helps demonstrate the idea in action. If someone told me five years ago that Dell (or any other large company) was a place I would find myself working, I would have looked at them like they had three heads. I am an entrepreneur who formed my career and view of myself off of building ideas from scratch. While I have had Fortune 500 companies as clients, I never saw myself as someone who would "go inside."

My first company was funded by a group of Dell executives, but after that company sold off its assets in the dot-com bust, I "fell away" from Dell for about ten years. Then, in 2010, I was invited into the Dell Women's Entrepreneur Network (DWEN), an invitation-only network of some of the top female entrepreneurs, CEOs, and visionaries in the world. I went to the event because one of my friends and colleagues, Heidi Messer, suggested I do so. Heidi sold her last company for $426 million, and I figured if Heidi thought it was important enough to go, then I would probably learn a lot from attending.

---

70 *Young People Want to Be Their Own Boss to Realize Their Ideas,* (Kauffman Foundation, 2007), http://www.kauffman.org/uploadedfiles/KF_Harris_Poll_Fact%20Sheet.pdf.

Attending the first annual DWEN event in Shanghai was a huge eye-opener for me. I got to see firsthand how a global corporation like Dell, a Fortune 50 company, was using its resources and assets to listen to and help women-owned businesses grow and succeed. Just a month after coming back from DWEN, the company I was running at the time sold. The experience made me stand back and look at my career to date, and ask myself the question, "What's next?" At that moment, I realized that I would dedicate my life to lining up my business, policy, and media initiatives to "Empower a Billion Women by 2020." When I think of female empowerment, I think of how, through supporting the unique, fresh perspective women bring, global sustainability can be realized. To do this, we must encourage women to be leaders in all types of organizations and to become self-sustaining for themselves, their families, their communities and ultimately, for the world. Instilling the entrepreneurial spirit within women increases their chance for success, regardless of their situation. A woman in the United States may define empowerment differently than a woman in an African village; however, the reality of empowerment can come to be through mentoring, education, and increased access to technology and other resources.

As entrepreneurs, we often make a commitment to our vision with an understanding that while we may not know exactly how to make it happen, we do have the knowledge and confidence to figure it out. I am no different. The only thing I knew, with a vision as big as reaching one billion women, was that I needed to create clout with organizations aligned towards similar causes.

Fast forward to June 2011, when I attended the second annual DWEN event in Rio de Janeiro. Once again, I found myself in awe watching this $60 billion-plus company listen to women share stories and explain how they could use Dell solutions to grow and innovate. It was out of these two DWEN experiences that I realized the power of a large company like Dell to be innovative and entrepreneurial. I also saw how they supported intrapreneurship by bringing to life ideas developed by Dell employees. A team at Dell saw the increasingly powerful role that female business owners were playing in driving economic growth, and their observations led directly to the creation of DWEN. "According to our network, what women entrepreneurs need most is access to networks, capital and knowledge," said Jennifer "JJ" Davis, who runs the Dell Women's Entrepreneur Network. "We created DWEN to help women entrepreneurs better achieve these things and leverage them to grow their businesses—both at home and internationally in fast-growth markets like China, Brazil and India."

The "aha! moment" came when I recognized the power that a collaboration with a company like Dell could have towards reaching my goal of empowering a billion women. In turn, I knew that by bringing "the outside in" with an entrepreneur's perspective as Dell's first Entrepreneur-in-Residence (EIR), I could bring a unique and valuable perspective to the company that could help them grow their customer base in an authentic way. From a business perspective, Dell's success meant success for all of us. With this thought in mind, I arranged a meeting with Dell President and Chief Commercial Officer Steve Felice. To my good fortune, and visionary thinking on his part, Steve and others at Dell had already been thinking about bringing in an Entrepreneur-in-Residence (EIR) to help them do exactly what I was thinking: bridge the ideas from the outside to programs and changes inside. As most great opportunities come together, there is a right place and time for everything and we were all on the same page. Subsequently, Dell made the decision to bring me on as their first EIR, which would change the way I viewed intrapreneurship forever. "In creating the EIR, Dell is expanding the ways we connect with, learn from and understand the needs of growing businesses so we can bring solutions and services to market that help them succeed," said Felice.

So, why is an EIR important? It's important to me because I got to see how intrapreneurship could be just as impactful and certainly just as critical as entrepreneurship. That same drive, creativity, and passion for growth that entrepreneurs have can also be used inside a company to benefit customers and team members. Below are some specific programs currently in place at Dell and other companies that foster innovation, entrepreneurial thinking, and ultimately job creation through new ideas and growth—ideas other businesses can model to foster intrapreneurship in their own organizations.

Bringing "the Outside In" with an Entrepreneur-in-Residence

The entrepreneur-in-residence (EIR) model is typically associated with venture capital firms or investors as a means for them to nurture a big idea and successful company, and then invest in the new venture at the end of the EIR's term. While Dell isn't a VC and EIRs aren't common in the technology sector, it is critical that the company continues to create technology solutions that can solve real business problems for its customers. In bringing me on as an EIR, Dell is expanding the ways it can connect with, learn from and better understand the needs of growing businesses, so it can bring solutions and services to market that help them succeed. By having me help drive strategy as the company's first EIR, Dell takes its ability to listen and act on what customers need to the next level.

Finding and Keeping Great Talent through Intrapreneurship and Career Development Opportunities

Dell recognizes the gift of finding and keeping great talent. They also recognize that to acquire top talent in today's competitive environment, they need to ensure that as a twenty-five-plus-year-old company, they can offer opportunities for significant career growth and personal development.

For example, one program I got to see was something called Transformation Idol, or TI (inspired by "American Idol"). TI is a program that was developed by two marketing and sales leaders inside Dell to inspire entrepreneurial and creative thinking. A couple times a year, they host a half-day challenge for employees who have dreamt up ideas to help Dell's business be more effective. Teams of employees come together after spending months preparing to take part in TI. They go through their presentations and at the end of the day, the leaders take a vote. The winner gets an opportunity to build on their ideas inside Dell with Dell's support (i.e. mentorship, resources, technology, and capital).

Growing and retaining top talent is a challenge that every company large or small faces. Google fosters intrapreneurship through an organizational structure of smaller teams that aim to give employees more autonomy. They're encouraged to spend time on outside projects, and not everything needs approval from top leaders at the company. This flattened system not only inspires and builds morale among employees, but it helps position Google as an innovative and desirable place to work. A similar policy exists at 3M, where management mandates that all researchers spend at least 15 percent of their time working on ideas outside of their normal tasks. This encouragement for researchers to push the envelope, make mistakes, and pursue new opportunities is what keeps 3M's commitment to innovation intact after all these years.

These ideas drive all these companies to continue to innovate and open up the doors for career growth and entrepreneurship, especially for employees newer to the workforce.

Creating Leverage and Jobs by Teaming Up with Other Organizations

Dell has gotten involved in Secretary of Labor Hilda Solis' Summer Youth Jobs Summit. This is an initiative led by the White House and the Secretary to create job opportunities for our country's youth. While attending the announcement for this program, former White House Chief Technology Officer Aneesh Chopra posed the question, "How can Dell help?" which opened the door for Dell to contribute towards the technical back end of the initiative's website, as well as share thoughts on mentorship in STEM (science, technology, engineering, and math). Additionally, Dell is working with members of the Administration, Congress and the U.S. Chamber of Commerce to create mentorship opportunities so that young people know HOW to prepare to get hired. There are jobs out there; it's finding them and getting hired that can be difficult.

Dell has a program already in place called Youth Connect. In the United States alone, Youth Connect has committed $3 million to help create over 20,000 jobs for students. By teaming up with the White House initiatives, Dell is able to further spread its message and get more young people involved in these programs. Partnerships provide a way to bring company initiatives supporting intrapreneurship (and entrepreneurship) to a wider audience of young people.

Another organization that has already assembled over $1 billion worth of commitments from dozens of partners including Dell,

Intuit, and Microsoft to accelerate job creation across the United States is the Startup America Partnership. Startup America recognizes that entrepreneurship is critical to the country's long-term success, so by bringing together some of the country's most successful companies, they're able to provide valuable resources to young companies with high-growth potential.

There are a lot of great companies out there that together are creating innovative opportunities through intrapreneurship to support women business owners and our country's youth. As the Entrepreneur-in-Residence at Dell, I have been able to see the power of these programs firsthand and the impact companies can have on young Americans. If I were a young person today, I would ask myself, "What am I doing to move myself closer to my dream and closer to the opportunities that will help me better my life? What steps do I need to take to get there?" For someone in the workforce or an entrepreneur, the question becomes, "What innovative ideas do I have that if I were to bring them to an established company, rather than approach them on my own, would increase my chance for success and create a mutual win-win as an intrapreneur?"

In summary, I'd like to go back to my earlier mention of John F. Kennedy. I think that to create the change the world needs, it comes down to a commitment from all sides to take mutual responsibility for success. I have seen that entrepreneurial thinking inside Dell has created an effective environment for growth and intrapreneurship. I have also seen that by teaming up with a large corporation and building for mutual success, it is possible for entrepreneurs to realize the biggest of ideas—even my idea to empower one billion women by 2020.

Peter F. Drucker, one of the best-known thinkers and writers on the subject of management theory, said it himself: "What we need is an entrepreneurial society in which innovation and entrepreneurship are normal, steady, and continual." And in today's world of ever-evolving technologies and market shifts, companies both small and large must be able to effectively respond to change and remain relevant in the face of the competition. Fostering a spirit of entrepreneurship among employees and encouraging innovation through intrapreneurship is almost a requirement for business success in today's complex business environment—and can also be a key to motivating employees, ensuring their job satisfaction, and retaining top entrepreneurial talent.

Ingrid Vanderveldt is the Entrepreneur-in-Residence for Dell, CEO of Green Girl Energy and Founding Organizer of the GLASS Forum (Global Leadership & Sustainable Success). Ingrid has designed and executed corporate, entrepreneurial and philanthropic programs to advance the economic success of women-owned and green-focused businesses, has worked with companies including Microsoft, Dell, Humana and SAIC. She was also the host and creator of CNBC's first original primetime series, "American Made." Visit her website at http://eir.dell.com/ingrid-vanderveldt or follow her on Twitter @ontheroadwithiv.

INGRID VANDERVELDT, LLC

entrepreneurs

New Bootstraps: Creating Twenty-First-Century Tools for a New Generation of Veterans

Jacob Wood and William McNulty,
Co-Founders, Team Rubicon

If the operating concept of a business entrepreneur is one who observes a situation and resolves deficiencies, or creates new opportunities where they have not previously existed, then the military is, in fact, preparing many veterans to fulfill just such a role. The prolonged engagements in Iraq and Afghanistan have generated unique initiative and truly unconventional thinking throughout the ranks. From the privates who began fashioning their own bolt-on armor to defend their vehicles against roadside bombs, to the generals who reduced a two-front conflict into a single fight by persuading the Sunni leadership to join the battle against al-Qaeda, all the branches of the military provide numerous examples of individuals who demonstrate entrepreneurial thinking and leadership in combat.

However, once these members of the armed forces become veterans and make the transition into civilian life, all levels of government and society as a whole fail to cultivate the traits, skills, and lessons learned in the military. The first challenge is to recognize veterans as being highly trained and specialized individuals, not a group of automatons incapable of functioning without orders. The second challenge is finding opportunities to engage what has been learned in the military by translating it into a civilian context, and to build upon the military experience rather than trying to dismiss or reform it.

For the purpose of meeting the latter challenge, practical new tools must be developed to assist veterans in putting their specializations and skills to use in civilian business life. While, in general, veterans are more likely to own their own businesses, and there are currently 2.4 million veteran-owned businesses and another 1.2 million businesses owned by veterans and non-veterans,[71] an unacceptably high number of men and women serve their country in the armed forces, only to return home to unemployment. A *Bloomberg-Businessweek* analysis of 2011 U.S. Bureau of Labor Statistics data put that number as high as 30.4 percent for the youngest returning veterans, aged eighteen to twenty-four.[72] These individuals are not incapable of working, but often find it impossible to identify meaningful work. To a certain extent, they have been trained out of the average workforce and the experience they have acquired has placed them beyond entry-level employment. Thus, the tools that are needed are ones that bring veterans together to share practical advice in how to define one's highest productivity, how to determine one's niche in the civilian business community, and how to use each others' experience and connections to build new veteran-owned, veteran-employing businesses.

---

71   "Survey of Business Owners – Veteran-Owned Firms: 2007," U.S. Census Bureau, last modified June 7, 2011, http://www.census.gov/econ/sbo/get07sof.html?17.

72   Dan Beucke, "Unemployment for Young Vets: 30%, and Rising," *Bloomberg Businessweek,* November 11, 2011, http://www.businessweek.com/finance/occupy-wall-street/archives/2011/11/the_vets_job_crisis_is_worse_than_you_think.html.

Team Rubicon: Bridging the Gap in Disaster Relief – Filling a Gap in Veterans' Lives

In 2010, after we had completed our service in the Marines, we were watching the news reports on the Port-au-Prince earthquake. We could see that none of the civilian aid agencies were prepared to respond to a disaster of that magnitude quickly. But we knew that the skills we learned in Iraq and Afghanistan and the experience we acquired under some extremely adverse conditions could be immediately applied in Port-au-Prince to great effect. As we prepared to travel to Haiti, against all conventional and media advice, we were rapidly joined by other veterans who saw precisely what we did—that we had been through similar and worse, and we had the capabilities to address the situation right away. These were capabilities that our civilian counterparts in the big aid organizations obviously lacked.

Over several weeks in Haiti, time and again, our veterans were the first responders to countless medical and life-safety emergencies. We were mobile and versatile. We were able to evaluate situations quickly and determine the best resolution based on the resources available. We served to bridge the gap between when the earthquake struck and when international aid organizations were eventually able to mobilize their bureaucracies and response mechanisms.

While we went to Haiti in order to render immediate aid after a natural disaster, we soon realized that the veterans who joined with us had been empowered by discovering a role wherein their military experience formed the invaluable foundation for a much larger project. This is how Team Rubicon was created. Subsequently, we have responded to the earthquake in Chile and the tornadoes in Missouri and Alabama. We have also sent teams to address humanitarian crises in Pakistan, Burma, and Sudan. In all of these missions, the veteran members of Team Rubicon have shown the sort of initiative and unconventional thinking that they learned in the military—and each of these missions has provided opportunities for them to put these traits to work for a greater good.

Building New Veteran Networks, Creating New Veteran Businesses

The first answer to the question of how to make veterans into entrepreneurs is to recognize that, in many cases, they are already entrepreneurs by training and experience. But this entrepreneurial skill must be redirected and applied in a civilian context. The key is not re-education, but identifying opportunities and effectively networking with other veterans. Team Rubicon came into being once a group of veterans all realized that an opportunity for service had presented itself. By coming together, these veterans have been able to undertake the task of translating their military skills into a civilian context with each other's assistance. In essence, these veterans already "speak military," so they understand each other perfectly well; thus, they are best suited to help each other learn to communicate all their insight and initiative into civilian terms.

The second answer to the question is self-reliance within the veteran community. The government can try to facilitate veteran business development with programs that reduce barriers to small business formation, increase support for entrepreneurship educational initiatives, and extend existing lending commitments like the SBA Patriot Express Loan Program. Proposed legislation like the Help Veterans Own Franchises Act[73] (now part of the AGREE Act) and a new GI Bill (the VET Act of 2011)[74] could move us toward eliminating financial barriers to business ownership. But the government cannot be the source of innovative practical solutions to

---

73 Help Veterans Own Franchises Act, H.R. 2888, 112th Congress (2011).

74 Veterans Entrepreneurial Transition Act of 2011, H.R. 3167, 112th Congress (2011).

veterans' real-world difficulties. And while nonprofit organizations perform highly valuable services for veterans in many different capacities, those seeking to engage and succeed in entrepreneurial business cannot rely on charities to lead the way. The entire mentality of depending on the government for assistance or hoping to find a philanthropic foundation to lend a hand must be dismissed in order to take up the challenge of building more veteran businesses. The initiative to construct a national network, to create a clearinghouse of ideas, and to build a new veteran business culture, must come from within the national veteran community.

If anything is holding veterans back from better employing their entrepreneurial skills, it is a lack of dynamic networking, and a lack of inspiring opportunities. From their first day of boot camp, members of the military learn, work, and solve problems as a group. They build on each other's strengths and they draw inspiration from the energy and dedication of the group. When their service is completed and they return to their home states, they are spread across all the United States. Thus, veterans lose the connections with fellow veterans and thereby lose the inspiration to find creative and innovative projects, opportunities, and solutions.

The connection must be restored for veterans to again tap the great potential they developed during their time serving in uniform. A peer-to-peer network for veterans is a necessity, not a convenience; and this community can create the synergy that will, in turn, renew the entrepreneurial inspiration and skill first learned in the military.

The Blueprint for a Veterans' Peer-to-Peer Network

In building Team Rubicon, we quickly discovered that networks expand spontaneously, but only when they have adequate platforms. We also learned that working with many enthusiastic and very different individuals can be productive only when there is a guiding vision and a leadership team ensuring faithfulness to that vision.

Hence, a successful peer-to-peer network must have these fundamental characteristics:

- Created by veterans themselves as an entrepreneurial venture
- Administered entirely separately from any governmental direction or dependence on larger national groups
- Structured to serve as a national, regional, and local platform that brings veterans together to share ideas, experience, and advice
- Guided by a comprehensive vision, mission, and purpose, focused on creating more veteran-owned and veteran-employing businesses
- Enabled to expand rapidly to accommodate growing sub-networks, to disseminate information and initiatives, and to meet new and unforeseen needs of a growing veteran business community.

Furthermore, the continuing interactions that such a dynamic network can produce and foster will be the source of ideas for new business ventures that capture veterans' imaginations and employ their unique skill sets. The shared experience of boot camp and deployment brings veterans to a certain level of like-mindedness that means they work best and most productively with others who have endured the same or similar mental and physical tests. In short, veterans speak a language unique to themselves; but this is not a handicap or an obstacle to working with others. Rather, it is a tremendous strength that should be built upon—bring these men and women together again through a peer-to-peer network, let them speak their language, let them draw inspiration from each other, and then the entrepreneurial productivity will issue forth.

A New Solution for a New Generation of Veterans

In previous generations, men of the same age and background, who came from the same town, would join the military together. When their service was completed, they would go home to that same town. They never lost touch with each other, and those so minded to build up local businesses and philanthropic organizations knew exactly where to go to tap energies and ideas complementary to their own.

Today, that sort of shared background is the exception, not the rule, in active-duty military units. And that sort of post-discharge physical proximity is very rare. Therein lies the critical lack that has resulted in veterans not undertaking entrepreneurial ventures as they did in the past. However, in an age of digital communication and social networking, there is absolutely no reason that an electronic peer-to-peer community of veterans cannot be constructed. Such a vital tool will empower veterans; it will generate the synergy on which veterans thrived when they were serving; and it will become a clearinghouse for ideas to develop and opportunities to seize.

The modern military has already laid the groundwork necessary for making young men and women into successful entrepreneurs. Upon return to civilian life, it is critical that the connections among those who have sweat and bled together be kept alive. With a dynamic network exclusively for veterans, their unique inspirations, energies, and skills can be harnessed and turned into an incredible engine for entrepreneurial business.

Jacob Wood graduated from the University of Wisconsin, where he played football, with a double major in Business and Political Science. He honorably served four years in the United States Marine Corps, deploying to Iraq in 2007 as an infantry squad leader and to Afghanistan in 2008 as a Scout-Sniper. He graduated Scout-Sniper School at the top of his class and in 2007 he was awarded the Navy and Marine Corps Commendation Medal with "V" for valor in the face of the enemy while in Iraq. Jake serves on numerous national veteran committees and speaks around the country at universities and conferences about veteran issues and social entrepreneurism.

William McNulty is a Marine who served in both the infantry and Intelligence. He has worked in support of the Defense Intelligence Agency, the National Security Council's Iraq Threat Finance Cell, and the Under Secretary of Defense for Intelligence. He holds a B.A. in Economics and Communication Studies from the University of Kansas and an M.A. in Government from The Johns Hopkins University. Visit Team Rubicon's website at www.teamrubiconusa.org.

PART II: SUPPORTING YOUNG AMERICANS' ENTREPRENEURIAL SPIRIT

Extending Self-Employment Assistance Programs to Entrepreneurs in All States

Senator Ron Wyden

I n June of 2008, Adam Lowry and Michael Richardson found themselves unemployed. The tech startup where they worked in Portland, Vidoop, had just closed its doors, and employees were being offered company laptops in lieu of back wages. Common sense would dictate that these promising young programmers should file for unemployment insurance and begin their search for new employment—which they did. In a way.

After working at a startup, Lowry and Richardson caught the entrepreneurial bug and wanted to build a business for themselves. In order to do it right, they needed to devote a huge amount of time to build the business from scratch—something that would have been hard to do if they were also searching full-time for full-time jobs, as the unemployment office required.

Instead, these two friends availed themselves of a versatile and often underused form of unemployment insurance known as Self-Employment Assistance. The program gives entrepreneurs like Lowry and Richardson the freedom to collect unemployment insurance while starting their own businesses. Together, the pair pooled their resources and launched Urban Airship. Today, Lowry and Richardson's company not only provides full-time employment for these two successful entrepreneurs, but also employs dozens of additional workers.

The current generation of young people—Millennials, as they are known—have a unique characteristic that, if cultivated, could result in huge benefits for the national economy. More so than many older generations, these young people want to start their own businesses and be their own bosses. Unfortunately, their entrepreneurial spirit is matched only by the economic hardship they are being thrust into.

The recession has had an outsized effect on young professionals and recent college grads. The quadruple whammy of skyrocketing education costs, unprecedented student loan debt, difficulty accessing capital and a safety net geared towards laid-off workers seeking traditional hourly-wage or salaried employment means that an entire generation of young people face unique and unprecedented labor market challenges. The result is that youth unemployment is the highest in the nation of any major demographic—hovering at a crushing 16.3 percent at the end of 2011.[75]

To make matters worse, the average college graduate has more than $25,000 in student loan debt. And that's for those who—through hard work, good fortune, or some combination of the two—were able to complete college. So here we have a highly motivated and highly educated demographic of Americans who are drowning in debt and can't find jobs. Shouldn't we be doing a better job helping them create their own?

---

75   Paul Taylor, et al., *Young, Underemployed and Optimistic: Coming of Age, Slowly, in a Tough Economy,* Pew Research Center, (Pew Social & Demographic Trends, February 9, 2012), 6, http://www.pewsocial-trends.org/files/2012/02/SDT-Youth-and-Economy.pdf.

How States Can Leverage Self-Employment
Assistance to Foster Entrepreneurship

Self-employment assistance (SEA) uses the framework of the existing unemployment insurance (UI) system to enable aspiring entrepreneurs to take their regular UI benefits and put them to work starting their own business. The program has been a tremendous success in my home state of Oregon and, if expanded, could play a powerful and low-cost role in our job-creation toolkit.

To understand SEA, it's necessary to first understand the general mechanics of the UI system. The federal government and the states work in partnership to run the system—all states and territories have an individual UI trust fund used to pay out weekly benefits to workers who have lost their jobs. The states administer their separate programs and set the eligibility requirements, benefit amounts and employer tax rates. The federal government sets broader guidelines, requiring employers to pay a minimum tax rate into their state UI trust fund on behalf of their employees.

Eligibility rules vary widely among states, but in most states, recipients are required to:

- Have become unemployed involuntarily through no fault of their own.
- Have earned a minimum amount in the time preceding the unemployment—known as the "base period."
- Be actively seeking full-time work.
- Accept a reasonable offer of work.

In most states, unemployed workers looking to start their own businesses would lose their unemployment benefits if they were not actively looking for another job.

Only a handful of states have used federal authority to create SEA programs and allow a small portion of UI recipients to draw down their weekly benefits as they work to start their own businesses. The benefits are in the same amount and for the same maximum duration as regular UI benefits, so there are no more costs to the government than there would have been otherwise. Furthermore, SEA participants are required to have a viable business plan and receive entrepreneurial training in order to qualify. This weeds out those seeking to game the system, and improves the likelihood of success for their new business.

Though this is a little-known program, the idea is not a new one—in fact, I have advocated for the expansion of SEA since I first learned of its success more than twenty-five years ago.

In the 1980s and 1990s, the Department of Labor (DOL) took part in a series of employment and training social science experiments, known as the UI Experiments that identified self-employment assistance as a cost-effective re-employment strategy. In 1987, Washington State was selected by DOL as the first site for a demonstration process which would test out a lump-sum payment SEA model based on a French program.

I proposed an amendment to the Budget Reconciliation Act of 1987 that would expand the demonstration program, and also require the DOL to test the feasibility of providing SEA payments in lieu of weekly or biweekly UI checks to beneficiaries in a system similar to what is in practice now. The "Wyden Demonstration," as it came to be known, was enacted into law, and Massachusetts was ultimately selected along with Washington State as the site for the UI Self-Employment Demonstrations.

The final report on the SEA Experiments as completed by the Department of Labor showed that both states' programs were successful and cost-effective for the participants—as well as society as a whole. The Washington program had a positive net benefit to participants (approximately $2,000) as well as society (approximately $700). Over the thirty-one-month observation of the Massachusetts program, participants had a net benefit of over $11,000, and a net benefit to society of over $13,000. Moreover, a cost-benefit analysis of the Massachusetts program from the government's perspective demonstrated over $2,000 in net benefits.[76] More specific results are summarized in the chart below:

Table 8.4 Summary of UI Self-Employment Demonstration Net Impacts

	Massachusetts			Washington		
	Treatments	Controls	Impact	Treatments	Controls	Impact
% self-employed since random assignment	58	47	12**	66	44	22***
Length of first UI spell (weeks)	26.5	24.5	–1.8***	19.3	11.6	–7.6***
Total benefit payments in dollars since random assignment (UI + lump sum payments in Washington)	7,400	6,567	–876***	6,750	5,442	–1,300***
Annual time in self-employment (months)	2.6	1.7	0.8*	3.4	1.1	2.3***
Annual self-employment earnings ($)	2,627	1,439	1,219	3,029	703	2,157**
Annual time in wage and salary employment (months)	4.4	4.1	0.6	5.2	4.5	–0.7**
Annual wage and salary earnings ($)	10,119	7,797	3,053**	9,920	8,414	–1,744**
Total time in employment since random assignment (months per year)	7.4	5.8	1.9***	7.8	6.7	1.1***
Total annual earnings since random assignment ($)	14,664	10,056	5,940***	14,259	13,173	205

NOTE: All impact estimates presented in this table are regression-adjusted impacts derived using ordinary least squares (OLS). * coefficient significantly different from zero at the 0.10 level (two-tailed test); ** coefficient significantly different from zero at the 0.05 level (two-tailed test); *** coefficient significantly different from zero at the 0.01 level (two-tailed test).
SOURCE: Benus et al. (1995).

306

Credit: Stephen Wandner, *Solving the Reemployment Puzzle*, W.E. Upjohn Institute for Employment Research, (Kalamazoo, MI: 2010), 306.

In June of 1992 and again in 1993, I introduced bipartisan and bicameral legislation to allow all states to pay SEA benefits to a small portion of a state's unemployed population in lieu of regular UI. This legislation was enacted into law as part of the North American Free Trade Agreement (NAFTA) in December of 1993, and became permanent law in 1998.

76 Jacob M. Benus, *Self-Employment Programs: A New Reemployment Strategy, Final Report on the UI Self-Employment Demonstration*, Unemployment Insurance Occasional Paper 95-4, (U.S. Department of Labor Employment and Training Administration, 1995), 23.

Next Steps for Advancing SEA Programs in All States

In spite of its proven success, only a handful of states have implemented SEA programs, and few individuals participate in programs that do exist. This is often due to a simple lack of information about the program's existence as well as a misalignment in the program evaluations upon which many states are judged. For example, programs funded by the Workforce Investment Act tend to be rated based on the extent to which participants receive wage and salaried positions thus those achieving success in entrepreneurial training do not count as "success stories" making states less willing to expand such programs. The swelling tide of youth entrepreneurship and prolonged inability of the public or private sector to create plentiful jobs in the current recession should encourage more states to give SEA a chance.

If anything, the success seen in Oregon should make for a compelling argument for SEA. According to a survey of SEA participants, nearly half of the successful SEA entrepreneurs in the state have created an average of 2.63 new jobs.[77] It is well-known that UI is an economic multiplier that goes far beyond the investment into the system, but with SEA, the unemployment insurance program can become a job multiplier as well. Let this generation embrace the entrepreneurial spirit, pool resources, and create jobs for themselves and others who are struggling to find work.

Under current law, states may only pay out SEA for the first twenty-six weeks of UI benefits. However, in times of elevated unemployment, the federal government has stepped up to provide additional emergency unemployment benefits. Earlier this year, legisla-

---

77 "Self-Employment Needs Role in Jobs Programs: View," *Bloomberg View,* August 23, 2011, http://www.bloomberg.com/news/2011-08-24/self-employment-should-play-a-bigger-role-in-jobs-programs-view.html.

tion I authored to allow states to create their own SEA programs was included in the payroll tax cut extension bill passed by Congress.

S. 1826, the Startup Technical Assistance for Reemployment Training and Unemployment Prevention (STARTUP) Act, allows states to pay out these additional federal benefits in the form of SEA.[78] It also instructs the Department of Labor to develop model language to help states gain awareness of the program and facilitate their enactment of permanent-law SEA programs. It gives states until December of 2013 to apply for their share of $35 million dollars to establish (or improve) their own self-employment assistance programs. Though $35 million may not seem like a huge incentive in the grand scheme of things, it can go a long way in the world of self-employment assistance and it is my hope that growing awareness of the potential of SEA coupled with these new federal dollars and model language from the Department of Labor will motivate more states to take advantage of the program and the new flexibility it offers. Aspiring entrepreneurs can only take advantage of this new program if their states enter into agreement with the Department of Labor, so outreach and awareness campaigns are critical.

Though this program can only directly benefit workers who have recently been employed in wage or salaried jobs—excluding recent college grads who have not yet fully entered the labor market—young people who have lost their jobs are among the best candidates for SEA. They are less likely to have families and own their own homes, making them more mobile and able to start a new business based on the demands of markets across the country. And with fewer financial obligations, the value of SEA benefits (the average UI benefit check is just $295 per week) can be stretched even further. The biggest hurdle we face now is awareness. Each state manages its UI programs

---

78 Startup Technical Assistance for Reemployment Training and Unemployment Prevention Act, S.1826, 112th Congress (2011).

differently and the legislation doesn't mandate that a state do this, it just gives them the means and the know-how to get their programs up and running. We need a concerted effort to show state officials the sheer potential of a program that invests in entrepreneurs and their capability to lift themselves and many others off of the UI rolls. That is why the example set by Urban Airship is so compelling.

Adam Lowry and Michael Richardson are now the lead engineers of one of the best-known technology startups to emerge in Oregon in many years. Urban Airship, the company they cofounded, enables "push" notifications and facilitates sales on iPhones, Androids, and similar mobile devices. In late 2011, the company announced that it arranged $15.1 million in strategic investment from Salesforce.com and Verizon, as well as the acquisition of a California-based mobile developer. Urban Airship is one of the many innovative new companies pushing the boundaries of the mobile technology and enabling a whole new industry of products to grow. As of November 2011, Urban Airship employed a work force of fifty-one, and continues to hire.

All of this may not have been possible if it weren't for Self-Employment Assistance. We owe it to the Lowrys and Richardsons of the world to give young entrepreneurs the means to create jobs for themselves—and to build businesses that create jobs for others. Most of all, we owe the next generation of bright, inspired young people a chance to turn unemployment into a track for success. It's time to get started.

Ron Wyden was first elected to Congress in 1980 to represent Oregon's 3rd District. In 1996, he was elected to the U.S. Senate in a special election, becoming the first U.S. Senator to be elected in a vote-by-mail election. He was sworn in on February 5, 1996, to the seat once held by his mentor, U.S. Senator Wayne Morse. Elected to his second full term in 2004, Senator Wyden received more votes over 1.1 million than any other candidate for office in Oregon's history. He was re-elected in 2010. Born in 1949 in Wichita, Kansas, Senator Wyden attended the University of California at Santa Barbara on a basketball scholarship. He later earned a B.A degree with distinction from Stanford University and received a J.D. degree from the University of Oregon School of Law in 1974. Following law school, he taught gerontology and co-founded the Oregon chapter of the Gray Panthers, an advocacy group for the elderly. He also served as the director of the Oregon Legal Services for the Elderly from 1977 to 1979 and as a member of the Oregon State Board of Examiners of Nursing Home Administrators during that same time period. In the U.S. Senate, Senator Wyden serves on the following committees: Finance, Intelligence, Aging, Budget, and Energy and Natural Resources. On the Energy Committee, he chairs the Subcommittee on Public Lands and Forests. On the Finance Committee, Wyden chairs the Subcommittee on International Trade, Customs and Global Competitiveness. Senator Wyden's home is in Portland. He is married to Nancy Wyden, whom he wed in September 2005. He and Nancy welcomed the arrival of twins, William Peter and Ava Rose, in the fall of 2007. Senator Wyden also has two children, Adam and Lilly, from a previous marriage.

A Loan Forgiveness Program That Gives Broke College Graduates a Chance to Start New Businesses (and Create New Jobs)

Aaron Smith, Co-Founder and Executive Director, Young Invincibles

In spite of all the stereotypes about unmotivated young people, a surprisingly high number of young adults see entrepreneurial activity in their future. Young Invincibles and Demos released a report and poll in 2011, *The State of Young America*, that provides a comprehensive look at the views and challenges facing young adults. Our poll found that 54 percent of young Americans aged eighteen to thirty-four either wanted to start or had already started their own businesses. And the interest in entrepreneurship was high among young adults from all backgrounds—63 percent of young African Americans and 64 percent of young Latinos said they wanted to start a business.[79]

Starting a business is the American dream for many Millennials. We have all heard about the high flyers, those young entrepreneurs with a high-tech startup, millions of dollars from venture capital investors, and an IPO around the corner, but needless to say, they

---

[79] *Young Invincibles Policy Brief: New Poll Finds More Than Half of Millennials Want to Start Businesses,* (Kauffman Foundation, 2011), 4, http://www.kauffman.org/uploadedfiles/millennials_study.pdf.

do not reflect the norm. When we went around the country and held fifteen focus groups—hearing from young adults ranging from community college students to construction workers to the unemployed—we consistently heard about the major barriers to starting a business instead. Many of these barriers, like difficulty accessing a small loan or the lack of education about running a business, reflect real failures of policy.

One issue in particular struck a chord. Student debt has surpassed $1 trillion, and not surprisingly, it is a real concern for millions of young people both in school and out. Yet few people have talked about how student loans may actually block risk-taking for many young people, including the two-thirds of college graduates who now carry student loan debt. But having tens of thousands of dollars in student loan debt alters both personal life choices—think marriage, starting a family—and career choices. Young people are far less likely to take a shot on starting a new business if they worry they won't be able to make their monthly payments. They may be missing an opportunity to follow their passion and succeed.

Student loans should not stand in the way of young people starting businesses. It is in our nation's economic best interest to remove barriers for would-be innovators. Furthermore, about three-quarters of outstanding student loan dollars are from loans held by the federal government, not private lenders.[80] The federal government should have an interest in making sure that the loans it makes to students do not become a burden to the overall economy.

Yet student loan debt is becoming a national crisis. A recent report from Moody's describes student loans as a bubble about to pop, similar to the sub-prime mortgage crisis, and with terrible

---

80 Tamar Lewin, "Burden of College Loans on Graduates Grows," *NYTimes.com*, April 11, 2011, http://www.nytimes.com/2011/04/12/education/12college.html.

possible consequences for the economy.[81] Today, nearly 9 percent of student loan debtors default on their loans,[82] and that percentage is expected to continue to rise given the escalating debt loads and scarcity of employment opportunities. To compound the problem, student loans are not dischargeable in bankruptcy (unlike other consumer debt), meaning that those who default on their loans could face a lifetime of financial troubles—including wage garnishment.

Bold policy reforms are required to address both the need to spur entrepreneurship and job creation, and to alleviate the student debt crisis. We need policy to unlock the potential of young people to be drivers of economic growth and innovation.

The Youth Entrepreneurship Act (YEA)

Young Invincibles and the Young Entrepreneur Council came together to address this challenge by creating and pushing for policies that incentivize youth entrepreneurship. We call this set of policies the Youth Entrepreneurship Act, and dozens of organizations have already signed on to our campaign to get these policies enacted into law.

The centerpiece of the Youth Entrepreneurship Act is a common-sense loan deferral, reduction, and forgiveness program that frees would-be young entrepreneurs from the debt burdens stemming from eligible federal loans, while at the same time creating as many as 100,000 new jobs in the first few years alone. The program, which is modeled after the current Public Service Loan Forgiveness (PSLF) program and uses the existing Income-Based Repayment (IBR) system, will ensure that loan payments and interest accrual are no longer barriers to business creation by graduates.

---

81   Cristian DeRitis, *Student Lending's Failing Grade*, Moody's Analytics, (July 2011), 55.

82   "Default Rates Rise for Federal Student Loans," U.S. Department of Education (press release), September 12, 2011, http://www.ed.gov/news/press-releases/default-rates-rise-federal-student-loans.

Both PSLF and IBR were originally part of the College Cost Reduction and Access Act, which was signed into law by President George W. Bush in 2007.[83] It was a strong step in the right direction for young people already burdened with debt. In a nutshell, PSLF forgives remaining loan debt after ten years for borrowers who work full-time for a qualifying nonprofit or government organization. Under IBR, federal loan borrowers pay a loan payment each month based on their income—lower income means lower payments. Borrowers who earn less than 150 percent of the federal poverty level will pay $0 per month. In addition, under the original IBR, loan payments were capped at 15 percent of discretionary income and the loan balance was forgiven after twenty-five years. IBR is also available to those who qualify for PSLF.

Student loan debt is clearly an issue that has the potential to cross party lines. President Obama recently modified the Bush-era version of IBR, capping payments at 10 percent of income and twenty-year forgiveness, and is marketing the IBR program aggressively to young entrepreneurs as part of a "Student Startup Plan."[84] YEA's proposal uses the same structure, but takes PSLF one logical step further—extending the financial benefits to entrepreneurs whose businesses meet certain qualifying benchmarks, not just government or nonprofit employees. Here's how it would work:

- **Year One:** In the first year, a potential entrepreneur will receive a deferral from paying principal or interest on their loans, as long as they enter income-based repayment while they start their business, take a business-planning course online, *and* certify that they are starting a new enterprise.

---

83   "Income-Based Repayment Plan," Federal Student Aid, U.S. Department of Education, last modified December 7, 2011, http://studentaid.ed.gov/PORTALSWebApp/students/english/IBRPlan.jsp.

84   "Student Startup Plan," U.S. Small Business Administration, accessed February 12, 2012, http://www.sba.gov/startupamerica/student-startup-plan.

Applications that demonstrate self-funding, where the entrepreneur is investing a percentage of their own income or family support in the project, will receive a "safe harbor" waive into the program, given that such funding is a strong sign of commitment toward a viable startup. At the same time, self-funding need not be a requirement for low-income entrepreneurs. Once the entrepreneur joins the program, there will be no accrual of interest in that first year.

- **Years Two – Ten:** The years that follow will provide staggered levels of forgiveness (10 percent in year two, another 25 percent in year five), followed by complete forgiveness for those who make it the full ten years.[85] Meanwhile, the young entrepreneur will remain in the income-based repayment system so as to minimize loan payments if their income remains low. The applicant will also have to provide documentation of ongoing minimum revenue to ensure that participants are indeed building their businesses.

The program will not be effective unless this information reaches the group of students who would take advantage of it. Therefore, we also propose that the college exit interview required for all federal loan recipients include a description of the loan forgiveness program.

Now, let's look at an example. Take Michael, who recently graduated from college and wants to start a small business, Home Craft Enterprises. Michael has $25,000 in debt, about average,[86] and takes out a mix of subsidized and unsubsidized Stafford loans. For

---

85 Another federal loan and forgiveness program, the Perkins Loan Program, uses similar staggered forgiveness for people pursuing occupations such as teaching.

86 "State by State Data," The Project on Student Loan Debt, 2010, http://projectonstudentdebt.org/state_by_state-data.php. The average is now $25,250.

simplicity's sake, his loans carry a 5 percent consolidated interest rate. Michael takes the requisite course, finds a local nonprofit mentorship program online, files with SBA, and consolidates his loans. He's still living at home, but he starts a small business selling homemade crafts online.

Under this new program, in the first year, he defers premium payments on the principal, which is about $2,500 a year, thereby saving $1,250 in interest payments for a total savings of about $3,750. He is able invest that extra $3,750 in expanding his website and promoting his crafts. The savings he has on his student loans, along with the knowledge that he will only be asked to pay what he can afford in year two, makes all the difference to Michael in getting his business off the ground. Importantly, this program also provides a powerful added incentive of rapid loan forgiveness that goes above and beyond IBR, and can help to convince entrepreneurs to start businesses sooner rather than later. From there, his business begins to grow, and he has the option of continuing in the income-based repayment program and working toward full forgiveness.

What is worth noting about young entrepreneurs like Michael is that they only need a small amount of capital to get started— meaning that the student loan relief program really can spur new businesses at a relatively low cost.

YEA Can Increase Innovation and Grow the Economy

This initiative ensures that young people enroll, pursue legitimate business ideas, continue on with successful enterprises, and do not accumulate unwieldy interest (and end up worse off if their businesses ultimately fail).[87] And the increasing revenue requirements

---

87   *Small Business Economy Report,* U.S. Small Business Administration, (2010). This data indicates that 7 out of 10 new firms survive for 2 years, half survive at least 5 years, 1/3 survive for 10 years, and 1/4 survive for 15 years or more.

demonstrate at least some baseline viability standard, ensuring that the investment in loan write-off yields long-term employment. The program also protects against any attempts at fraud by small projects created solely for loan forgiveness purposes.

Additionally, requiring income-based repayment (IBR) ensures that the owners are actually paying what they can afford, particularly if they do launch one of the more successful "gazelle" firms and end up earning significant income. In other words, if an entrepreneur makes millions, they will pay off their loans themselves, which is only fair. Finally, the IBR requirement avoids disincentivizing innovators who fear failure might result in the inability to make payments on premiums or the accrual of interest.

The initial interest forgiveness and staggered total forgiveness percentages mean that young innovators are not deterred from starting at all or from continuing to pursue an idea that may take a few years to gain steam, as is often the case. And giving benchmark rewards means that they are not dissuaded from entering the program at all due to the prospect of failing before they hit the ten-year mark.

In terms of cost, we predict that this program will be both affordable in the short-term and revenue-positive in the long term. To predict enrollment, we used a range of take-up possibilities, assuming anywhere from a moderate increase in new business creation to an increase to similar levels of entrepreneurship from older age cohorts not burdened with such debt.[88] Given that assumption, and the number of young people who graduate with debt, we predict that the program will cost between $300 million and $1 billion over ten years (an average of $30 to $100 million per year, with lower costs

---

88   Robert W. Fairlie, *Kauffman Index of Entrepreneurial Activity*, (Kauffman Foundation, May 2010). Based on this report's data, about 0.24% of young adults (age 20-34) currently start a business, compared to 0.4% of older adults, yet young adults historically have expressed greater interest than older adults in starting a business.

in the first few years). At the same time, depending on participation, the program could create anywhere between 25,000 and 125,000 new jobs in the first five years alone.[89] And those numbers do not include young adults who choose to enroll but would have pursued their ideas even without the program—when we add in those young entrepreneurs, the total participation level results in anywhere from 65,000 to 215,000 jobs. Moreover, income and corporate tax revenues produced from these new firms and employees could offset the program's cost over ten years.

Ensuring that young, debt-ridden graduates are not prevented from pursuing new ideas and growing our economy is one of the most effective ways that we can encourage new business generation during these tough times—and beyond. Doing so also facilitates business investment with capital otherwise wasted on debt repayment, which can have a multiplier effect and create other jobs throughout the economy.

Removing student loans as a barrier to starting a business, combined with increased access to capital and a broader educational commitment, will help create an innovation-driven economy that puts young people back to work. We see loan forgiveness as a smart first step to kick-start a potentially transformative movement of young people creating businesses. And in a time of Washington, DC gridlock, this idea appeals across party lines by leveraging relatively few government resources to produce an enormous societal gain— growing the economy and the middle class at the same time.

The policy also reflects our uniquely American passion for big thinkers and risk-takers, and our high hopes for a younger genera-

---

89   Michael Horrell and Robert Litan, *After Inception: How Enduring is Job Creation by Startups?*, (Kauffman Foundation, July 2010). According to this 2010 report, small businesses typically each create about four jobs, and about 80% of those jobs typically remain after 5 years. Moreover, while half of small businesses will fail after five years, some percentage will grow substantially. Therefore, these numbers could even be conservative.

tion full of potential—one that has grown up understanding new markets and new technology. By supporting policies like YEA, we can put young people back to work, give young adults their shot at the American dream, and create jobs in a new economy.

 **Aaron Smith** is co-founder and Executive Director of Young Invincibles. Aaron is a native of Yonkers, New York, an honors graduate of Swarthmore College ('04), and a cum laude graduate of Georgetown University Law Center ('10). Aaron has appeared in the *NY Times*, *Washington Post*, CNN, MSNBC, NPR, Politico, and PBS NewsHour, among other media outlets, discussing a variety of issues impacting young Americans. In December 2010, he testified before the Senate Commerce Committee on the problems with "mini-med" plans and how they fail to provide affordable health care for young workers. Aaron also served as a consumer representative in the National Association of Insurance Commissioners, where he worked with Insurance Commissioners from around the country to ensure strong consumer protections in the health care industry. Aaron believes strongly in the power of young Americans to change the world. Learn more about the Youth Entrepreneurship Act at http://www.youthentrepreneurshipact.com/.

TOGETHER, INVINCIBLE.

How Legalizing Crowdfunding Will Jump-Start American Entrepreneurship

Congressman Patrick McHenry

Remember when the American dream was the envy of the world? When hard-working, innovative men and women had the means to start a business to support their families that they could pass to the next generation? I do. My family lived it. My father started a company with nothing but a credit card and five hungry mouths to feed.

America's greatness is based on the fact that my family's story was not unusual—thousands of other successful companies were started by entrepreneurs willing to mortgage a home or borrow from family and friends to get their business off the ground.

The environment for entrepreneurs has changed a lot since I was a kid. Most recently, the global financial crisis that unfolded in 2008 caused capital markets to tighten, making everyday forms of credit difficult to obtain. This had adverse effects on labor markets, triggering unprecedented unemployment rates in the United States and handing our youth the worst job market in generations.

These market realities, coupled with new regulations out of Washington increased startup costs, drove down the number of newly created employer businesses by 23 percent from 2006 to 2012.[90]

Familiar with the fact that small businesses historically create over 60 percent of the new jobs in this country, it was clear to me that something had to be done to get startups going again to pull the economy out of the doldrums.

Before you throw a pity party for America, it is wise to ask how a country whose markets are the envy of the world could slip so quickly. The answer is simple: We became complacent.

As the United States became easygoing about retaining its title as the world's number-one destination for capital and growth, developing countries took plays from our economic playbook to jump-start their own economies.

The result has been a tremendous decline in the number of US initial public offerings (IPOs)—from a 1990s average of over 500 per year to only sixty-three in 2009.[91]

This severe drop was directly correlated to our seismic loss of new jobs, seed money for startups, and overall net investment in our economy.

While America had seen recessions before, it was clear this was different.

To understand why the number of new startups in the United States has declined, one must recognize the latest obstacles entrepreneurs face when raising capital.

Conventional wisdom tells us that new businesses follow a fairly defined pattern of financing. First, an entrepreneur uses his or her savings and help from family and friends to start a business. Then,

---

90   E.J. Reedy and Robert E. Litan, *Starting Smaller, Staying Smaller: America's Slow Leak in Job Creation*, (Kauffman Foundation, July 2011), 4, http://www.kauffman.org/uploadedFiles/job_leaks_starting_smaller_study.pdf.

91   "Hoover's IPO Scorecard Reveals First Year-Over-Year Triple-Digit Percentage Increase in More Than a Decade," Hoovers.com (press release), January 11, 2010, http://www.hoovers.com/about/press-releases/100003124-1.html.

after the business begins to generate revenue, it approaches venture capital, angel investors, or banks to spur strong profits and growth. After that period passes, the business either decides to go public via IPO or is acquired through an M&A.

As simple as that sounds, recent studies show that, in reality, most startups finance themselves through lines of credit, such as a credit card or home equity, to get off the ground.

Unless you lived under a rock from 2008 until today (2012), this presents a problem that is twofold: few people have access to credit lines sufficient to start a business, and many have seen the equity in their homes wiped out due to a housing crash. It goes without saying that bank lending has been severely restricted in the past few years.

The result of these realities is plain and simple—countless young, ambitious entrepreneurs are facing the most risk-averse lending market in generations as they look for capital to expand and compete on the open market.

Crowdfunding: The Missing Puzzle Piece

To directly address these market realities facing American entrepreneurs, on March 22, 2011, Darrell Issa, Chairman of the House Oversight and Government Reform Committee, blasted a thirty-three question letter to the Chairman of the Securities and Exchange Commission, Mary Schapiro. It was one of those letters that not only spurs dialogue between the Hill and a federal regulator, but also among market participants and everyday Americans.

Serving as chairman of the House Oversight Subcommittee for issues related to financial services and banking regulations, I had the luxury of reading this letter before the ink had dried. I soon realized I was flipping through the pages of a letter that would transform the way Congress prioritized capital formation.

Approaching the end of the letter, one particular question caught my eye: "Has the SEC considered creating exemptions that would enable unaccredited but sophisticated investors in the U.S. to invest, with reasonable limitations, in unregistered securities issued by small start-ups under what is being called 'crowdfunding?'"

At that moment, I said to myself, "crowdfunding," and thought it sounded both new and familiar. I was very familiar with the work Muhammad Yunus and this concept seemed to have similar objectives to the microlending principles he brought about. The basic idea was to raise money through small contributions from a large number of people, creating a hybrid of microfinance and crowdsourcing. Although very different, I realized the connection campaign fundraising shares with crowdfunding.

This begged the question: Why not extend to smaller entrepreneurs, who traditionally have great difficulty obtaining capital, the same fundraising opportunities that are extended to Members of Congress, Senators, and even President Obama, who, after raising hundreds of millions of dollars in the 2008 election, put together the most successful crowdfunding machine in United States history?

Crowdfunding appeared to be a missing piece in our economy's puzzle. Like everyone else in our information-driven society, I Googled "crowdfunding" to see what I could learn about it.

Within minutes, I read about ad executives who were thwarted by the SEC after organizing investors who wanted to buy the Pabst Blue Ribbon (PBR) beer company. I also explored funding platforms, such as Kickstarter and RocketHub, which enabled fans of artists and musicians to support their next big projects.

Later that week, I visited other sites, such as Kiva and Indiegogo, and was impressed each step of the way. I learned about a woman in Jordan who needed funds to open a preservatives store, and a man in South America who sought two thousand dollars to jump-start a tire company. The requests were small, yet the returns for the lendees were enormous and would forever change their lives. I was becoming a diehard fan of crowdfunding, especially since it utilized online technology to increase small-business access to new sources of financing. Social networks were not just for keeping up with friends—they could become marketplaces for everyday investors and entrepreneurs.

While I was encouraged by existing forms of crowdfunding that relied on philanthropic or principle-only return models, I knew that something bigger could exist for our nation's future generation of entrepreneurs seeking investors to finance their big ideas. I presumed that if people were willing to help an idea that made them feel good, surely there existed a strong level of interest for platforms that offered equity and the potential to make a return on one's investment.

As data continued to prove that our economic recovery was modest and vulnerable, I knew time was of the essence. If our nation's tech savvy-youth were not able to fully capitalize on their entrepreneurial potential, we would continue to lose market share to international competitors.

Years earlier, America lost its manufacturing edge, resulting in a loss of jobs that many predicted would cripple communities for decades. I was determined to not let that happen to America's entrepreneurial edge, and crowdfunding was a way to retain our prowess.

The Entrepreneur Access to Capital Act

Strongly pursuing crowdfunding as a policy initiative, I asked my staff to reach out to academics, entrepreneurs, and market participants familiar with capital formation to compile a list of obstacles that they often confronted.

After countless meetings, conferences, and Congressional hearings, I finally had legislation drafted for the first crowdfunding bill. I was ready to take it to prime time.

However, as I looked to introduce the bill the same week my Subcommittee announced a hearing on crowdfunding, something unexpected happened—President Obama announced his support for crowdfunding during his jobs speech before a joint session of Congress. While the speech was received with mixed reviews, everyone in the crowdfunding world heard the President's single remark—"We're also planning to cut away the red tape that prevents too many rapidly growing startup companies from raising capital and going public"—as a sign that reform was a priority.

The President's Startup America Initiative confirmed those hopes with a blog post that specifically supported crowdfunding for small businesses. Within days of the President's speech, I introduced the first official piece of crowdfunding legislation: H.R. 2930, the Entrepreneur Access to Capital Act.

Of course, since Washington was still mired in political gridlock, I knew that navigating the legislative process in a bipartisan manner would be key to getting the bill through Congress.

In a legislative body with Members of Congress who still used pagers to find out when votes were to take place, education would clearly be the first step. On September 15, 2011, my Subcommittee held an enlightening hearing that included a witness from the SEC, a successful entrepreneur, and Dana Mauriello, an individual who attempted to launch a crowdfunding platform under existing SEC regulations.

As each witness spoke, Members and staff began to gain interest in crowdfunding, a form of capital formation that was foreign to them that very morning.

Ms. Mauriello, despite her struggles with outdated and onerous SEC regulations, laid the foundation for a key title to my crowdfunding legislation—addressing the burden of state-by-state securities.

Specifically, due to the complexity of having to deal with fifty different state securities laws, Dana quickly found that if you had one investor from Connecticut, you could only have ten investors in Colorado. The regulation on its face was senseless and opened the eyes of Congress to the reality that America's securities were outdated.

From that day onwards, the Subcommittee and entire House of Representatives, in addition to President Obama, learned that a workable crowdfunding platform must preempt blue sky laws to efficiently and effectively connect investors and entrepreneurs from across the country. While this provision met some resistance by a handful of groups and Members of Congress, advocates of crowdfunding understood that educating policymakers is the best way to influence legislative policy.

If anything, the resistance by opponents or Members of Congress who were tentative towards the new idea was a blessing in disguise. It fueled the fire in crowdfunding advocates to better explain the obstacles put before them by government regulators and to pressure Congress to produce securities regulations that suited a twenty-first century economy.

For crowdfunding supporters, the Subcommittee hearing was a great success and attracted important allies from influential Democrats on the House Financial Services Committee. Our bipartisan commitment to meaningful investor protections strengthened the crowdfunding bill throughout the legislative and committee process.

This bipartisan effort led to an unexpected event—unanimous approval by the House Financial Services Committee for the Entrepreneur Access to Capital Act (H.R. 2930).

If that was not enough, immediately before the United States House of Representatives announced that it would vote on H.R. 2930, President Obama declared his official endorsement for the crowdfunding bill. That evening, H.R. 2930 earned the support of 407 Members of the House of Representatives, an astounding bipartisan victory.

The Crowdfunding Breakthrough and Tomorrow's Challenges

For most bills, simply receiving a vote in either the U.S. Senate or U.S. House is a victory. However, I knew crowdfunding was not any other bill and that the American people and economy could not wait for another year or longer for it to happen. My thoughts were shared by the White House and others on Capitol Hill.

Thus, after pushing the legislation though the House and Senate, on April 5, 2012, crowdfunding proponents and I were invited to the White House to see President Obama sign into law crowdfunding legislation that was based on policy I introduced just six months earlier.

Although a few Senators misinterpreted the spirit and promise of crowdfunding by inserting burdensome provisions and amplifying SEC rulemaking authority, I was proud of the overall product that landed on the President's desk. As the President signed the JOBS Act, securities legislation prompted by Chairman Darrell Issa's letter to the SEC just one year earlier, I became more confident than ever that the United States would once again hold the title of the world's most dynamic and entrepreneurial marketplace.

The United States was founded by people who took a chance. Founded by people who sailed across oceans with the idea of a better life for themselves and their children. That spirit still lives today—in every state, city, neighborhood, and home across America.

When I first felt a calling to government, I made a promise to myself to defend principles that would better serve our citizens and strengthen economic opportunity for all.

Over the last year, Congress learned a lot from our nation's young entrepreneurs about what the government can do to enhance opportunities for innovation and job creation, resulting in legislation that improves our way of life and global competitiveness.

As long as our government remains committed to seeking out and promoting policies that empower young entrepreneurs and jumpstart marketplaces of information, I am more hopeful than ever that America's future will be in the right hands to carry on our economic tradition as the home of innovation and the land of opportunity.

 *Patrick McHenry* is serving his fourth term in the United States Congress where he represents the citizens of North Carolina's 10th District. In the 112th Congress, McHenry serves as a Deputy Republican Whip, helping to manage the legislative priorities of Congressional Republicans on the House floor. Congressman McHenry is a member of the House Financial Services Committee, which deals with federal legislation related to the securities market, banking, insurance and real estate. He is also a member of the House Committee on Oversight and Government Reform, where he serves as Chairman of the Subcommittee on TARP, Financial Services and Bailouts of Public and Private Programs. As a Subcommittee Chairman, Congressman McHenry is at the heart of the Oversight and Government Reform Committee's effort to make the federal bureaucracy more accountable for how it spends the American people's money. Prior to being elected to Congress in 2004 at the age of 29, Patrick McHenry represented the 109th District in the North Carolina House of Representatives. He also served as Special Assistant to the Secretary of the U.S. Department of Labor, a post he was appointed to by President Bush. Patrick McHenry is a graduate of Ashbrook High School in Gastonia, N.C. and Belmont Abbey College, where he earned a Bachelor of Arts in History. Congressman McHenry and his wife Giulia live in his hometown of Cherryville, N.C. and worship at Saint Michael's Church.

Warts and All: A Plea for Better Media Coverage of Startup Culture

Donna Fenn, Author of Upstarts! How GenY Entrepreneurs are Rocking the World of Business

When I started working at *Inc. Magazine* as a young researcher/reporter in 1983, most of my journalist friends thought I was crazy. I had moved from Washington, DC, where I had been working for *The Washington Monthly*, a small but highly respected magazine that covers politics and government, to Boston to work for *Inc.*, which was then just a few years old and hardly at the epicenter of what my peers considered serious journalism. "Why do you want to write about entrepreneurs?" I remember one of them asking. "No one cares about them."

And to be perfectly honest, I didn't care much about entrepreneurs either back then. I had moved to Boston to be closer to home (the Berkshires, in western Massachusetts) and I wanted a job at a monthly magazine. There were two choices: *Inc.* and *Boston Magazine*. There happened to be a job opening at *Inc.*; I interviewed for it, landed it, and took it, despite not knowing (seriously!) the difference between profits and revenues. I learned quickly under the tutelage of the some of the best editors—and best people—I have ever had the privilege to know, and before I knew it, I was hooked.

Stories about entrepreneurs are inherently dramatic. The heady startup days when no one sleeps, the last-minute shift in strategy, the demands of greedy venture capitalists, the partnership that went horribly wrong, the company that failed only to pave the way for the one that was a huge success—it all made for great reading. Unlike politicians who love to spin the facts, and big company executives who wouldn't say a word without their pubic relations people hovering nearby, entrepreneurs were willing to tell all. And even more enticing for journalists, they seemed to revel in their missteps and failures.

Slowly but surely, the rest of the world realized what *Inc.'s* founder, Bernie Goldhirsh, knew all along—that being an entrepreneur was an incredibly rewarding, impactful, cool, and potentially life-altering pursuit. I like to point out that Gen Y, or Millennials, as they're often called—born between 1977 and the early 1990s—grew up when the pubic perception of what it meant to be an entrepreneur was radically changing. Back when the Millennials' Baby Boomer parents were growing up, people rarely described themselves as entrepreneurs, and to utter the word as a description of someone else was to suggest that the concerned party was less than honorable—someone with a get-rich-quick scheme. And so Gen Y is really the first generation to grow up with inherent respect and admiration for people who start and grow their own companies.

It's no wonder; they had a very impressive group of entrepreneurial role models who were treated like rock stars by the press: Steve Jobs, Richard Branson, Anita Roddick, Howard Schultz, and Oprah Winfrey, to name just a few. Later, of course, the superstars of their own generation—such as Mark Zuckerberg of Facebook, Chad Hurley, Steve Chen, and Jawed Karim of YouTube, Dennis Crowley and Naveen Selvadurai of Foursquare, and Andrew Mason of Groupon—came roaring onto the entrepreneurial landscape, riding a technology wave that made starting a business faster, cheaper, and easier than it had ever been. The media fell in love with these young tech stars. And why not? Who doesn't love a story about a geeky guy in a college dorm room, hovering over a keyboard, writing code, plotting to best the arrogant frat boys, and ultimately developing a product that literally changes the world?

The problem is that the Mark Zuckerbergs of Gen Y have been held up by the media at large as the gold standard for young entrepreneurs. And this creates the perception that if you are young and drawn to entrepreneurship, then you must certainly be a white male planning to launch a tech company. It also sends a message to budding young entrepreneurs that you must be an awesome coder and have an idea so big that you are able to raise millions in venture capital funding. In fact, nothing could be further from the truth, but you'd never know it from what you read in the press.

When I wrote my second book, *Upstarts! How GenY Entrepreneurs are Rocking the World of Business*, I interviewed young entrepreneurs in a variety of industries. I found them everywhere—starting companies that were challenging the status quo, breathing new life into tired industries, taking what they had learned in mundane jobs and using that experience to start innovative new companies. My first book, *Alpha Dogs: How Your Small Business Can Become a Leader of the Pack*, chronicled the success of eight highly successful companies in completely lackluster industries, and sent a clear message that it's not what you do, it's how you do it. Ultimately, I think the story of how one man turned a single bike shop into a $10 million company without taking a penny in outside investment (I'm talking about Chris Zane of Zane's Cycles) is far more inspiring and instructive than a story about a team of tech wizards from MIT or Stanford who raised $10 million from venture capitalists and still have no revenue model, let alone profits (I'm talking about…well, take your pick!).

Sure, the latter story is fun and aspirational. But the bottom line is that most companies are not started in Silicon Valley, they don't raise venture capital (only about 4 percent of all startups raise VC money), and they won't be acquired for ridiculous sums of money. And so the young CEOs who typically become media darlings are the ones whose stories are of the least practical value to their aspiring peers.

What most young entrepreneurs need is advice and inspiration from peers who have been there and done that, and the more relatable those peers are, the more effective they will be. So the media has to dig a little deeper and work a little harder to find companies that may not be household names, but whose stories also offer drama and illustrate success strategies that are useful and replicable. Here are just a few examples of young entrepreneurs who are tremendous role models for their peers, and who started businesses that may well be the "Alpha Dogs" of tomorrow:

- Nick Friedman and Omar Soliman, based in Tampa, started College Hunks Hauling Junk and became wildly successful by branding and professionalizing their junk hauling company in a way that their tiny competitors had never dreamed of.
- Rachel Weeks, the founder of School House, addressed the lack of fashion-forward college apparel for women by starting a clothing manufacturing company in her native North Carolina, where she's contributing to the growth of US manufacturing jobs.
- Brian Adams of Restoration Cleaners in Houston knew nothing about the dry cleaning industry but perceived an unmet need in the restoration of mold, fire, and water-damaged goods. Restoration is now a multi-million dollar company and Adams has started his own venture accelerator.

- Morgan First and Tyler Balliet founded The Second Glass to help introduce the wine industry to a new generation of young consumers who simply did not respond to the industry's stuffy, outdated marketing tactics.
- Joe and Bob McClure resurrected their family's pickle-making tradition and started McClure's Pickles in Detroit. Now, the family cuts and brines over 800 jars of pickles a day and their products have national distribution in Whole Foods, Williams Sonoma, and a variety of specialty stores.

Don't get me wrong—I love tech companies and their stories as much as the next business journalist. But what I love even more is a compelling success story—warts and all—about someone who took a relatively ordinary idea and turned it into something extraordinary. Those are the kinds of stories that are most likely to strike a cord with the vast majority of young people who think they might like to start a business. Few people look at Mark Zuckerberg and say, "If he can do it, so can I." But Tony Hsieh of Zappos? The guy sells shoes, but in a thoroughly extraordinary way. That's my kind of role model.

In *Inc.'s* early days, every reporter was encouraged to evaluate story ideas by first asking a very simple question: "What's the payoff for the reader?" In recent years, as the emphasis has shifted from print to online, I think the question most often asked by editors everywhere is, "How much traffic will this generate?" And so there's increasing danger that we reject important stories in favor of SEO-friendly ones. If that trend continues, we'll miss out on an opportunity to tell the stories of the best and brightest of a new generation of entrepreneurs.

So my suggestion—my plea, actually—is for editors (print and online alike) to fight for the resources to cover entrepreneurs the way they deserve to be covered. We want to know about the heady startup days when no one sleeps, the last-minute shift in strategy, the demands of greedy venture capitalists, the partnership that went horribly wrong, the company that failed only to pave the way for the one that was a huge success. That's what inspires young people to start companies of their own, not another five-hundred-word riff on "Five Ways to (fill in the blank)." And frankly, the stories that dig deep and bring to life the drama and tension that always comes with starting a company are the kinds of stories that get people like me— someone who never dreamed of writing about business—hooked on the world of entrepreneurship and the incredible people who hold the future of our economy in their hands.

Donna Fenn is the author of two books: *Upstarts! How GenY Entrepreneurs are Rocking the World of Business and 8 Ways You Can Profit From Their Success* (McGraw-Hill, 2009); and *Alpha Dogs: How Your Small Business Can Become a Leader of the Pack* (Collins, 2005). A business journalist for more than 25 years, Fenn is a contributing editor at *Inc. Magazine* and senior editor for Inc.com's 30 Under 30 Coolest Entrepreneurs feature. With Scott Gerber, she is co-founder of YEC Mentors, an initiative of The Young Entrepreneur Council. She is also an experienced international keynote speaker. She has been a blogger on BNET/CBSi, a columnist on Lifetuner.com, and her work has appeared in *The New York Times, Newsweek, Working Woman, Parents, Reader's Digest*, and *The Washington Monthly*, among other publications. She was a correspondent for The Associated Press in Riyadh, Saudi Arabia from 1988 to 1992. She now lives in Pelham, NY with her husband, Guian Heintzen, and is the proud mom of a Tulane grad and a Cornell junior.

ACCESS TO CAPITAL

Ten Ways the Private Sector Can Increase Small Business Owners' Access to Capital

Ami Kassar, CEO and Founder, MultiFunding

The American economy runs on a simple, powerful, and critical dream: Someone decides that they would like to start a company. They're tired of working for the man, and they want to do it on their own.

America's number-one priority today must be to give entrepreneurs the encouragement, resources and support that they need in order to build, sustain, and nurture their businesses. After all, small businesses (as defined by the U.S. Small Business Administration) have generated 65 percent of all net new jobs in the United States over the past seventeen years.[92] This figure doesn't just represent the next big startup idea coming out of Silicon Valley. It includes every employer from the local corner store, to a manufacturing plant, to a consulting company—to name a few. Every one of them creates jobs, rents a building from a landlord, buys equipment, pays taxes, and keeps the economy growing. I'm not just talking about new businesses, either—every existing business out there needs support as well. They all need to be helped, one business at a time.

---

[92] "Frequently Asked Questions," U.S. Small Business Administration's Advocacy Small Business Statistics and Research, accessed February 18, 2012, http://web.sba.gov/faqs/faqIndexAll.cfm?areaid=24.

This essay is about how we as American leaders and fellow business owners can help keep this dream alive. The recession decimated many financing options for entrepreneurs who want to start and grow a business. But even as the credit crisis eases, many small business owners still suffer from its lingering effects—for example, they may no longer have collateral like real estate to help qualify for traditional bank loans, or perhaps their credit card limits have been reduced.

In my opinion, there are five critical issues set off by the great recession that are currently threatening the American dream:

- Banks (especially big ones) are holding onto our money for dear life and not lending it out to small businesses. According to the FDIC, as of December 30, 2011 American banks held just over $8 trillion of domestic deposits and $606.1 billion of small business loans. At the beginning of the recession, domestic deposits were $5.7 trillion and small business loans were $680 billion.[93]

- Housing values have dropped dramatically throughout the recession. This has created a collateral crisis is making it tougher than ever to get loans. The banks say "sorry" because so many entrepreneurs don't have equity left in their houses that they can use as collateral.

- Fortune 1000 companies are taking longer than ever to pay their small business suppliers. Recent National Federation of Independent Business (NFIB) research shows 40 percent of small businesses are receiving payments at a slower pace. On average, they're getting paid forty-eight days after the invoice date, a six-day increase since 2010, and up ten days since 2006.[94] This cash-flow crunch forces small

---

93   All data is compiled from 2011 bank call reports available at www.fdic.gov.

94   "Late Payments to Small Businesses on the Rise," National Federation of Independent Businesses, 2011, http://www.nfib.com/video?video=1054527906001.

business owners into high-interest and expensive factoring arrangements that are making the alternative financiers rich—and hurting small businesses.

- Small business owners and entrepreneurs have compromised on accurate accounting and bookkeeping in order to focus on building products, delivering services, and keeping their doors open. This fundamental lapse is making it more difficult than ever for them to get financing.

- There is so much confusion in the small business community about borrowing money that many business owners are afraid to apply for a loan at all and don't know where to turn. In a recent study conducted by our firm, MultiFunding, we learned that 73 percent of those small business owners in need of a loan during the last year have not applied yet.[95] Amazingly, each business owner we surveyed believed that if they had access to the capital they needed, they would add an average of eight employees each.

As business leaders, we must find ways to overcome these hurdles and do everything in our power to keep the entrepreneurial dream alive in America. Entrepreneurs create jobs and valuable products or services. They spur economic growth. Here are ten actions we, as Americans, can put into place right now to help entrepreneurs.

Importantly, not one of these ideas requires the government to do anything. If we wait for them, we'll be in gridlock forever. Our future is up to us.

1. Hold banks accountable for their small-business lending records.

Small business owners need a system to help identify banks that are

---

95 "MultiFunding's Second Quarterly: Small Businesses Aren't Applying for Loans," Multifunding, August 11, 2011, http://www.multifunding.com/uncategorized/multifunding%E2%80%99s-second-quarterly-small-small-businesses-arent-applying-for-loans/. The survey was conducted in conjunction with Lieberman Research Worldwide, surveying 5,000 small business owners.

friendly to them and genuinely interested in their business. That's why we at MultiFunding have put together a bank report card for every bank in America and given them a grade for their commitment to small business lending.[96] The grade is calculated based on the ratio of the banks' deposits to its small business loans. The grades change quarterly based on the lending activity of the banks, and are calculated as a ratio of the banks small outstanding small business loans divided by their deposits.

As consumers of banking products, let's choose to have our banking accounts and savings accounts at the banks in our community that are taking our deposits and turning around and lending them back to entrepreneurs who are hiring our neighbors and creating jobs. These are the banks that deserve our business and our support.

2. Use "individual future earnings" as a form of collateral. A lack of collateral is one of the toughest hindrances facing young entrepreneurs who need access to capital. So we would like to suggest a loan agreement that would look something like this: If after X amount of years, the loan has not been paid back or goes into default, the lender has the right to take an ongoing percentage of the borrower's earnings until the obligation is paid off. We could use the same mechanisms and infrastructure that we use to enforce child support payments to get the job done.

There would be risk in this form of collateral for a lender. They would have to look at the historical earnings and income tax returns of a small business owner, and forecast future earnings.

3. Create a collateral-exchange platform. Depreciated real estate values and stock accounts make it tougher and tougher for the small business owner to find the collateral they need to get the loan. At MultiFunding, we often ask our clients if they have a family member

---

96   Available at bankinggrades.com.

or friend whom they could ask to put up some collateral for the loan. And more often than not, the answer is no. Either everyone they know is also strapped, or they are simply too embarrassed to ask.

The collateral crisis creates an opportunity. A lot of these companies that can't come up with the collateral have strong, cash-flowing businesses. Many are in the service industry and don't have many tangible assets on their balance sheets.

We would love to see an exchange platform where folks with collateral could offer to put it up in exchange for warrants or upside in a particular business that they like. The idea is that a small business owner in need of collateral would post their business plan, their collateral need, and offer some upside in exchange for it. The investor would put up the collateral (and take the risk if the company blows up), but not have to put up cash.

4. Let's find a Fortune 1000 small-business leader. A lot of the blame about the current lending meltdown is pinned on big banks. And while we believe that they hold plenty of responsibility, a good amount of the financial crisis that small business owners are facing is the result of their customers taking a long time to pay them. When their customers are Fortune 1000 companies, there is absolutely no excuse for this.

It is amazing to us how mammoth corporations are taking one hundred days or more to pay their small business suppliers, who risk losing their business with them if they complain. This slow payment is forcing many small business owners into very expensive factoring arrangements to finance the big companies.

We challenge a CEO of a Fortune 1000 company to take a leadership position and make a commitment to pay all of its suppliers within thirty days. This would hopefully create a domino effect and others would follow. This decision would have little to no impact to the bottom line of the top companies, but would make a dramatic and decisive difference to the small business owners.

5. Create a committed-to-pay-on-time platform. As part of this effort, we would like to see an Internet entrepreneur come up with a platform where small business owners can publically display how long it's taking the big companies to pay them. This scorecard will hopefully put pressure on the big companies to pay faster and improve small business liquidity.

In turn, we could all support big businesses that support small businesses. Are the big corporations that you buy your cable TV, cell phone services, and other products small-business friendly? They're demanding payment from you in thirty days, but are they paying their small business suppliers in thirty days? We should demand answers and support those big corporations who take care of small businesses.

6. Offer mini audits for small businesses. One of the toughest challenges that small businesses owners face when looking for financing is that their books aren't in order. They're so busy taking care of clients, building their products or rendering their services that the bookkeeping slips on the list of priorities. Slow bookkeeping can result in bad business decisions and backed-up taxes. And when it comes time to applying for a loan, gridlock follows.

Small business owners can't afford full-blown audits like big businesses get. It's not practical. But what if we could have a "mini audit" or an "audit light?" A small business could earn the certification if their accountant reported or certified that the business is current on all of their tax filings and has a bookkeeping system in place that they can at any time produce financial reports within thirty days. And perhaps once a year, there would be a check to make certain that the fundamentals of the balance sheet and income statement make sense.

Small businesses would have an incentive to get this certification if banks and lenders promised that loans coming in with this certification would get first priority in the lending queue. And more private investors might be willing to make equity investments in small businesses if they knew that the books were in order.

7. Apply game theory. We would love to see a company like Intuit offer a meaningful weekly prize to a lucky small business owner who is picked in a lottery and who can, within one hour of being notified, provide accurate and complete financial reports for their business and show that they are current on all of their taxes.

Let's give small business owners an incentive to get their books in order, and add a little game theory to it. The idea is pretty simple. A company like Intuit randomly selects one business a day and calls them. It's an instant audit. If that business owner produces current financials that make sense within one hour, and is current on all of his taxes, the business wins a prize. And if they can't, they're out of luck. The hope would be that small business owners would rush to get their houses in order.

8. Let's put accounting students to work. Every business school in America makes it a requirement for their students to donate some time every week to a local business to help with their accounting systems. While many internship programs exist, they often focus around the students going to CPA offices. We would like to see the students go out into the field and help small business owners who need the help. This could be topped off with a professional group like the American Institute of CPAs joining forces to let a local accountant mentor the student.

9. Certified mentors should be a factor in lending decisions. A significant body of research has shown that mentors can and do influence small business success. In fact, the likelihood of approval for a commercial loan more than doubles when young entrepreneurs receive non-financial support, including mentorship and business training, and 55 percent of young entrepreneurs around the globe agree that their business is more successful as a result.[97] We would like to propose that we find an organized fashion to let a lender feel more comfortable lending money to a company if they know that the company is being mentored. There are good mentoring programs in the market today. These include programs like SCORE, small business development centers (SDBCs), and other private-public initiatives. But participation in these programs today doesn't give a company points at the closing table.

Perhaps a bank or lender could pilot a program where they set standards for a "certified mentor." If a company matches up with one of these mentors and proves it in their loan application, this might compensate for other factors such as lack of collateral. This pilot might be done with an existing mentor program. The challenge is to find a way to link it to the loan process.

10. Improve basic financial education. Confusion abounds in lending markets and opportunities for small business owners and entrepreneurs. The different loan products that are available are often confusing to navigate through and understand. Entrepreneurs need help in sorting out the options, and making sure they understand what they're signing up for when they accept a loan program.

The need for clear transparency in lending is amplified by the growth of programs like factoring and merchant cash advance loans during the great recession. We need programs and websites to help a small business owner to be able to clearly understand a loan program they are signing up for, to make certain that they're not being scammed or misled about the terms.

---

97   *Global Youth Entrepreneur Survey 2011*, (The Prince's Youth Business International, 2011), 8, http://www.youthbusiness.org/pdf/YouthEntrepreneurshipSurvey2011.pdf.

We believe that we're scratching the surface for this need for education at MultiFunding, but it's not enough. We need plenty of resources pointed towards this need. But we're hopeful that these ideas will propel debate and drive action about how to improve the lending situation for small business owners and entrepreneurs across America. Some of them are controversial, and some might make you think. The point is that we have to find out-of-the-box ways to think about how to get capital into the hands of our entrepreneurs at reasonable and fair prices. Without it, our economy will remain "stuck" for a long time, and this will impact all of us.

Ami Kassar, CEO and Founder of MultiFunding, is a nationally renowned small business advocate and leader. He's committed to ensuring that small business owners have the best possible access to the capital they need to help grow and manage their businesses. Kassar appears in the national press on small business issues and blogs regularly on these topics at www.slingshotcafe. net. He has developed a national reputation for confronting and challenging the largest banks in America for their lending records to small businesses. He's assembled research reports that have become a critical component of the national debate about small business lending. In addition, Kassar is a regular speaker at universities and small business events across the country on topics including entrepreneurship and access to capital. Kassar earned his MBA from the University of Southern California and graduated with a B.A. in American Studies from Brandeis University. He currently lives in the suburbs of Philadelphia with his wife, two children and his corgi-spaniel.

How to Create More Profitable, Sustainable Businesses in America

Carissa Reiniger, Founder and
President, Silver Lining Ltd.

How do we fix young America? I want to ask a slightly different question: How do we fix the economy, through young Americans? I believe the answer is to get as many young Americans as possible to build profitable, sustainable small businesses.

Notice that I did not say that we get as many young people as possible to start businesses—I said *build profitable, sustainable businesses*. Of the 27.5 million businesses that are considered small businesses in America, only about six million had any employees at all in 2007.[98] We have got to see an increase in the number of small businesses that are healthy, have revenue, and are employing people.

I have worked with over ten thousand small business owners in the last seven years, and I am continually shocked at how hard they fight to keep their businesses alive. They are extremely passionate and committed, they work harder than anyone I know, and yet very few are making any real money. There is an ongoing struggle to keep it all together, never mind grow.

---

98   "Frequently Asked Questions," U.S. Small Business Administration's Advocacy Small Business Statistics and Research, accessed February 18, 2012, http://web.sba.gov/faqs/faqIndexAll.cfm?areaid=24.

At Silver Lining, we talk all the time about something that we call the Cashflow/Capacity Catch-22. When you talk to a small business owner, they will tell you (if they are telling the truth) that they are way too busy and are having cash-flow issues. They lack time and money. And if you get them to talk about it, they will start to say that if they had more time, they could make more money. But if they had more money, they could generate more time: the Cashflow/Capacity Catch-22.

Ironically, if you want to grow a small business, you need to inject additional time and money, the very two things that the majority of small business owners don't have enough of. When you realize that the two things required for growth are the two things that no small business has enough of, it becomes pretty simple to see why more small businesses are not growing. Not only are they not growing, but they often stay stuck for their entire time in business. Or, worse, an external factor comes in and forces them to shut down. They have run out of funding and a loan is getting called. A spouse threatens to leave them if they don't create more stability. They can't take the stress anymore.

Businesses are not failing because the business can't succeed. Businesses are failing because the owners can no longer persevere through all the trials of growing a small business. We have to not only convince young Americans to start companies, but we have to help them succeed. While I think that this is an extremely complex problem with a ton of work needed to truly solve it, there are three things that we can do now that will have an immediate impact.

1. Get real about small business.

While I am a true believer in free enterprise, creating your own economic reality, and the idea that an increase in small business is a solution to economic recovery, I have a very strong opposition to the way that most governments and academic institutions are promoting entrepreneurship.

I was in an airport a few years ago, and as I walked to my gate, I saw a series of advertisements promoting a new MBA program for entrepreneurship. The first was of a man sitting in a huge penthouse apartment, at night, overlooking a city skyline. The second was a guy sitting on the beach with the ocean in front of him and his laptop on his lap.

Talk about false advertising. Fact: It is hard to grow a small business. I truly believe that one significant reason so many small businesses fail is that founders have not been adequately prepared for what it takes to grow a business. When we consider that half of all small businesses fail after five years, we have to ask ourselves why. [99]

Let's get real about small business. Let's prepare young America for what it is really like and let the ones who can't wait to start go for it, and stop the rest from embarking on a journey that they ultimately won't end up finishing.

2. Make it respectable to start a small business.

Small businesses are everywhere. Your local coffee shop, your dry cleaner, your mechanic or your accountant, for example. These businesses are not sexy. They are not being written about and profiled in the news. They are not "changing the world" or "disrupting a space" or "raising ten million in capital."

But if you look at the collective power that the entire group of American small businesses have, they are the most impressive people around. They employ about half of all private-sector US employees, and they pay 44 percent of total US private payroll.[100] More impor-

---

99   Ibid.

100   Ibid.

tantly, up until the last decade, small businesses contributed to over 50 percent of the national GDP—but that rate has been steadily declining.[101] In other words, this group is one of the most important groups of people that we can be thinking about, supporting and getting young people involved with. If we don't, we don't just risk their future, but the country's future as well.

And yet, how many young people do you hear talking with pride about starting a little business that they are going to bootstrap themselves? We have created such an extravagant image of what entrepreneurial success looks like that most young people want to raise millions and make millions. We need to help them understand that their contribution as a small business owner is important, necessary, and respected. The small businesses of America are fighting every day to keep economy moving, keep people employed, and keep our country in business.

Economic opportunities will not necessarily open up for more young Americans simply because we uncover the next technological innovation. But if every single small business hired just one more employee next year, it would literally change the country.

We need the world to recognize and give due respect to the small business owners of the world. If we do not start to profile them, talk about them, and communicate how important they are, why would any young person choose to start or get involved? But imagine, instead, if everywhere you turned people were thanking small businesses for what they did for the economy and the country. It would create a climate where our best and brightest young people would think that there was simply no better choice than to start a small business—or go work for one.

---

101   John Tozzi, "Small Business's Shrinking GDP Contribution," *BloombergBusinessweek*, February 16, 2012, http://www.businessweek.com/articles/2012-02-17/small-businesss-shrinking-gdp-contribution.

3. Create productive collaboration among small business owners.

We need to decrease the isolation that most small businesses face. Instead of every small business being a small, inconsequential island, we must connect them in such a way that represents the reality of their collective power.

If you look at almost every resource available for small businesses, they have been created by and are being delivered by large corporations or by the government. The irony that most small business resources are coming from people who have never been small business owners seems to be lost on most of the world. Small businesses want to help each other—we just have to make it easier for them to do so.

Aggregating small businesses for the sake of a bigger listserv, a social network, or something that will ultimately just be a drain on small business owners' time is not helpful. Bringing small businesses together so that the collective is significantly more powerful than the sum of its parts is doable and necessary. If you think about how much money small businesses collectively spend, how many service providers they source from, how much energy they spend trying to figure out who to talk to and what to buy, it is significant. If you think about how much small businesses sell and how extremely varied they are in their service offerings and experience, you start to understand the scope of possibility if we just had small businesses supporting each other.

There is no better small business expert than an actual small business owner with expertise on a specific topic. We have a business culture where we continually sit back and wait for the next product release from that new tech startup or the corporations we buy from or the government program that we are thinking about getting involved in. I think it's far more interesting and exciting to think about what would happen if small businesses bought from each other, shared with each other, and truly started to figure it out together.

Practically speaking, there need to be much better ways to facilitate these connections. Based on our experience at Silver Lining, when you build ways for small businesses to support each other, they absolutely will. So, let's do more of it. I am absolutely convinced that if we want to create real opportunities for young people, or change the world that young people live in, we need to take a much deeper look at small businesses. And I have zero doubt that with an increase in small business success, we would see a huge positive impact in the economy—and a huge step towards a better America.

Carissa Reiniger is dedicated to small business. Her first business, Silver Lining Ltd. (www.silverlininglimited.com), was inspired by her passion to see more small business owners making money doing what they love. At Silver Lining, Carissa created the SLAP™ (Silver Lining Action Plan), a business method that helps small businesses set and hit their financial goals. Silver Lining has helped over 10,000 small businesses grow and recently released SLAPcenter.com, which will allow Silver Lining to grow as the company helps thousands more small businesses grow. Carissa speaks often on entrepreneurship, has written two books, *Inspiring Entrepreneurs: How to Build Your Business To Its First Million* and *I Will* and is a featured columnist or has been featured in the *New York Times, Globe and Mail, Huffington Post, National Post* and more. Carissa has been a small business spokesperson and partner with leading Fortune 500 companies such as RIM, Staples, Intuit, HP and UPS, working with these large companies to help more small businesses grow. She is a Founding Partner and Director of Fundraising for Gen Y Capital Partners.

Microlending in the United States

Jessica Jackley, Co-Founder, Kiva and ProFounder

Young America doesn't need to be fixed. What does need fixing, however, are the systems that make it exceedingly difficult, confusing, expensive, and sometimes outright impossible to invest in many young Americans' entrepreneurial potential. As timing would have it, my first draft of this very essay included a long rant about how certain laws—laws that limited our ability to do this—must change. Happily, since then, we've celebrated the passage of the JOBS Act in Congress, which has removed several of the most significant legal and regulatory barriers that had made crowdfunding investment capital so difficult in the past.

So, what now? The hard work really begins. What we need to do next is create the right platforms, mechanisms and opportunities to make it accessible and easy for entrepreneurs to access the capital and community support they need to start thriving businesses right here in the United States.

A lack of access to startup capital has an insidious effect on young entrepreneurs. When communities cannot easily invest in their own rising entrepreneurial stars, those entrepreneurs who can will seek funding and support elsewhere. This may mean tapping the angel and venture capital community, or getting a bank loan, or turning to other sources of capital that could demand more than their fair share of ownership and control. For the entrepreneurs who cannot access capital elsewhere, they may simply start off more slowly, though they'll be held back by a lack of access to resources they need. As for the rest? Some will never get a chance to try.

In all cases, the lack of participation by the entrepreneur's community sends a message: "We aren't able to help you." This creates a disconnect between budding entrepreneurs and the people who may have had the best potential to encourage and validate them through the tough path they have chosen as entrepreneurs. Over time, they may lose sight of their own incredible potential to live entrepreneurial lives and create lasting, positive change. And the would-be investors? Their capital isn't put to use at all, or at worst, it's put to use invested elsewhere, perhaps feeding the growth of behemoth public corporations that may not align much at all with their own values or create long-term, sustainable benefit to their communities.

But both microlending and crowdfunding offer real, viable solutions—one with a track record in the US and the developing world, and one that's just now been given the opportunity to blossom more than ever before. The next step in fixing young America is to put platforms in place that benefit both investor and entrepreneur.

When I co-founded Kiva.org in 2005, we first focused on the developing world; I had no idea how much our work there would teach me about entrepreneurship right here in the United States as well. As background, Kiva is the world's first person-to-person microlending website. On Kiva, people can lend $25 or more to hardworking entrepreneurs in need. Since its founding, and as of the publication of this essay, Kiva has facilitated nearly $300 million in loans to hundreds of thousands of borrowers around the world.[102]

---

102 "Statistics," Kiva, accessed March 17, 2011, http://www.kiva.org/about/stats.

Kiva has taught me many lessons. I learned how powerful it is for an individual to see herself as an entrepreneur and real change-maker, how a supportive community of funders from around the world helps to validate and encourage this conception of oneself, and how the provision of appropriate capital (in the case of entrepreneurs on Kiva, a small loan) from this community allows borrowers to accomplish great things with their microenterprise endeavors—even lifting themselves and their families out of poverty over time.

When Kiva launched partnerships in the United States in June 2009, I became fascinated with the startup and small-business communities right in my own backyard. As it does with the rest of its programs, Kiva works through existing lending organizations that can find great borrowers, administer loan funding, collect repayments, provide support and education to clients, and more. After a thorough application and due diligence process, Kiva forms partnerships with select lending institutions, giving them an account on the Kiva site to post profiles of entrepreneurs in need of a loan. Kiva calls these select institutions "field partners." The worldwide community of Kiva lenders can then browse those profiles, choose someone, and lend $25 to that specific entrepreneur or group of entrepreneurs. Over time, with a nearly 99 percent repayment rate, lenders receive their money back and can re-lend again and again.

These field partners are central to Kiva's model, and in truth, they are the real champions and the real experts in microlending in the communities where they work. Some begin as small, grassroots organizations, and may evolve into official organizations and financial institutions, whether nonprofit or for-profit. Some began as programs at larger banks that take on a life of their own. For example, Kiva New Orleans chose ASI Federal Credit Union as its partner in the area; according to a September 2011 article in the *Credit Union Times*, every one of the 14 initial program loans first added to the website upon the program's launch were funded within 24 hours (to the tune of $125,000).[103] I believe these lending programs are key to empowering microenterprises and small businesses in certain impoverished areas of the United States (like New Orleans) just as they have been in the developing world, especially those programs that emphasize empowerment, education, women, and other values that Kiva holds dear.

However, lending is just one way to support these ventures that are so crucial to the US economy and the set of possible paths available to each of us. Other vehicles are needed to ensure that all entrepreneurs have access to the resources they need to succeed.

Entrepreneur by entrepreneur, my fascination became focused and the idea for ProFounder, my second startup, was born when my co-founder Dana Mauriello and I saw two classmates from the Stanford Graduate School of Business try to gather investments from dozens of fellow classmates. When these entrepreneurs asked their lawyers to structure this investment deal, they were told that it was impossible for their classmates to invest even $1,000 each because they are unaccredited investors. When pushed, the lawyers spent months—and tens of thousands of dollars of the entrepreneurs' money—to structure a deal that would include only thirty-five of the dozens and dozens of interested classmates. In the end, they were able to net $15,000 of what could have been many times more. We were struck by the incredible inefficiency of this arrangement; abundant capital existed in these entrepreneurs' community, but there were tremendous legal and administrative barriers to accessing it.

We started ProFounder to solve this market inefficiency and make it possible for entrepreneurs to unlock the abundant

---

103   David Morrison, "Kiva New Orleans, ASI FCU Team Up to Rebuild a Ravaged City," *Credit Union Times*, September 7, 2011, http://www.cutimes.com/2011/09/07/kiva-new-orleans-asi-fcu-team-up-to-rebuild-a-rava.

capital in their communities. We called this method of financing "community funding," and created a platform that allowed entrepreneurs to utilize their social networks for investment capital in a way that is be simple, inexpensive, efficient, and legally compliant for all involved. We chose to focus our efforts on supporting small businesses and startups in America, because we feel that these businesses have the most limited resources—but limitless ideas and potential to create innovation and economic value.

We're proud of both the impact we've had on individual entrepreneurs who have accessed capital and grown their businesses using ProFounder's platform, as well as our influence on crowdfunding regulatory reform in Washington.

Despite our progress, the regulatory environment prevented us from pursuing the innovations we felt would be most valuable to our customers, and we made the decision to shut down the company in February 2012. We then put all of our energy into working with Congress to write and fight for the support of the crowdfunding bill included in the JOBS Act. To everyone's surprise, within weeks, both the Senate and the House passed the JOBS Act, and Dana and I were even invited to witness the signing of the bill into law on April 5th, 2012. The bipartisanship Congress showed in pushing these changes through in such a short time has given me renewed hope that more platforms like Kiva and ProFounder can and will be created in the law's wake. This common-sense legislation dramatically changes the way entrepreneurs do business in the US, and gives investors the opportunity to participate and support those entrepreneurs in unprecedented ways. I believe we will see the direct positive impact immediately.

After democratizing access to capital for all entrepreneurs and making crowdfunding (for investment capital) legal, we can now move forward with the seeds that have already been planted. All of the pieces have been in place—the relevant technology, social networks, and desire from would-be funders all exist--and now the law is as well. Allowing entrepreneurs to raise small rounds of funding from their friends, family and community will unlock incredible amounts of capital and create millions of jobs,[104] for young Americans today and in the future. More importantly, the engagement and participation of investors is going to be unleashed, leading to even greater success for crowdfunded ventures.

Jessica Jackley is a social entrepreneur focused on empowering other entrepreneurs in the US and around the world. Jessica currently serves as a Venture Partner with Collaborative Fund, focused on investing in creative entrepreneurs who want to change the world through emerging technologies. Before this, Jessica was a Founder and CEO of ProFounder, a pioneering crowdfunding platform providing tools for small business entrepreneurs in the U.S. to access start-up capital and harness community involvement. Earlier in her career, Jessica was a Founder and Chief Marketing Officer of Kiva, the world's first p2p microlending website. Jessica has been recognized for her work in many ways and has received the 2011 Economist's "No Boundaries" Innovation Award, the 2010 USA Network's Character Approved Award, and was voted as a finalist for *TIME's* 100 Most Influential People in 2009, among other honors. Convinced that social change happens across all sectors, Jackley has worked in public, nonprofit, and private organizations including the Stanford Center for Social Innovation, Amazon, World Vision, Village Enterprise Fund, Project Baobab, Potentia Media, and others. Jessica lives in Los Angeles with her husband, author Reza Aslan, and their twin sons.

---

104   According to one source, www.legalizecrowdfunding.org, at least 1.5 million jobs would be created.

Teaching Our Kids to Write Software

Scott Schwaitzberg, Advisory Board Member, Academy for Software Engineering

O ver the past several years, the technology and digital media sector in New York City has grown tremendously; technology sector employment has grown by an estimated 30 percent in the past five years, even as private sector employment has decreased overall.[105] The City of New York has been at the forefront of nurturing and supporting that growth. In the immediate term, the City has alleviated real estate pressure through a series of startup incubators. In the long term, the City has expanded and sustained the innovation and talent pipeline through its partnership with Cornell and Technion to create a first-class applied sciences campus on Roosevelt Island.[106]

However, there have been no major city programs to engage New York City's public school kids in the startup sector or prepare them for careers in this fast-growing part of New York's economy. To solve this, with support from the city's startup community, the Department of Education will open the Academy for Software Engi-

---

105   Alan Feuer, "On the Move, in a Thriving Tech Sector," *NYTimes.com*, November 19, 2011, http://www.nytimes.com/2011/11/20/nyregion/on-the-move-in-new-yorks-thriving-tech-sector.html.

106   Oliver Staley and Henry Goldman, "Cornell and Technion Chosen by NYC for Engineering Campus," *Bloomberg Businessweek*, December 20, 2011, http://www.businessweek.com/news/2011-12-20/cornell-and-technion-chosen-by-nyc-for-engineering-campus.html.

neering in the fall of 2012, a public high school focused on training the next generation of software engineers. The new high school will be located in Union Square, the heart of the city's startup sector, and will help create the next generation of innovators and entrepreneurs.

In mid-2010, the New York City Mayor's Office gathered a few civic and business leaders from the startup world to brainstorm on whether we were, and how we could proceed in, preparing our kids for careers in the technology startup sector. As a member of the Mayor's staff, I had the privilege of participating in this discussion and developing policies based on their feedback. That group unanimously felt that the children of New York City public schools were missing out on a key opportunity to learn how to write software. Well-prepared high school students are not only capable of learning basic computer science and software engineering, but exposure and training in the field can put students with a relatively wide range of academic achievement on the path to a successful career post-high school or post-college. Demonstrating this in New York City would provide a model of technology education for schools across the United States.

Goals of Expanded Software Engineering

Beyond the vocational and economic development benefits, software engineering also provides a unique pedagogical opportunity to leverage technology and algorithmic problem solving across other subjects. Training students to use computational tools and algorithmic thinking gives them the opportunity to apply it to many other subject areas, from biology to music to physics. Students who learn software engineering or computer science will be more engaged and more prepared to identify and execute creative solutions. It may be the closest we can come to teaching "clever."

Expanding software engineering training at the high school level helps achieve two goals:

- To provide students for whom college is not appropriate with the skills for a successful and well-paying career
- To prepare college-bound students for successful experiences in engineering programs.

A major challenge to achieving these goals is that large-scale "computer science" curricula in New York City tend to be vocational in nature, with a focus on technology in three ways: basic productivity tools (keyboarding, Microsoft Office, website design), tech support (e.g. Making Opportunities for Upgrading Schools and Education, a.k.a. MOUSE), and hardware optimization (e.g. Cisco Academy).

These programs are important and valuable, but create only limited opportunities for economic mobility. Keyboarding and productivity tools are critical to operate in the modern workforce, but not sufficient as gateways to technology careers. Programs like MOUSE that extend beyond basic computer literacy give students confidence and valuable life skills and can inspire them to learn more, but do not offer enough training by themselves. And hardware optimization programs offer a clear career path in technology, but one that is limited to only most basic elements of the technology stack (and has potential to be automated out of existence).

Curricula with a real focus on writing software are rare and small-scale. In New York City, only Stuyvesant High School has such a program, and graduates approximately one hundred students per year (out of a class of eight hundred-plus) with substantial training in computer science.

After reviewing the options available to New York City students, it became clear that a new high school would be necessary both to directly train interested students in the field and to act as a center of excellence for teacher training and program development across the city. Due to generous financial support from Fred Wilson, Managing Partner of Union Square Ventures, the Department of Education was able to rapidly accelerate the school development process and target an opening date of September 2012.

Developing the Academy for Software Engineering

There are three major elements to designing a school like the Academy for Software Engineering: target population, curriculum development and linkage to industry.

1. **Determine your target population.** Determining the target population for a school requires delicately balancing two challenges: One, ensuring that incoming students will be sufficiently prepared to master the materials; and two, reaching a diverse population of students that genuinely expands the overall engineering talent pool. Depending on the school district, there are different selectivity mechanisms to choose from; in New York, our choice boiled down to creating a "screened" school with specific academic criteria tied to admission, or an "unscreened" school with no academic criteria included in the admissions process. Creating an academic "screen" can increase the likelihood that every student will be successful, but can limit the diversity of the student body and the portability of the program to more typical academic environments.

   The Academy for Software Engineering seeks to replicate the experience of at-home discovery and learning of software engineering skills that a student with limited means may not be able to have at home. As a result, the Department of Education chose to make the school "limited unscreened," meaning that students must show a commitment to school by attending an information session and meeting with leadership, but upon doing that, the selection process would essentially be via lottery. While the "limited unscreened" model can pose challenges, especially in bringing students to the same baseline early on, the opportunity to offer top-quality software engineering education to a diverse student population makes solving those challenges worthwhile.

2. **Develop a curriculum for a diverse population.** The curriculum will be designed to teach a diverse population of students how to make software in a traditional high-school setting. While it's still being developed, the curriculum will be based in part on the successful computer science program in place at Stuyvesant High School, but modified to expand into the entire high school curriculum and to allow for varying levels in student achievement (Stuyvesant is one of New York's elite test-based admission schools). The curriculum will emphasize building block tools for software development (rather than rigid adherence to a specific programming language), extensive math and logic training, group-based practical projects, and cross-disciplinary application of software tools (in English, biology, etc.). Academy students will learn how to ship working code, and apply it to their academic lives.

In order to build this curriculum, the Department of Education assembled a team of experts, including Mike Zamansky, the founder and developer of the Stuyvesant High School CS program, Professor Evan Korth, who has done extensive research into teaching high school age students to use computer science to solve cross-disciplinary problems, and several others. Identifying local experts in the field of computer science education is critical to create an effective program and to do so quickly.

3. **Link the school to community industry.** In order to provide students with a program that prepares them for the actual needs of the digital industry, the Department of Education assembled an advisory board of engineers from innovative technology companies. Advisors from Google, Stack Exchange, Foursquare, Kickstarter, eBay, 10gen, Makerbot and more are participating in the design of the Academy via the advisory board. Incorporating feedback from current leaders in the world of software early on allowed us to tailor the curriculum effectively and build The Academy from the ground up to prepare New York City students to work at (or create the next) innovative technology companies.

    The advisory board is also critical for the last major piece of the puzzle: linkage to industry. The students' experiences will be defined by exposure and interaction with practitioners of software engineering. Internships, mentorship programs, guest lectures, hackathons and observation— New York City is uniquely positioned to provide its students with these real-life opportunities as part of an everyday high school experience.

Finally, the school will be located in the Union Square neighborhood, at the heart of the technology and innovation sectors of the city. It's important to find a location that allows easy access for engineers and entrepreneurs to volunteer at the school, and for students to intern and explore the companies in the immediate vicinity. The latter is critical for creating an immersive experience that includes observing current practitioners and learning by doing. The Academy for Software Engineering will provide students from across the five boroughs access to companies and job opportunities that would have otherwise been out of reach.

Scaling Software Engineering across the City

Creating a single new software engineering high school is not the end, but the beginning. The Academy for Software Engineering will have only five hundred students (across four grades) at maturity. But the school will be the central pivot point for training thousands of students across New York City. The school will serve as a vital test bed for developing curricula and tools to teach students how to write software. The Academy's software engineering curriculum and program is designed with portability and replication as a key element from day one.

The Academy will also serve as a training ground for computer science and software engineering teachers. These teachers, armed with tools and syllabi, will serve as ambassadors for software engineering across the city. Success of these programs and teachers will allow principals in many of the other four hundred-plus high schools around the city to incorporate them into their own schools. Depending on student demand, the Department of Education may also open more software engineering-focused high schools in other boroughs.

Conclusions

Technology is the future of our economy, and New York City is leading the way to prepare our kids for careers and success within it. The technology industry has come together to provide financial, technical and technological support to train the next generation of entrepreneurs, hackers and lead engineers. And the city is working at a startup pace to conceptualize and execute this vision, moving from idea to a fully functioning school in twelve months. Thousands of children will be prepared for a high-paying twenty-first-century career who otherwise would never have had access, and once again, New York will have built a model for the rest of the country to look toward and replicate.

Scott Schwaitzberg is a Vice President at Activate, where he works with media companies to create and improve their digital business and strategy. Prior to Activate, Scott served as Deputy Chief of Staff to the Deputy Mayor in the Bloomberg Administration in New York City, where he was responsible for multiple technology partnerships and other special initiatives, including launching free Wi-Fi in New York City Parks and creating a high school for software engineers. Before entering public service, Scott was an Engagement Manager at McKinsey & Company working with clients in the technology, financial services and social sectors to develop growth strategies and reduce costs. Scott sits on the Advisory Boards of Catchafire (an social enterprise web startup), Blue Engine (an education nonprofit) and the upcoming Academy for Software Engineering in New York City. He is a graduate of The University of Texas at Austin with a BA in Plan II and Economics and a member of Phi Beta Kappa.

Success Starts in Seventh Grade:
Empowering Student Entrepreneurs through Experiential Learning, Crowdfunding and Technology

Slava Rubin, Co-Founder and CEO, Indiegogo

The best way for students to become entrepreneurs is through practice and experience. LeBron James became a basketball star because he practiced and played basketball regularly from an early age, not because he watched Michael Jordan on television. Similarly, students wishing to enter the entrepreneurial world must engage in experiential learning, taking advantage of the modern technology that is now available through the Internet and digital devices. I would like to invite students to use crowdfunding platforms to launch one new business idea every year from seventh grade through college—that's ten businesses before graduation. This process would help lower the barrier of entry to the business world, accelerate the pace of learning in the classroom, and help young people become fluent in the language of entrepreneurial thinking—an asset not just to entrepreneurs, but also to the employers of tomorrow's innovative companies.

Why Teach Entrepreneurship

Most kindergarten teachers inspire kids to become doctors, lawyers, astronauts, or firemen, but few teachers today mention the possibility of becoming an entrepreneur in the early years —at least, not outside of extra- or co-curricular programs. It is time to break this mold and make entrepreneurship a desirable profession from day one.

In the entrepreneurial world, there are many benefits to starting early and practicing often. The options for new student-led business ideas are endless—from cupcake shops, to babysitting services, to providing web content for mobile apps, to designing and building video games. Imagine a student with ten years of practice in entrepreneurship before even entering the workforce. She would have already learned by doing, gained confidence in her skills, and grown from her mistakes. Instead of being buried in the chapters of old and outdated textbooks, students can be stimulated by their own creativity, which is what they will eventually rely on to find product-market fit in today's innovative world. And students can flex and develop all the muscles needed for teamwork, leadership, communication, and ultimate success—skills that will serve them well in any future workplace.

The idea of requiring middle-school-to-college-age students to create a business a year might seem like a fantasy due to the considerable institutional barriers, from budget constraints to teacher and curricular limitations, or simple bureaucracy. But there are ways to make this plan a reality. Co-curricular programs such as FBLA (Future Business Leaders of America) or NFTE (Network for Teaching Entrepreneurship) have led the way thus far, and what we need now is a more integrated approach. In addition to providing a new source of capital formation for young entrepreneurs, crowdfunding platforms can be leveraged as an educational tool for students looking to take their first steps as entrepreneurial thinkers.

Don't take my word for it—there are students who have already successfully used crowdfunding platforms to their advantage, including my own, Indiegogo. If students begin young and build a campaign a year on crowdfunding platforms, they can learn the skills and practice they need to confidently create their next new business (or entrepreneurial idea) by the time they graduate high school or college.

Why Use Crowdfunding and a Business a Year to Teach Entrepreneurship?

Historically, there have always been significant barriers to starting a business. From idea formulation, to research and development, to launch, to selling, to fulfillment, each step can require a significant investment of time and resources. Today, the entire process of building a business can be captured in a single online crowdfunding campaign.

Although crowdfunding sounds like a new term to many people, the concept actually dates back to when the United States acquired the Statue of Liberty. In 1884, the Americans received statue itself as a free gift from the French. However, Americans still needed to raise funds to build a base for the statue. Since the city of New York was 50 percent short on their $300,000 target, Joseph Pulitzer put *The New World* newspaper (the historical predecessor to the *New York Times*) to creative use and called on readers to make small donations. Pulitzer was able to convince over 120,000 individuals to contribute $0.83 on average. This was an incredible feat, considering the funders received no tangible profit, tax deduction, or recognition for their donations.

Fast forward to today. Entrepreneurs can harness digital tools to share their message faster and capture funding more efficiently than ever before. It is not just crowdfunding that is accelerating the speed of entrepreneurship, either, but also the quickly evolving support tools for digitally savvy entrepreneurs—from Facebook to Paypal, mobile payment apps to QR codes, YouTube to FourSquare. Although crowdfunding platforms have barely been on people's radars in the past five years, they are projected to transact billions of dollars in years to come.

Let's take Emmy's Organics[107] as an example of successful crowdfunding. This gluten-free dessert company needed capital to improve their packaging so they could sell their product in supermarkets. After being rejected by a local upstate New York bank, the twenty-two-year-old founder Samantha Abrams used Indiegogo to raise the $15,000 that she needed to grow her business.

Samantha created a personalized three-minute video outlining her message and her "ask," in addition to a written four-paragraph pitch supporting the ask. She determined the pricing of her perks (each level of donation on Indiegogo guarantees funders certain benefits, called perks) to ensure there was enough margin left over after fulfillment to pay for the packaging upgrade that was the primary purpose of her campaign. Her perks included a single serving of macaroons at the $25 donation level and a customized tote bag full of gluten free desserts at the $100 donation level. And she promoted the campaign both online and offline, getting a crash course in Internet marketing and public relations—via email, Facebook, Twitter, promo parties, word of mouth, and even local papers. During the course of her campaign, Samantha attracted 102 customers, each one validating

---

107   See http://indiegogo.com/EmmysOrganics.

her business idea by spending money, proving demand, mitigating risk, and providing their customer data.

Throughout the campaign, Samantha provided updates so that the funders were a part of her success. This campaign wasn't simply about transactions and dollars; rather it was about developing a lasting and engaging relationship with the customer, all in the course of a few short weeks. It would take years of experience for entrepreneurs to match the hard and fast lesson Samantha received in scaling her business throughout the course of her crowdfunding campaign.

Today, Emmy's Organics sells its products in supermarkets in twenty-six states around America. And in late 2011, Samantha's crowdfunding campaign was mentioned in a White House blog post about President Obama's American Jobs Act.[108]

Making It Happen

The key to making this initiative successful would be to incorporate the "business a year" concept directly into the school curriculum. Each crowdfunding campaign can be done in under sixty days (in fact, the campaigns that are most successful on Indiegogo have a thirty- to sixty-day duration). As part of an annual curriculum, the class can be built out into four distinct parts, each approximately two months in length. Consider the following roadmap:

- **Section 1: New theory and principles** – In the first quarter, the teacher can focus on the fundamental theories of building a business and the basics of crowdfunding.

- **Section 2: Research and planning the idea/campaign** – In the second quarter, the students can brainstorm ideas, do

108   Aneesh Chopra and Tom Kalil, "The President's American Jobs Act: Fueling Innovation and Entrepreneurship," U.S. Office of Science and Technology (blog post), September 8, 2011, http://www.whitehouse.gov/blog/2011/09/08/president-s-american-jobs-act-fueling-innovation-and-entrepreneurship.

research for their new company, and build the specifics of their campaign.

- **Section 3: Running the crowdfunding campaign** – In the third quarter, the students can actually run the campaign, engage donors, post updates, and use social media to widen their reach.
- **Section 4: Campaign follow-up and learnings** – In the fourth quarter, there is time to review the experience, chart progress, identify gaps, plan improvements, and set goals for the following year.

Students and teachers can keep a journal from year to year to track challenges and improvements. With an accumulation of data over several years, teachers can provide customized guidance and target areas for future improvement.

To accommodate students' evolving understanding of business and to keep the process interesting from year to year, students can focus their ideas around a different theme each year: local (e.g., newspaper for high school sports); community service (e.g., recycling oil from fast-food companies); online (e.g., a mobile app to learn math); offline (e.g., carpooling to school); and global (e.g., language education via Google+ Hangouts). This would not only give focus to the arc of learning, but would also touch upon the major marketplace challenges young entrepreneurs actually face by highlighting some of the biggest challenges in American business. Furthermore, the hands-on process and market research can be an outlet for learning in more traditional subjects—basic economics, mathematics, computer science, and even writing and history.

Below are some examples of young people successfully using crowdfunding:

- **Luminaid:** Two graduate students from Columbia University in New York were able to design and prototype an inflatable solar light. They needed $10,000 for their production run. In addition to their entrepreneurial ambition, these students had a social mission and incorporated a "buy-one, give-one" philosophy into their marketing and perks. They were able to raise over five times their goal ($51,000) and send 1,100 lights to communities in third-world countries.

- **New Left Media:** Two college students from Ohio were able to raise nearly $22,000 (nearly double their $12,000 target) to continue their production of issue-oriented micro-documentaries. A total of 363 funders joined the effort to ensure this independent voice continued to be heard.

- **Open Source Display:** A seventeen-year-old student was able to take computer components and a soldering gun to create sub $100 visual display boards. He exceeded his funding target and used his mother's bank account to receive funds since he was under eighteen.

- **My Sucky Teen Romance:** A seventeen-year-old film phenom from Austin wrote and directed a high-school vampire story. She was twice successful in raising funds from her fan base, comprised of friends and strangers. In the process, she was featured on *Ain't it Cool News*, won awards at South by Southwest 2011, and had her film acquired for distribution.

Tomorrow's Technology Today

Crowdfunding is just one specific way to call students to action in the entrepreneurial field. But there are many opportunities to use the latest innovations to improve entrepreneurship-focused education.

President Obama stated that by the year 2020, he hopes the United States will be a world leader in education, with the highest proportion of college graduates in the general population of any country in the world. To help achieve this goal, the Department of Education unveiled the National Education Technology Plan[109], designed to incorporate advanced technologies into the classroom at all levels of education.

Technology is filtering into our education system and is making the classroom a different place than it was just a decade ago—and a more open one. But even the tools we use for business and socialization every day are valuable in the classroom:

- **Social media** for sharing information and keeping the dialogue going outside the classroom – Facebook, YouTube, Twitter, blogs, Blackboard, et al.
- **Web video conferencing** to learn about cultures via students from other countries, learn languages from the experts, or simply share an experience – Skype, Google+, et al.
- **Tablets and mobile devices** to keep books and notes easily up to date. Forget the days of carrying ten pounds of books, now simply sync to the latest book or notes each week – iPad and other tablets
- **Interactive whiteboards and collaboration spaces** give an opportunity to easily save and share different lessons – Basecamp

---

109 "National Education Technology Plan 2010," U.S. Department of Education, accessed February 25, 2012, http://www.ed.gov/technology/netp-2010.

- **Video games for education** to help make the learning process more engaging. While focusing on the content alone can be dry and unexciting, a more exciting and diverse presentation can help students embrace new topics—think of it as a digital field trip. For example, Gamestar Mechanic, a video game to teach kids how to make video games, has already been leveraged in classrooms throughout the United States.[110]

- **Personalization** will eventually play a big role in each student's education. Just like Amazon accumulates data from your clicks and purchases to provide better product recommendations, so too will teachers and schools be able to better customize a curriculum per student based on previous classroom experiences and aggregated test results—although interestingly, the exposure of more data and data mining will probably lead to challenges across stakeholders, as evidenced by the upset over the dissemination of teacher performance data in the New York City public school system in February 2012.

Hundreds of years ago, no one taught math in schools. Seventy-five years ago, no one taught foreign languages in schools. Forty years ago, no one taught computer science in schools. The time has come for the entrepreneurial language to become a regular part of school curricula. Like math, Mandarin, and coding, entrepreneurial instinct is a new language that can best be learned through action.

---

110   Heather Chaplin, "Digital Media in the Classroom Case Study: Gamestar Mechanic," *Spotlight on Digital Media and Learning*, April 19, 2011, http://spotlight.macfound.org/featured-stories/entry/digital-media-in-the-classroom-case-study-gamestar-mechanic/.

Slava Rubin is CEO and co-founder of Indiegogo (www.indiegogo.com), the world's funding platform, which provides anyone with passion the opportunity to fulfill their dreams and fund creative, entrepreneurial, or cause campaigns. Since its founding in 2008, the site now distributes millions of dollars each month to campaigns globally. In 2011, Indiegogo was named one of the partner companies for Startup America, President Obama's initiative to stimulate entrepreneurship in America. Recent speaking engagements include Skoll World Forum, TEDx, SXSW, CMJ & Internet Week NY, while press includes *New York Times, Wall Street Journal,* Good Morning America, Oprah, BBC, and CNNMoney. Prior to Indiegogo, Slava was a Strategy Consultant leading growth initiatives for clients ranging from MasterCard to Goldman Sachs to Fedex. He started Music Against Myeloma, an annual charity event raising funds and awareness to fight this rare form of cancer. Slava is also an advisor to several startups. Slava is a member of Renaissance Weekend and the KIN Global Summit (Kellogg Innovation Network). He is a former member of the Young Leadership Fund of Chicago and currently an advisor to multiple Jewish non-profits in NYC. Slava graduated with a B.S.E. from the Wharton School of Business. He loves food, film, travel, and the World Cup.

Programming Our Future

Zach Sims, Co-Founder, Codecademy

I n August of 2010, I was one of the first employees at a small startup called GroupMe. One year later, the company sold to Skype for tens of millions of dollars. The story seems familiar— a duo of young entrepreneurs started the company and modeled it on a problem they had. They worked nights and weekends and hired a team to help make their vision a reality. Hundreds of thousands of users used GroupMe to keep in touch with their friends. And within a year, they built an incredible amount of value—not just for their investors, but for their users as well.

GroupMe is one of thousands of examples of businesses created in today's information economy that use technology to solve a problem. As I grew up watching startups, I always remained transfixed by the notion that anyone—no matter how old or where they were from—could create something new and magical using the Internet and technology. Yet, for some reason, I never focused on just how they created what they were building.

More often than not, technology businesses are started by engineers or programmers. They create thousands of jobs for people like them: the creators of software and web applications. But all too frequently, web entrepreneurs in the United States are stymied by the difficulty of hiring engineering talent. They are unable to realize their visions because of the startling shortage of qualified computer programmers like them.

I saw these concerns firsthand in the summer of 2011. I started a company with a friend from Columbia and was accepted into the Y Combinator incubator program. The few computer science classes I had taken while at Columbia had left me in constant need of a refresher—I spent much of my time learning and relearning programming concepts by reading books and videos. My co-founder Ryan, a programmer since his early teens, wondered why I hadn't learned to program when I was in middle school or high school. He, on the other hand, had spent years teaching programming while at Columbia, founding a club that has educated more than five hundred students on the basics of programming.

My problem learning programming is a problem faced by millions around the world. In the process of building our startup, Ryan and I realized that we could solve a more pressing need: the lack of great education for our future software developers and technology founders. We founded Codecademy, the easiest way to learn to code, as a result.

Just How Important Is Computer Science?

Learning programming is not just an easy way to build your own creations and companies—it's also one of the best routes to securing a high-paying job. A 2011 report by The White House stated, "Long-term prospects for employment in networking and information technology (NIT) occupations in the United States are exceedingly strong." [111] They neglected to even mention current opportu-

---

111   President's Council of Advisors on Science and Technology, *Designing a Digital Future: Federally Funded Research and Development in Networking and Information Technology*, Executive Office of the President Report to the President and Congress, (December 2010), 87, http://www.whitehouse.gov/sites/default/files/microsites/ostp/pcast-nitrd-report-2010.pdf.

nities—computer-engineering majors are the highest-paid college graduates. Their average salaries topped $70,400 on average in 2011. And salaries have steadily been increasing by more than one percent a year.[112]

Computer science is not just this generation's most important academic major today—it will continue to be so for the future. The Bureau of Labor Statistics reported that the "employment of computer software engineers is expected to increase by 32% from 2008-2018, which is much faster than the average for all occupations."[113]

The empirical evidence clearly shows that talented programmers have their pick of job opportunities after graduation (or after becoming independently skilled). The news is filled with pictures of the perk-filled Googleplex and Facebook's new headquarters. Programmers aren't just paid well—they're pampered.

Coming Up Short

Computer science should be the most enticing college major—it's challenging and helps you become a builder and, just as importantly, virtually guarantees a high-paying job upon graduation. Yet, for some reason, the United States still doesn't graduate enough people to fill the jobs it creates in the technology sector every year. Instead, we try to import talent—more than 40 percent of the 214,271 H1-B visas granted in 2009 were for workers in "computer-related occupations."[114] These are jobs that could just as easily be filled within

---

112   *NACE Salary Survey: Starting Salaries for New College Graduates January 2012 Executive Summary*, (Bethlehem, PA: National Association of Colleges and Employers, January 2012), 4, http://www.naceweb.org/uploadedFiles/NACEWeb/Research/Salary_Survey/Reports/SS_January_exsummary_4web.pdf

113   Bureau of Labor Statistics, U.S. Department of Labor, *Occupational Outlook Handbook 2010-11 Edition*, "Computer Software Engineers and Computer Programmers," last modified December 17, 2009, http://www.bls.gov/oco/ocos303.htm.

114   *Characteristics of H-1B Specialty Occupation Workers*, Fiscal Year 2009 Annual Report, (U.S. Citizenship and Immigration Services, April 15, 2010), ii, http://www.uscis.gov/USCIS/Resources/Reports%20and%20Studies/H-1B/h1b-fy-09-characteristics.pdf.

the United States—we simply aren't graduating enough qualified people to take some of our most coveted jobs.

The problem doesn't just lie with college. Unfortunately, there is no solid track for students of any age level in the United States to become programmers. In fact, the K-12 education system is offering even less computer science education in our classrooms than was previously available. From 2005 to 2009, the number of secondary schools offering introductory computer science courses dropped 17 percent. The number offering Advanced Placement (AP) computer science dropped 35 percent.[115] Not only are we not graduating enough programmers—we're not educating the CS teachers of tomorrow, either.

The Computer Science Teachers' Association notes that there is a "serious shortage of information technologists…at all levels."[116] This is reminiscent of my own high school experience. While in school, I learned basic HTML and CSS from books I borrowed at the library and from online tutorials. Yet when it came time to exercise this knowledge, school wasn't the place to do it. High schoolers often self-studied for the AP comparative government and macro- or microeconomics exams, but very few managed to take the AP computer science classes.

The current infrastructure—both inside our classrooms, and out—isn't designed to support a future generation of technologists and programmers.

---

115   Cameron Wilson et al., *Running on Empty: The Failure to Teach K-12 Computer Science in the Digital Age,* (The Association for Computing Machinery and The Computer Science Teachers Association, 2010), table 1, 6, http://www.acm.org/runningonempty/fullreport.pdf.

116   Allen Tucker et al., *A Model Curriculum for K-12 Computer Science: Final Report of the ACM K-12 Task Force Curriculum Committee,* (Computer Science Teachers Association, October 2003), 3, http://www.acm.org/education/education/curric_vols/k12final1022.pdf.

More than Computer Science

As our world becomes increasingly more complex and technological, it's become even more important to understand the technologies that we involve in our daily lives. We wake up in the morning, often to alarms set on our iPhones, and run to the computer to check our email or get ready for the day. We're rarely apart from technology for long, whether it's email, video, texting, or something else.

A few weeks ago, a journalist related a story to me about struggling with not understanding the technologies he used on a daily basis. Afraid of his overreliance on his Global Positioning System (GPS), he began learning celestial navigation. He needed to prove that he could still navigate without the aid of the computer. Clearly, it would have been much more valuable (and probably easier) for him to just figure out what makes a GPS work instead.

A few computer scientists and education experts have realized that what once was "computer literacy" now needs to be "computer fluency." Computers are becoming an integral part not just of our daily lives, but of almost every academic and professional field as well. Now, there are computational biology and computational statistics fields, to name just two interdisciplinary fields. In the words of Jeannette Wing in *Communications of the Association for Computing Machinery* journal, "Computational thinking has already influenced the research agenda of all science and engineering disciplines."

Learning the broad strokes of computing helps not only to understand the basics of technology and programs, but also how to use computing more effectively in other fields. The new digital literacy is computer fluency—we need to understand the tools we use on a daily basis in order to more efficiently and effectively use them.

Navigating outside a Broken System

The government has looked into addressing the problem before, and there are signs that governments elsewhere are recognizing the scale of the problem we face with the tremendous shortage of developers. The United Kingdom has implemented a new program that is already teaching computer science in schools across the country. The United States, however, has been relatively silent about the importance of programming.

As a result, entrepreneurs are filling the gap. My co-founder Ryan and I, for instance, created Codecademy, an interactive way of learning to program online. In the six months since the site has been live, it's been reached by more than one million people in hundreds of countries. More than 50 percent of the site's audience is international. One program, Code Year, is designed at raising awareness of the importance of programming. Code Year reaches around 350,000 people every Monday with a new interactive programming lesson. New York City Mayor Mike Bloomberg is among the site's users, and the White House has partnered with us to create a condensed version of Code Year called Code Summer.

While the government may be best equipped to manage public education in many circumstances, time is of the essence in both creating and maintaining programming curriculum. The Internet is rife with programming tutorials created by developers for other developers—programming is one of the few places where peer-to-peer education has already taken root and educated a generation.

The education of the future will harness what's already been created but more importantly, will create structure for furthering education worldwide. Platforms will rise that enable teachers—maybe not in the traditional classroom sense—to teach millions on the web, as open courseware initiatives and online learning platforms are already starting to do. Programming has already seen a bit of this with Codecademy and companies like Udacity and Khan Academy, which allow professors to reach millions of people through online videos, exercises and peer-to-peer platforms.

Replacing Teachers

Ramping up the number of computer science educators takes time, but using tools on the Web make it easy for anyone to learn programming (or anything else) without the aid of a teacher. These new tools make it easy for a national programming movement to take root. In February of 2012, we launched Code Year meetups to get people to meet each other in their community who were also learning programming.

Meetups occurred at 7:00 p.m. in more than 250 different cities and ranged in both size and agenda. One thing, however, united them—an understanding that programming is the key both to a better job and a better future. They all came together outside of a formalized learning structure and use each other for peer support and Web learning as the teacher. Great teachers no longer are confined to the classroom, while top learners now become facilitators of better learning and community.

Learning by Doing

One of the benefits to using technology to teach technology is that it makes learning by doing a feasible possibility. Tons of great developers learned their craft not by cracking open books but by picking projects and learning how to build them. The act of creation—and the difficulty in finding out how to create something well—are equally powerful motivators on the path to programming.

Not coincidentally, these are also core entrepreneurial skills—and the best and brightest programmers go on to found or become associates at companies, large or small, that change the world and fill gaps in the marketplace.

The web allows us to replicate many of those feelings. With Codecademy, for instance, people are learning to code *by coding*, not by reading or watching videos. Better yet, they're using learning that's built for the twenty-first century—it's modularized so it can be consumed in short periods of time, and it's easy to review and share with friends.

With technology increasing the possibilities of simulation, we no longer just have traditional education opportunities available outside of the classroom—we have entirely new opportunities.

Let's Program the Future Together

Programming is incredibly vital to our twenty-first-century economy—and not just to programmers. Learning to code helps people build a more cognizant understanding of the world around them and can help them to automate and improve their daily lives. And it creates higher-level job opportunities for un- and underemployed young people, some of whom will go on to found their own companies, or work for companies (in every industry) that now rely on technology to move forward. Sadly, our education system falls short in producing an adequate number of computer science graduates, and our K-12 education system shows little sign that it will fix the problem.

The answer, fortunately, lies with the Internet and entrepreneurs—a new generation of education entrepreneurs have started businesses like mine to help teach a new generation the most important skill they can learn at low or no cost, allowing any budding young entrepreneur or programmer to take part regardless of location or education. Let's make sure we support them—and learn how to code while we're at it.

Zach Sims is the cofounder and CEO of Codecademy, the easiest way to learn to code. More than a million people have used Codecademy since its launch in August 2011 and the site has been featured in publications like the *New York Times, Wall Street Journal,* and CNN. The company raised $2.5 million from Union Square Ventures and others. Code Year, the company's attempt to get people to learn to program in 2012, resulted in 400,000 new users including New York City Mayor Michael Bloomberg and a partnership with The White House. Zach dropped out of Columbia University to found Codecademy and previously worked at GroupMe (sold to Skype), drop.io (sold to Facebook), and AOL Ventures.

Codecademy

ECOSYSTEMS

Three Steps for Fostering Entrepreneurial Ecosystems in B and C Cities

Jeff Slobotski, Co-Founder and Chief Community Builder, Silicon Prairie News

Roughly four years ago, while I was working for a technology company based in New York, I experienced firsthand the entrepreneurial ecosystems of San Francisco, New York, Boulder, Boston and other cities, and I was intrigued by what I saw. There is something unique about each of these cities' cultures that brand them to individuals outside of the area. They are filled with people armed with an amazing sense of drive and inspiration, who push forward with new ideas and launch new businesses each day.

Then I'd return home to Omaha, Nebraska and see these same individuals in our region, but they were heads-down and siloed, working on their own initiatives alone and largely unaware of what was going on around them. At the time, there was no outlet for telling the stories of the entrepreneurs and creatives working hard in our own backyard.

This was the inspiration for Silicon Prairie News, a website we started as a simple way to highlight and document the individuals doing unique things in our own neighborhoods. Since its official launch in July 2008, Silicon Prairie News' mission has been to work on building and connecting our community. We initially started in Omaha, and are now focusing our activity in the Des Moines and Kansas City regions as well. Our focus continues to be on highlighting and connecting the emerging entrepreneurs and innovators in our communities through stories, interviews, and events in order to foster an entrepreneurial ecosystem of our own.

Our goal isn't to build Omaha and the Silicon Prairie into the next "Silicon Valley;" instead, we are focused on taking the strengths and assets that are unique to our region, and building upon them. What has made Silicon Valley, New York or even Boston, Austin or Boulder different are not the same things that will make the Omaha, Des Moines and the Kansas City regions successful—and the same is true for other emerging communities throughout the country. That the theme of the third annual Kauffman Foundation "State of Entrepreneurship Address" in 2012 was local and state growth is no accident—as interim president Benno C. Schmidt remarked, making it easier to start and grow new companies locally is both easier than accomplishing change at the federal level and more practical.[117] If we want to change American cities, we need to start by increasing connections in our own backyards.

Three Key Components for Nurturing an Emerging Entrepreneurial Ecosystem

As we continue building the Silicon Prairie, we have found there a few key components that are vital to nurturing any emerging entrepreneurial ecosystem. Three of the key ingredients are:

---

117 "A Roadmap for State Growth," Kauffman Foundation, February 9, 2012, http://www.kauffman. org/uploadedfiles/soe_2012_remarks.pdf.

1. A community champion(s) who is dedicated to seeing the community grow to new heights;

2. A consistent and motivating platform or outlet to share and highlight the continued work throughout the year;

3. And lastly, consistent opportunities for the community to gather in person for collaboration and brainstorming.

1. Grow the community.

With the continued access to individuals, markets, and ideas around the globe through technology and social networks, there's no reason that the Midwest can't be internationally recognized as home to the next global businesses.

One of the first steps we identified as being pivotal to developing and consistently building our community is to identify a community champion, or a small group of individuals who are passionate about architecting the community. If something is not being done, then it falls upon you to create the change you want to see. My background and areas of study are not in sociology or anthropology, but in finance and banking. That being said, I saw a need to start talking about the interesting and creative entrepreneurs that were within our own backyard, and started doing something about it.

Once things started moving forward, I met other committed individuals in the city and community who were equally as passionate towards creating a community for like-minded innovative thinkers that already existed in Omaha.

It's amazing what you can accomplish when you start—even if you start small, the act of actually starting is something most people never do at all. Stay committed and bought in to the work for the long haul; the work of building communities isn't something that comes to fruition overnight, or even over the course of a year.

Lastly, remembering the idea is to empower others to believe and get involved in something bigger than themselves—or any one person or organization—and allow others to receive the credit and recognition when it's due.

We are just in the beginning stages of building the community here in the greater Omaha area and the Silicon Prairie. The last three and a half years have been filled with numerous positive events and milestones within the community, but I get more excited about what the city and region will look like in three, five or even fifteen years from now.

I love the quote, and believe wholeheartedly in its truth, from US anthropologist Margaret Mead, who said: "Never doubt that a small group of thoughtful, committed citizens can change the world. Indeed, it is the only thing that ever has."

2. Create a platform to highlight and share the work of others.

The next step in building a community is to have a distribution channel in which to share information about the community through events, profiles or stories of what's taking place on a consistent basis.

For us this was, and continues to be, the Silicon Prairie News website. I started Silicon Prairie News in July of 2008 after I had been blogging on a personal site on the things I was noticing while traveling around the country. I realized that we had a number of innovative, creative, and interesting companies and people right here in Omaha, but there was no "go-to" spot to discover or read more about the projects and businesses in which they were involved. Thus the need to create a platform, which over time, has become the site for those interested in reading more about the innovative, high-growth and entrepreneurial ventures within the region.

A few key takeaways include the need to challenge yourself as a community to maintain some level of frequency in updating and engaging the broader community through the website or platform you choose. Whether this means a post every two weeks or every two days, work to develop a dependable level of engagement with your community. This can include events as well. In the early days of launching Silicon Prairie News, we noticed that many of the site's readers were engaging with one another on Twitter, but had never met in person. Therefore we organized smaller, frequent meetups throughout the year just to get people in the same room and work to connect people not only online, but offline as well.

Another takeaway is that the tool itself doesn't matter—a Tumblr blog versus a Facebook Group versus an email newsletter—as much as the fact that you must identify what will work best for your community. And most importantly, stick to it. It may seem that no one is engaging in the beginning, but if you stay consistent, and remain open to adapting to what the community believes is most important, you'll unlock the energy and potential that community members have when they start to realize they are part of something larger.

3. Leverage in-person events for collaboration and brainstorming.

In addition to the site itself, we realized that there was great value in connecting individuals offline. Getting people together via events and other gatherings helps forge relationships that have the best chance at future success.

After holding frequent smaller events including BarCamp, Startup Weekends and general meetups, we hosted writer and author Sarah Lacy in Omaha while she was on tour for her first book, *Once You're Lucky*. We had over 120 people show up for the event. The key here wasn't the number of people that participated in the event, but the fact that, for the first time, we had entrepreneurs sitting alongside investors, professors and others who had never me, let alone talked with one another about what they were working on.

The success of this event inspired us to do something bigger, and that's where the Big Omaha event came in. Our goal was to bring entrepreneurs who inspired us into the region. Gary Vaynerchuk was someone I was inspired by personally, through what he had built, his genuine hustle and his tremendous level of caring. After Gary agreed to come in to Omaha for the event, we continued to assemble a growing list of innovators. Today, our goal is to bring the nation's leading entrepreneurs and social innovators into Omaha each year to share their inspiration and stories with entrepreneurs hailing from over two dozen states and countries.

The first year we expected to have maybe 100 to 200 people come in for the event. By the time of the event, we had over 400 people registered. Each year its reach continues to expand, and last year we had over 600 attendees from roughly twenty-five states across the United States.

The benefits of an event like Big Omaha are multifaceted. We are able to connect the innovators and entrepreneurs here, within the region, to show them they are not alone, while at the same time garnering encouragement and motivation from successful entrepreneurs outside the area.

Importantly, presenters return to their cities outside of the region with a new sense of awareness and understanding of what's taking place in the Midwest. This builds bridges within the region, while connecting us with opportunities around the United States—and around the world.

Each year, the event gets bigger, and we're starting to see a ripple effect from relationships and ideas that began just a few short years ago. Here's a telling comment from a previous attendee: "Big Omaha wasn't just about Omaha. It was about taking your passion and turning it into everyone's passion ... Big Omaha proved that the Midwest can be just as innovative and tech-savvy as any other region of the US."

No longer must we settle for the idea that you have to be located in a certain city or region to launch a business or push forward with an idea.

The Future of Omaha and Cities Like It

We realize that this is a long-term play, and although we can see incremental changes in the short term, it will take years of dedication and hard work for our region to fully support the efforts of the entrepreneurial community.

That said, we have already seen some of the fruits of our work. Additional startups are launched each month, an increased amount of funding is being raised as well as invested, and we're seeing a consistent awareness from individuals both inside as well as outside of our region about the companies being built here.

Today, I believe that both Omaha and the greater Midwest are poised to harvest amazing results in businesses and innovation. We have all of the key components to launch ideas: capital, entrepreneurs, mentors, and key stakeholders. The challenge is in working to accelerate the connection points between each, so that individuals are not only aware of the opportunity that exists here, but able to execute on moving things forward.

As a result of the incredible creative work of our community's thought leaders, combined with access to critical resources, the perception of the Midwest has shifted from that of an agricultural-based economy to one with a strong financial and insurance base (thanks to companies like TD Ameritrade, First National Bank, Mutual of Omaha, ConAgra Foods and Warren Buffett's Berkshire Hathaway, to name a few) and a unique culture and creative energy.

Whether it's the work of Conor Oberst, Bright Eyes and the other talented artists on the SaddleCreek Records label, or Rachel Jacobson and her work in opening Filmstreams in 2007, a nonprofit theater dedicated to enhancing the cultural environment of the city through film, or restaurateurs like Clayton Chapman and Paul Kulik, who opened The Grey Plume and Boiler Room to national acclaim, there's a new culture emerging. And I believe the same can happen in your city.

Here in the Midwest, we're just getting started. Using these lessons learned to share, inspire and motivate other communities to create their own unique communities (or ecosystems) is just one of the things we hope to accomplish over the next several years. My family and I are proud to call the Midwest home, and have chosen to plant our roots here and become not just consumers of our city and community, but creators and contributors. We are inspired by the opportunity to not only show the next generation that you can dream big, but at the same time, show that the environment is conducive to supporting and nurturing ambitious ideas and the changemakers who will execute them.

 *Jeff Slobotski* is the Co-Founder and Chief Community Builder at Silicon Prairie News, an Omaha-based company dedicated to highlighting and supporting entrepreneurs and creatives, and a emerging model for grassroots entrepreneurial ecosystem development within the Omaha, Des Moines and Kansas City regions. In addition to blogging about members of the region's creative class, Slobotski helps organize events to connect these individuals such as the Startup Job Crawl and the Big Omaha and Thinc Iowa conferences which are focused on startup culture, entrepreneurship and innovation. Big Omaha brings together more than 600 entrepreneurs

and innovators from across the U.S. Slobotski's work has been high-lighted by CNN.com, Fast Company, Kiplinger Finance, author Seth Godin, Frontier Airlines' inflight magazine, Mixergy.com and numerous other publications. Slobotski lives in Omaha with his wife Molly and their three sons, Cayden, Logan and Joseph. You can follow him on Twitter at @slobotski and read all about the happenings on the Silicon Prairie via SiliconPrairieNews.com.

Replicating New York City's Growing Technology Startup Sector

Brad Hargreaves, Founding Partner, General Assembly

S econd only to, "How do I get into a startup?" there's one question I get asked more than anything else: Why has New York City's startup ecosystem grown so remarkably over the past four years? And it is usually followed by a corollary: How can other cities copy this success, if at all?

It is worth mentioning that some of the perceived growth of the New York City startup ecosystem isn't actually growth at all, but rather increased network density and visibility. The proliferation of accelerators, meetups, coworking spaces and other organizations has given anyone identifying as an entrepreneur a platform to meet. The remarkable response from the technology community in opposition to SOPA and PIPA legislation in early 2012—including over a thousand people joining a street protest organized by the New York Tech Meetup—could simply not have happened in 2007, even if all those entrepreneurs had been present in New York City.

But the number of new companies has grown, and grown remarkably: From 2007 to 2011, the number of startup financings in New York has grown 40 percent, significantly more than any other market.

This is not representative of a broader national trend. Other than Washington, DC—which I will address later—all major technology centers in the United States saw less than a 20 percent change in venture financings from 2007 to 2011. In other words, the perception has largely been true—New York's startup ecosystem has experienced real growth, and it's unique.

Change in the Number of Venture Financings, 2007-11[118]

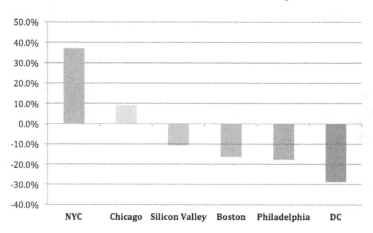

In early 2011, I attended a dinner hosted by New York City's Economic Development Corporation (EDC) for the technology community. Over steak and asparagus in midtown Manhattan, the City asked the assembled entrepreneurs and venture capitalists what problems they were facing with New York's startup environment. The EDC came armed with a number of likely targets in mind—the availability of financing, the regulatory environment, commercial rent, and more. But the attendees weren't interested. The technology community wanted more talent. Entrepreneurs needed more developers, designers, online marketers and salespeople, and they needed them now.

---

118   PricewaterhouseCoopers and National Venture Capital Association, *MoneyTree™ Report*, (2011), https://www.pwcmoneytree.com/MTPublic/ns/index.jsp.

New York City's passion for technology entrepreneurship can be traced to the single largest event in the city in the past five years: the rapid contraction of the financial industry in 2008-9. New York's unemployment rate rose from 4.7 percent in early 2008 to 8.9 percent by mid-2009.[119] The financial sector was hit particularly hard, losing a total of 46,900 jobs during the recession. Banking in particular lost almost 13,000 jobs, a 13.3 percent decline.[120] But there was a silver lining. Unlike the collapse of the automotive industry in Michigan, the contraction of finance in New York put a unique kind of individual into the unemployment line: software programmers.

Unlike welders and machinists, software programmers are uniquely suited to start new companies. Over the past ten years, the cost—in time and money—of starting a new technology company has dropped significantly. Whether a technology company is developing new products, selling those products in a new way, or helping people live longer and better lives, the first step in a company's development often involves writing some software—the realm of programmers.

But the vast majority of software programmers don't start their own companies. Instead, they join existing companies, helping those companies grow. And the demand for programmers doesn't just apply to web startups, but to all varieties of technology companies, from biotech to clean energy to hardware companies, which all need to build software in order for their technology to function.

When the finance industry stopped hiring, it not only sent programmers into the job market, it re-directed thousands of skilled

119 "Local Area Unemployment Statistics," Unemployment Rates for the 50 Largest Cities, Bureau of Labor Statistics, U.S. Department of Labor, last modified February 29, 2012, http://www.bls.gov/lau/lacilg09.htm.

120 Mark Heschmeyer, "NYC Financial Industry Facing Another Round of Huge Layoffs," CoStar Group, October 12, 2011, http://www.costar.com/News/Article/NYC-Financial-Industry-Facing-Another-Round-of-Huge-Layoffs/132767.

college grads from finance into technology. As a magnet for recent graduates, New York benefited significantly.

Like New York, the change in fortunes of DC's tech startup ecosystem can arguably be traced back to a macro event—in this case, 9/11. As the Global War on Terror ramped up, government departments such as the National Security Agency and Department of Homeland Security were flush with cash. Since war and security are increasingly becoming more technical and quantitative, that cash increasingly went to paying high salaries to software programmers.

This hypothesis is reinforced by conversations with key stakeholders in the DC technology ecosystem. "The DC region suffers from a specific malady unlike any other in the country—or perhaps the world," says Peter Corbett, the organizer of the DC Tech Meetup and the founder of iStrategy Labs, a DC-based marketing and technology-consulting firm. "Our best and brightest young engineers often join contracting shops or government agencies where they can make a healthy salary with near zero risk to the stability of their employment. That means they're not likely to join startups or create the next big successes that end up employing thousands of people."

While the explanation I've offered here may be true, it isn't particularly helpful for anyone seeking to encourage technology entrepreneurship in a given area. After all, no city would be willing to shrink a successful industry just to release programmers into the job market—nor would that be wise. Thankfully, talent doesn't have to be a zero-sum game. Rather, cities should seek to *create* more software engineers in the job market either by attracting or retaining recent computer science graduates, or retraining the existing labor force.

It's not difficult to identify the skills that need to be taught. Technology job postings are everywhere, and the most sought-after skills—in rough order of importance—are web development, user experience design, web design, sales, online marketing, and opera-tions. And other than sales and operations, these skills are rarely taught in even the most vocational four-year universities. Even top computer science graduates, who have been taught the core concepts of programming, typically need at least three months of training in modern web technologies, version control and collaborative program-ming to be useful to a technology company. Unlike larger companies, startups do not have in-house training programs to bridge this gap.

There are a number of organizations positioned to provide this kind of training, although few currently offer it. Accredited educa-tional institutions are often unresponsive to employer needs, although this is not always the case. Pittsburgh's Carnegie Mellon, for instance, has been a thought leader in developing cutting-edge programs in fields ranging from game design to medicine, programs that have been instrumental in the reinvention of Pittsburgh's economy. But more often than not, the responsibility for this kind of training falls on technology community organizations, meetups and user groups. In New Haven in mid-2011, students banded together to start offering the practical training that local universities wouldn't, with part-time instructors in an ad hoc program training sixty students in web development languages.[121] And in some cases, encouraging technology training on the part of cities can be as simple as providing space for the local Java and Python user groups.

But once a city trains a legion of engineers, how does it keep them around? First and foremost, the best retention tools come from the people to be retained. If a small city simply takes one thousand people immediately out of college and trains them to be engineers, it is likely that a majority will be gone within a year, having moved on to deeper job markets in New York, San Francisco or Boston. But if

---

121   Amy Friedman, "Harvard Alum Creates 'Hack' Program at Yale," *The Harvard Crimson*, October 12, 2011.

that same city were to train a thousand thirty-five-year-olds, retention would likely be far higher—those people already have families and other bonds that keep them close. People need community in order to stick around.

What if a city could build that sense of community among all members of the technology community, not just those with families? Specifically, could a city help people in an ecosystem form the connections that help prevent them from moving elsewhere? Alongside training, fostering community remains one of the most challenging yet promising components of building an entrepreneurial ecosystem. To do it right, a few things need to be true:

- **Key stakeholders are bought in.** Robust partnerships are a necessity, not an option. Universities are especially critical stakeholders, as local computer science and design graduates can build the base of a technology talent pool. Even the largest technology companies have difficulty identifying top candidates and getting visibility in university career fairs, where booths are often allocated to the highest bidders regardless of reputation, geography or industry. Economic development groups like the NYC Economic Development Corporation or public-private partnerships with universities are great groups to spearhead these efforts.

- **Just-in-time learning is available.** Education shouldn't stop with core skills training. Rather, continuing education opportunities need to be available across the board to tech-savvy workers, who typically love to continue picking up the newest technologies. This kind of learning also serves the secondary purpose of keeping the workforce up-to-date, ensuring that new innovations are harnessed effectively, rather than disruptively, to the local economy.

- **Geographical critical mass can be found.** A technology community won't ferment if it is spread evenly over one hundred square miles of metropolitan area, especially if mass transit options are limited. Even in densely populated New York City, the technology community is clustered around a few streets in the middle of Manhattan Island and Brooklyn. It rarely takes more than fifteen minutes to walk to a class or meeting, making it easier for personal connections to be built within the ecosystem.

Government intervention can't make a city's technology community boom. But by removing barriers and encouraging talent development, economic development organizations and governments can put a city in a position to succeed and attract technology companies, jobs and venture investment.

Brad Hargreaves is a Founding Partner at General Assembly, an urban campus for technology, design and entrepreneurship. As an entrepreneur Brad has created products and companies that bridge online and offline worlds including GoCrossCampus, Aloysius Properties and General Assembly. Prior to founding General Assembly, Brad was an Entrepreneur in Residence at Tipping Point Partners, an early-stage investor and incubator in Tribeca. Brad attended Yale, where he co-founded Yale's first university-run entrepreneurship initiative. He writes about entrepreneurship, New York City and life at http://bhargreaves.com.

How Building an Entrepreneurial Movement Can Revive a City in Decline

Tim Williamson, Co-Founder and CEO,
The Idea Village

Late one evening in 1999, at the stylish Loa Bar in downtown New Orleans, a movement was ignited. Five local entrepreneurs were having a conversation about how to reverse the last forty years of fundamental economic and social decline in our city. New Orleans was in a downward spiral, failing in all relevant areas of community vitality: education, jobs, health and crime. As a result, there was an exodus of talent; from 1990-2000, over 41,000 twenty-three to thirty-five-year-olds left the State of Louisiana.[122] This "brain drain" created a vacuum of innovative thinking to redirect the economy and to address social issues. The cycle needed to be broken.

Collectively, we believed in the power of entrepreneurship as an agent of change. The solution to building a healthy and sustainable community was to attract and retain entrepreneurial talent. The thinking was that this group of individuals would build new networks, attract diverse talent, create quality jobs and generate new wealth. We believed that they, the entrepreneurs, would become the city's new lead-

---

122   Raymond J. Brady, "An Anatomy of Weakness: A Comparative Analysis of the New Orleans Metropolitan Statistical Area Economy over the Period 1969 – 1999," Louisiana Workforce Commission, August 2001.

ership by identifying innovative solutions to the community's challenges. Unfortunately, the local leadership was rooted in the traditional practice of investing in conventional industries and practices; they deemed supporting entrepreneurship a risky venture. In fact, one leader's response to our request to support entrepreneurship was, "What if it fails?"

That statement sparked the movement. We found the core problem. He was our Goliath.

Motivated by the shortsighted vision, we decided to challenge the status quo. Each of us contributed $2,000 towards a $10,000 business plan contest, best idea wins. The media caught wind of the project, and news spread quickly—entrepreneurs emerged pitching their big ideas and professionals began contacting us with offers of in-kind support, leading to a grand prize worth over $125,000.

To this day, I am still amazed by the profound impact that a small amount of money can have to catalyze action. We hit an unexposed nerve in a still-fledgling community of people who believed in the sense of possibility. This small act connected a group of emerging leaders to invest time and money in the infrastructure to support and retain entrepreneurial talent. We found the believers.

The Idea Village, as the movement officially came to be known, formalized as an independent 501(c)(3) nonprofit organization in 2002 with a mission to identify, support and retain entrepreneurial talent in New Orleans. What began as a small group of local entrepreneurs has evolved into an engaged global network of over 1,746 CEOs, professionals investors, MBA students, corporations, entrepreneurs and civic leaders who have invested over 42,000 hours of mentorship and $2.7 million in seed capital to 1,101 New Orleans entrepreneurs. This network has helped create and sustain over 1,006 jobs and $83 million in annual revenue. We have solidified long-term relationships with thought leaders from Google, salesforce.com, Economic Development Administration, Harvard, Stanford, TPG,

Goldman Sachs, and the Hearst Foundation, to name a few. Though The Idea Village has a solid track record of providing technical assistance to local entrepreneurs, the organization's greatest accomplishment is its success at nurturing a network of diverse partnerships to define, create and sustain an entrepreneurial movement. The Idea Village's mantra *"Trust Your Crazy Ideas" connects the network.*

As we look to the next decade of our effort, The Idea Village is focused on sustaining this movement by installing the necessary systems that properly engage the growing networks and open up access to entrepreneurial talent in different stages of development and diverse industries. Our vision is that the fundamentals of entrepreneurship—passion, resiliency and persistence—are a permanent fixture in the New Orleans culture.

Creating an Entrepreneurial Movement: A Five-Step Game Plan

The Idea Village story is genuine, but not so unique that it cannot be implemented elsewhere. We were able to grow an entrepreneurial movement by being at the right place, with the right people, at the right time. We utilized a depressed economic situation to connect pivotal players, who, in turn, advocated the need for an innovation agenda that could create transformative economic change. New Orleans has produced incremental and significant results.

The following road map outlines five steps we used that other communities can adapt to foster their own entrepreneurial movement:

1. **Identify the issue.** Community leaders need to identify the real issue that is prohibiting their community from attracting and retaining entrepreneurial talent and create a vision to address the issue. The issue could be crime, corruption or leadership. This vision must be larger than the individuals themselves and serve the needs of a greater, more diverse

population. In New Orleans' case, the real issue was insular networks created over decades. A vision was hatched to create a new network to attract and retain talent, an "idea village." Entrepreneurship is about change and change will be resisted.

2. **Find the leader.** Leaders who embrace this new vision must identify an entrepreneur to take the lead in building a network of private, public, and university leaders who are able and willing to embrace and advocate on behalf of the vision—a call to arms. This individual must understand entrepreneurs, be passionate about creating community change and open to diversity in the form of people and ideas. A successful leader will build trust among the diverse network and be the honest broker by hearing new ideas and approaches—even if they compete with the existing vision. The leader should also be able to help identify key community influencers in business, government and university sectors who have wide appeal and trust to help validate the vision. For this reason, it is important that the values of the key supporters reflect those of the organization. If there is imbalance the movement will suffer. This step requires the right leader who is willing to invest considerable time with no significant financial upside. According to a 2001 report, *Building Entrepreneur Networks*, "...when trying to build networks to promote cultural change, communities need to be in it for the long haul. Typical network programs may require a commitment of at least three to four years before significant progress can be achieved."[123] Movements need the right leader, a long-term vision, and patience.

3. **Organize the network.** At this stage, the entrepreneurial network leaders have been identified and momentum has

---

123   *Building Entrepreneurial Networks,* (National Commission on Entrepreneurship, December 2001), 22.

been created with local buzz. The network now must become well organized, or it will fail to evolve into a movement. The leader of the network is quickly faced with the challenge of ensuring that the network remains both active and focused. To ensure that the group remains focused, the leader can create an organizational structure or series of activities that can unite the players by proactively channeling their energy to produce achievable results. Activities can include the creation of new programs, events, networking sessions, technical assistance, outreach or any other function that is relatively easy to perform and which yields results. Immediate results are important, as the process of securing low-hanging fruit helps to both unite and focus the network. Try new crazy ideas that will engage a diverse group of leaders.

4. **Evolve the network.** Now that the network has been organized, the leader needs to attract new members and advocates who support the original vision but better reflect the changing landscape. It is important for both movement leaders and participants to understand that structure needs to change as the ecosystem in which they operate evolves. Recognize the need to reach out to new leaders, advocates and general supporters. If the organization fails to do so, it will suffer from a stale existence that does not accurately reflect the more dynamic nature of the entrepreneurial community they are trying to serve. For this reason, it is also important that the leader embraces new ideas and possibly new competition. A successful network is one that can figure out ways to grow the total pie by interacting with the competition to better leverage each other's assets. Focus on growing the ecosystem, not your organization.

5. **Sustain the movement.** To ensure sustainability, systems must be installed to sustain the engagement of the network and increase the diversity of entrepreneurial talent participating. In order for entrepreneurship to become part of the culture of the community, there needs to be a way for everyone to participate. In New Orleans, we have organized the programming into an "Entrepreneurial Season" that begins each July and ends in March with New Orleans Entrepreneur Week. Modeled after the community-wide Mardi Gras season, we are able to balance the common ideals of our diverse partners to meet the needs of the local entrepreneurial base. *The Entrepreneur Season* provides a pathway to extend the network past its traditional comfort zone and enlist new people with new ideas who buy into the movement and the benefits it generates for the community. The leader must be sensitive to the fact that new members may require organizational change, and for this reason, it is important for the movement's leader to lead from behind by validating new opinions and elevating others in the ecosystem. Entrepreneurship is a tool to connect the community.

Funding Requirements of the Five-Step Process

Like a startup business, creating a movement requires committed mentors and a nominal amount of startup funding. Private independent resources are needed initially to support the creation of the entrepreneurial network, and to help support or offset the cost of hosting events, training, and any other programs the organization may create. It's helpful to treat the startup phase of a network like an entrepreneurial venture, encouraging the network to grow organically through relationships and trust, rather than relying on capital expenditures and consulting reports. The Idea Village was seeded with $10,000. Initial resources were donated by founders and interested partners, which allowed us to remain independent in the early stages.

Large capital expenditures on incubator space and nonprofit seed investment funds are not necessary in the beginning. Organizations should utilize limited funding to support program management associated with creating, sustaining and expanding the network, as the viability of the network determines the success or failure of the movement. As the network grows, real estate developers, professional service providers and private capital will be attracted to the community.

Once the network gains traction, then an infusion of private and public capital can be utilized to scale the movement, but there should always be a portion of the budget driven by self-generated income to keep the leaders of the network focused on building strong relationships.

New Orleans at a Tipping Point

Today New Orleans is at a tipping point and the movement that started in 2000 is showing measurable results. The August 2009 issue of *Entrepreneur Magazine* described New Orleans as a blueprint of economic recovery through entrepreneurship, and in April 2011, an article in *Inc.com* called New Orleans the "coolest startup city in America." A 2011 *Forbes* article named New Orleans the "#1 brain magnet in the country" and the "#2 best big city for jobs." During the second annual New Orleans Entrepreneur Week in March 2010, noted author and historian Walter Isaacson said, "New Orleans is a brain magnet instead of a place that will suffer a never-ending brain drain."

Dynamic entrepreneurs leading new ventures like Receivables Exchange, ISeatz, Turbosquid, Naked Pizza, Federated Sample, Sucre, AudioSocket, Kickboard, Cordina, Lifestyle Revolution Group, and Schedulist are validating that entrepreneurs can grow successful companies in New Orleans. New entrepreneurial hubs are sprouting up in critical neighborhoods, capital is being invested in new ventures and leaders from education, community development, water and the creative industries are solving critical issues through entrepreneurship. New models for healthcare, public education, physical infrastructure, food and creative media are being incubated and developed. Entrepreneurs are emerging as the next generation of leaders and mentoring the next generation of entrepreneurial talent. The downward cycle has been broken and new networks have formed.

Historically, great cities have been led by entrepreneurial leaders who felt a strong connection to their community. There is something special happening in New Orleans as we are in the midst of reinventing a great American city. The next generation entrepreneurial leaders are being developed here and the movement is scaling to other communities. New Orleans can provide a roadmap for other communities seeking to become a magnet of talent.

But now is the time to start. First step: Find the entrepreneurs in your community and start a movement.

 *Tim Williamson* is the co-founder/CEO of The Idea Village, a private 501(c) (3) non-profit organization founded in 2000 with a mission to *identify, support and retain entrepreneurial talent in New Orleans.* An entrepreneur by trade and by training, Mr. Williamson has successfully started and operated five entrepreneurial ventures in four different cities and has been a steadfast advocate for making New Orleans a vibrant entrepreneurial community. Mr. Williamson is a frequent speaker on entrepreneurship and strategies to build an entrepreneurial ecosystem. A graduate of the Stanford University Executive Program for Non-Profit Leaders, New Orleans Regional Leadership Institute, and CABL's Louisiana Leadership program, Mr.

Williamson was honored among *CityBusiness* "Power Generation," *Gambit* "40 under 40" and 2009 YLC Role Model. Mr. Williamson also earned the Junior Achievement Rising Star Award, received *"Heroes of the Storm"* award in 2008 and served as a Fleur-de-Lis Ambassador. Mr. Williamson received a B.S.M. in Finance from Tulane University in 1987.

A Three-Part Strategy to Catalyze a Startup Renaissance

John Harthorne, Founder and CEO, MassChallenge

In March 2009, the economy hit rock bottom. The Dow fell below 7,000 and virtually every economic metric was at a record low and trending worse. In under a year, more than a decade's worth of economic gains were destroyed. House values plummeted. Credit dried up. Jobs and businesses disappeared at a frightening pace, and media pundits talked of the next great depression, ten years of stagnation, and the fall from grace of the Western world.

I was a strategy consultant at Bain & Company at the time. I had graduated from MIT just a little less than two years earlier, after completing my MBA at the Sloan School of Management. I wanted to launch a startup when I graduated, but I didn't have a compelling opportunity, and I needed to pay down student debt badly—so I went into consulting instead. From day one, however, I plotted my escape with the Harvard Business School grad at the desk next to me, Akhil Nigam.

In 2009, the world needed growth badly—preferably in the form of new businesses and new jobs, and lots of them. While at school, I ran the MIT Global Startup Workshop (GSW), a conference on how to use catalytic events to promote entrepreneurial activity. I also won the MIT $100K Business Plan Competition with two engineers working on a medical device. Akhil had founded a successful startup before going to HBS and was knowledgeable about venture investment and trends in the industry.

Together, we developed a plan that we thought could empower America's young people to save the world from its downward spiral.

So we left Bain to issue a "massive challenge" across the globe to generate high-impact, high-growth startups to address the world's most pressing problems and bring growth back to the global economy. Thus, MassChallenge was born.

Everything, Now, More: The Startup's Resource Race

"Entrepreneurship is the pursuit of opportunity without regard to the resources currently controlled."

Howard Stevenson, Harvard Business School, in *Breakthrough Entrepreneurship*

Entrepreneurs start with an opportunity in mind and figure out how to fund, build, market, and sell it as they go. That means they are constantly seeking resources. To succeed, entrepreneurs need access to legal, strategic, financial, and operational advice. They also need to secure talented co-founders, facilities and technology, funding, promotional opportunities and customers.

The stereotypical startup is launched in a garage or in mom's basement, with none of these resources. Because they are new to the startup community, first-time founders don't necessarily know how or where to find these key resources, and the community doesn't know which of the newcomers are worthy of support—so founders must first locate resources and then prove themselves worthy before receiving help. And that process needs to be repeated, for multiple resources. All the while, the clock is ticking because big opportunities are short-lived, and because founders need to eat and pay bills.

So there is a filtering and matching problem between high-potential startups and competent resources that creates major inefficiencies in the early-stage startup market, and there is also a limited amount of time for the founder to secure those resources. This resource race significantly reduces the speed and rate at which early-stage startups launch and succeed.

A Plan Comes Together

Akhil and I both felt that the key to promoting startup growth would be to connect high-potential startups at scale with the resources they need to launch and succeed. In the US generally, and in Massachusetts specifically, all of these resources exist in abundance, so they don't need to be cultivated. This really is primarily a filtering and matching issue. But that still isn't a trivial task, especially on a large scale, and Akhil and I were both relatively unknown in the community. How could we identify and connect all the best startups and all the best resources? And why would anyone listen to us?

We developed a three-part strategy:

1. Design a massive startup accelerator based on input and support from experienced leaders

2. Leverage the power of competition to enable scale and legitimacy

3. Galvanize community support by promoting value creation over value capture.

1. Design a massive startup accelerator based on input and support from experienced leaders.

Mentorship and access to resources are the most important drivers of success for startups, so we spent a lot of time designing our accelerator. Because we wanted to have a national and global impact, we built it to be massive from the beginning. We wanted to support at least one hundred startups each year and to provide all of them with free office space, world-class mentorship and training, access to funding and media, and much more.

Most accelerators support a much smaller number of startups, typically fifteen to twenty at a time. As far as we know, nobody else has ever attempted to accelerate 125 startups at one time in one place. To get started, we sought out a few of the most influential people in the startup community by tracking them down at events and via mutual contacts. We told them we were going to launch the largest-ever startup accelerator, but we acknowledged their expertise and our inexperience and we asked a lot of questions. How could we raise the requisite funding? How could we engage quality mentors? How could we source the best quality startups? We also asked each person whether they would be willing to support our efforts and requested five more introductions. Then we integrated the most consistent and logical answers into our plan and moved on to the next set of meetings, sharing the commitments of support and insights we had gathered to date.

Our passion and commitment was absolutely critical at this stage. A key breakthrough came for us when we met with Desh Deshpande, the most respected and iconic entrepreneur and mentor in the Boston startup community. He liked our pitch and saw our passion. When we finished explaining our plan, he had only one question for us: Had we already quit our jobs? We had, and with that demonstration of commitment, he agreed to make a commitment himself by introducing us to a dozen of the top people in the startup community. Those introductions radically accelerated our progress.

Having gathered the input and support of the community's leaders, we set out to secure funding and other resources. Desh, and eventually Massachusetts Governor Deval Patrick, agreed to announce our plan together at an event for leaders of the startup community. We hadn't yet worked out the details, and didn't have anything close to the resources required to effectively execute. We were honest about that to the community, but we announced our vision as a fact. We declared dates and outlined a budget and a fund-raising timetable. The response from the community was overwhelming, and we've never looked back since then.

Thanks to the collaborative energy of the Boston startup community, we were able to launch the largest-ever startup accelerator based primarily on a commitment to our vision and a willingness to listen. We integrated the wisdom of the community into our design and eventually engaged a popular mentor and experienced entrepreneur, Karl Büttner, to refine and manage our accelerator activities.

2. Leverage the power of competition to enable scale and legitimacy.

It's one thing to get a room full of people to profess their support based on the endorsement of a few iconic leaders. It is more difficult to secure and maintain that support in practice, and even more challenging to manage it at scale without sacrificing quality. To address those challenges, we embedded our accelerator inside the framework of a competition. MassChallenge awards $1 million in cash prizes annually to the world's highest-impact startups. The competition acts as our sourcing mechanism and helps us identify the highest-potential startups. The 125 finalist startups in the competition enter our three-month accelerator program where they have unrivaled access to key resources, and then final judging occurs after the accelerator period to determine which startups win a share of the $1 million in prize money.

The competition format has many advantages. We use it primarily to:

- Attract attention and engagement
  - Startups enter seeking prize money and prestige
  - Investors and resources engage seeking high-quality startups
- Enable the community to identify high-potential startups quickly
  - Deadlines and organized processes facilitate quick results
  - Public judging is more transparent and legitimizes results
- Celebrate and connect the best entrepreneurs and resources
  - Showcasing founders as heroes creates pull demand for more

A community-based startup competition essentially crowd-sources the "filtering problem," not only identifying the highest-potential startups explicitly through judging, but also identifying the most active and supportive experts in the community by leveraging a volunteer model for their engagement. And then the judging process automatically showcases the entrants to the very resources they are seeking—addressing the matching problem even before the accelerator begins. It also offers rapid, formal feedback from experts to all entrants, helping early-stage founders make improvements to their plans and pitches even if they don't advance to the accelerator stage. And it does all of this at relatively low cost.

As a strategic model, competitions are very versatile and highly leveraged. Whether you're fundraising for a cause, promoting an activity or hobby, or trying to increase sales at a company, competitions are a great way to foster engagement, identify high performers and celebrate success.

3. Galvanize community support by promoting value creation over value capture.

It seemed clear to us that greed played a major role in the economic meltdown, and that major components of the US and global economy had become too focused on how they could each maximize their individual profit, without seriously considering how they could foster sustainable growth for everyone's benefit (including their own).

We saw this reflected clearly in the startup community. Startups are vital for value creation in the economy. Startups are new businesses by definition, and as innovators, startups sometimes invent or redefine whole industries. In fact, startups have produced essentially all of the net jobs in America over the last few decades.[124] Most of those jobs come from high-growth firms, sometimes called gazelles—but gazelles represent only about 5 percent of all startups.[125] Too many founders work out of a basement, must stand in line to access critical resources, and are often required to surrender significant ownership rights in return for modest support, preventing them from ever realizing their growth potential. We were concerned that many of the community's stakeholders were too focused on maximizing their own profits to worry about how the ecosystem was generating new growth as a whole.

We wanted to do our part to help re-emphasize sustainable value creation. We decided to launch MassChallenge as a nonprofit and

---

124 "Job Growth in U.S. Driven Entirely by Startups, According to Kauffman Foundation Study," Kauffman Foundation, July 7, 2010, http://www.kauffman.org/newsroom/u-s-job-growth-driven-entirely-by-startups.aspx.

125 Martin Neil Baily, Karen Dynan, and Douglas J. Elliot, "The Future of Small Business Entrepreneurship: Jobs Generator for the U.S. Economy," Policy Brief #175, *Brookings*, June 2010, http://www.brookings.edu/papers/2010/0604_innovation_small_business.aspx.

committed not to take any equity from the startups we support or place any restrictions on them. It's difficult enough for founders to launch a successful startup, so we agreed to help reduce their friction and cost without a personal demand in return.

Something pretty amazing happened when we made that decision. The community rallied around our tiny, unknown organization with an overwhelming outpouring of support. Donors offered significant time and money to ensure our success as an organization. Joe Fallon, a developer on the Boston waterfront, donated 27,000 square feet of prime office space in a brand new building for use as the accelerator headquarters through 2014. Turnstone furniture donated hundreds of thousands of dollars worth of tables and chairs. Massachusetts Governor Deval Patrick and Boston Mayor Thomas Menino spoke highly of our efforts on multiple occasions, providing us with critical legitimacy and media reach, and the state provided essential seed funding. The Blackstone Group and Microsoft provided major grants as well, and two of the country's most successful entrepreneurs aided us with detailed advice and introductions: Desh Deshpande and Josh Boger.

It turned out that being true to our values was not only more rewarding than angling for our personal profit, it was also more effective. We contributed our vision to the community as sincerely as we could, and the community responded with overwhelming support that enabled us to create one of the most effective accelerators of all time. But don't take my word for it. Check out our results.

MassChallenge Results

MassChallenge accelerated 111 startups in 2010 during our first-ever program—more than any other accelerator ever. We accelerated another 125 startups in 2011, another world record. Those 236 startups express higher satisfaction with MassChallenge than Apple customers express with Apple. Nearly 80 percent of MassChallenge startups answered 9 or 10 of 10 when asked how likely they are to recommend MassChallenge to another early-stage startup, and over 95 percent answered 7 or above. Based on public, comparative data that places MassChallenge in the top five brands in the United States based on customer satisfaction.

Furthermore, the 111 startups MassChallenge accelerated in 2010 raised over $103 million of new funding within twelve months of joining MassChallenge, and they have raised many millions of dollars more since they crossed the twelve-month mark in August 2011. They have also added jobs at a breathtaking pace. The 111 startups increased their total employee count from under 300 when they started MassChallenge to more than 800 in less than twelve months.

So the 2010 class of MassChallenge startups:

- Have raised well over $1M each on average
- Increased funding by >850 percent within 12 months of MassChallenge
- More than doubled in size, from 296 to 805 employees in 12 months.

Next Steps: Increase Scale and Impact

Thanks to the support of the community, MassChallenge is already the largest-ever startup accelerator and competition, and we already support many of the world's highest-impact startups. We remain eager to increase our scale and impact even more though. To do so, we will need to improve our technology infrastructure, expand our reach via global partners, and increase global awareness of our activities. These processes are all under way.

Key Takeaways

Our official mission at MassChallenge is to catalyze a startup renaissance. We believe that launching or joining a startup is the best way to express your soul in the business world. We wanted to bring that experience to everyone, so we created the largest-ever startup accelerator. To design and launch it, we sought advice from the leaders of the community, and we secured their support by demonstrating our passion and commitment. To make the accelerator work at scale and ensure quality and legitimacy, we integrated a community-based competition framework. Finally, and most importantly, we founded MassChallenge on a core set of values and remained true to those values—that enabled us to secure and sustain deep community engagement.

If there's one key takeaway from this essay, that is it—start by understanding your core values and how you think the world should be. Contribute that vision to your community sincerely and you will be both happy and successful.

Imagine if all of America's young people were to do that. Wouldn't we catalyze a startup renaissance?

John Harthorne is the Founder and CEO of MassChallenge, a startup competition and accelerator designed to catalyze a startup renaissance by connecting high-impact startups from around the world with the resources they need to launch and succeed. In the first 12 months since joining the 2010 MassChallenge accelerator program, the inaugural group of 111 MassChallenge startups raised over $100 Million in outside funding and created nearly 500 new jobs. The 2011 MassChallenge competition received over 730 applications from 34 states and 24 countries. In January of 2011, President Barack Obama identified MassChallenge as one of America's most effective startup accelerators. The application period for 2012 opens on March 1 and closes on April 11. John received his MBA from the MIT Sloan School of Management in 2007. While at school, John received Grand Prize in the 2007 MIT $100K Business Plan Competition and received the 2007 Patrick J. McGovern Award for impact on quality and visibility of entrepreneurship at MIT. He also led the 10th annual MIT Global Startup Workshop (GSW) held in Trondheim, Norway. Learn more about MassChallenge at: www. masschallenge.org, follow them on Twitter @masschallenge or visit www.facebook.com/masschallenge.

Help Us #FixYoungAmerica

What's next? Simple: you.

As the diverse and often thought-provoking essays in this book clearly show, fixing young America is not some utopian, rhetoric-filled dream—at least, it doesn't have to be. But we will only succeed in our mission to #FixYoungAmerica if all Americans come together to share and implement their own solutions to youth unemployment, whether that means mentoring a young person, starting a business plan competition in your community, or simply joining the conversation.

We have only touched on a fraction of the solutions in this book. We know there are many more out there—and we need your help to get them on the table and into the hands of our politicians and decision makers. Visit www.FixYoungAmerica.com to find out how you can support our campaign and become part of the answer as we #FixYoungAmerica together.

Share your own ideas to #FixYoungAmerica:

- **Pass the baby.** Come up with an idea to #FixYoungAmerica and share it with your network using our Pass The Baby module on FixYoungAmerica.com.
- **Help us get into the heads and hearts of every politician, student leader, and changemaker in America** by sharing what you've learned here with your family, friends, colleagues, local leaders and social media networks using the #FixYoungAmerica hashtag.

- **Blog or write about your own story or solution** and share the link on facebook.com/fixyoungamerica. We will include the best new essays in a digital addendum to this book, so that this conversation continues well into the future.

Thank you for helping us #FixYoungAmerica. Together, we can and will succeed.

Scott Gerber
Founder, Young Entrepreneur Council
New York, NY

BIBLIOGRAPHY

"Accredited Investors." U.S. Securities and Exchange Commission. Last modified October 17, 2011. http://www.sec.gov/answers/accred.htm.

Altchek, Christopher. "Hillary Clinton Outlines Global Youth Engagement Plan to Tunisian Millennials." *Policymic*. February 25, 2012. http://www.policymic.com/articles/4651/hillary-clinton-speaks-about-global-youth-engagement-to-tunisian-millennials/latest_articles.

American Growth, Recovery, Empowerment and Entrepreneurship Act, S. 1866. 112th Congress, 2011.

"A Roadmap for State Growth." Kauffman Foundation. February 9, 2012. http://www.kauffman.org/uploadedfiles/soe_2012_remarks.pdf. Alpha?

The Aspen Youth Entrepreneurship Strategy Group. *Youth Entrepreneurship Education in America: A Policymaker's Action Guide*. The Aspen Institute, 2008. http://www.americaspromise.org/~/media/Files/Resources/NFTE%20-%20policymakers_action_guide_2008.ashx.

Baily, Martin Neil, Karen Dynan, and Douglas J. Elliot, "The Future of Small Business Entrepreneurship: Jobs Generator for the U.S. Economy," Policy Brief #175, *Brookings*, June 2010, http://www.brookings.edu/papers/2010/0604_innovation_small_business.aspx.

Benus, Jacob M. *Self-Employment Programs: A New Reemployment Strategy, Final Report on the UI Self-Employment Demonstration*. Unemployment Insurance Occasional Paper 95-4. U.S. Department of Labor Employment and Training Administration, 1995.

Beucke, Dan. "Unemployment for Young Vets: 30%, and Rising." *Bloomberg Businessweek*. November 11, 2011. http://www.businessweek.com/finance/occupy-wallstreet/archives/2011/11/the_vets_job_crisis_is_worse_than_you_think.html.

Brady, Raymond J. "An Anatomy of Weakness: A Comparative Analysis of the New Orleans Metropolitan Statistical Area Economy over the Period 1969 – 1999." Louisiana Workforce Commission, August 2001.

Brandeis University Research. Network for Teaching Entrepreneurship,1993-98. http://www.nfte.com/sites/default/files/brandeis_university_research_0.pdf.

Bridgeland, John M., John J. Dilulio, Jr. and Karen Burke Morison. *The Silent Epidemic: Perspectives of High School Dropouts.* Bill & Melinda Gates Foundation, March 2006.

Building Entrepreneurial Networks. National Commission on Entrepreneurship, December 2001.

Bureau of Labor Statistics. U.S. Department of Labor. *Occupational Outlook Handbook 2010-11 Edition.* "Computer Software Engineers and Computer Programmers." Last modified December 17, 2009. http://www.bls.gov/oco/ocos303.htm.

Chang, Angie. "Mentorship and Networking Especially Important for Women Entrepreneurs (Stories of Leadership)." *Women 2.0.* November 7, 2011. http://www.women2.org/mentorship-andnetworking-especially-important-for-women-entrepreneurs-stories-of-leadership/.

Chaplin, Heather. "Digital Media in the Classroom Case Study: Gamestar Mechanic." *Spotlight on Digital Media and Learning.* April 19, 2011. http://spotlight.macfound.org/featured-stories/entry/digital-media-in-the-classroom-case-study-gamestar-mechanic/.

Characteristics of H-1B Specialty Occupation Workers. Fiscal Year 2009 Annual Report. U.S. Citizenship and Immigration Services, April 15, 2010. http://www.uscis.gov/USCIS/Resources/Reports%20and%20Studies/H-1B/h1b-fy-09-characteristics.pdf.

Chopra, Aneesh and Tom Kalil. "The President's American Jobs Act: Fueling Innovation and Entrepreneurship." U.S. Office of Science and Technology (blog). September 8, 2011. http://www.whitehouse.gov/blog/2011/09/08/president-s-american-jobs-act-fueling-innovation-and-entrepreneurship.

"College Students Aren't Getting Entrepreneurial Skills; Schools Need to Focus on Giving Start-Up Experience, According to New National Poll." *Reuters* (press release). May 13, 2011. http://www.reuters.com/article/2011/05/13/idUS151878+13-May-2011+PRN20110513.

Cone, Judith. "Teaching Entrepreneurship in Colleges and Universities: How (and Why) a New Academic Field Is Being Built." Kauffman Foundation. Accessed February 17, 2012. http://www.kauffman.org/entrepreneurship/teaching-entrepreneurship-in-colleges.aspx.

The Conference Board, et al. *Are They Really Ready to Work? Employer's Perspectives on the Basic Knowledge and Applied Skills of New Entrants to the 21st Century U.S. Workforce.* 2006. http://www.p21.org/storage/documents/FINAL_REPORT_PDF09-29-06.pdf.

"Country Note: United States," in *Divided We Stand: Why Inequality Keeps Rising.* OECD. December 5, 2011. http://www.oecd.org/dataoecd/40/23/49170253.pdf.

David H. Koch Charitable Foundation Evaluation Results: New York City. Network for Teaching Entrepreneurship, 1998. http://www.nfte.com/sites/default/files/research_koch_ny_0.pdf.

"Default Rates Rise for Federal Student Loans." U.S. Department of Education (press release). September 12, 2011. http://www.ed.gov/news/press-releases/default-rates-rise-federal-student-loans.

DeRitis, Cristian. *Student Lending's Failing Grade.* Moody's Analytics. July 2011.

Dobbs, Richard, James Manyika and Charles Roxburgh. "What business can do to restart growth." McKinsey & Company. September 2011. http://www.mckinsey.com/Features/Growth/What_business_can_do_to_restart_growth.

Drucker, Peter. *Innovation and Entrepreneurship.* New York: HarperCollins Publishers, Inc., 1985.

The Economic Impact of Franchised Businesses, Volume 2. Prepared by PricewaterhouseCoopers for the International Franchise Association Educational
Foundation. January 31, 2008. http://www.franchise.org/upload-
edFiles/Franchisors/Other_Content/economic_impact_document /
EconomicImpactVolIIpart1.pdf.

"Employee Engagement Report 2011." BlessingWhite. January 2011.
http://www.blessingwhite.com/eee__report.asp.

"Employment and Unemployment Among Youth Summary." Bureau of Labor
Statistics, U.S. Department of Labor. August 24, 2011.
http://bls.gov/news.release/youth.nr0.htm.

"Entrepreneurship Competency Model." U.S. Department of Labor. Employment and Training Administration. Accessed February 18, 2012.
http://www.careeronestop.org/competencymodel/pyramid.
aspx?ENTRE=Y.

Entrepreneurship in American Higher Education. Kauffman Foundation, 2006.
http://www.kauffman.org/uploadedfiles/entrep_high_ed_report.pdf.

FactSheet: High School Dropouts in America. Alliance for Excellent Education, September
2010. http://www.all4ed.org/files/GraduationRates_FactSheet.pdf.

Fairlie, Robert W. *Kauffman Index of Entrepreneurial Activity*. Kauffman Foundation,
May 2010. http://www.kauffman.org/uploadedfiles/kiea_2010_report.pdf.

Feuer, Alan. "On the Move, in a Thriving Tech Sector." *NYTimes.com*. November
19, 2011. http://www.nytimes.com/2011/11/20/nyregion/on-the-
move-in-new-yorks-thriving-tech-sector.html.

Framework for 21st Century Learning. Partnership for 21st Century Skills.
Accessed February 14, 2012. http://www.p21.org/storage/
documents/1.__p21_framework_2-pager.pdf.

"Frequently Asked Questions." U.S. Small Business Administration's Advocacy
Small Business Statistics and Research. Accessed February 18, 2012.
http://web.sba.gov/faqs/faqIndexAll.cfm?areaid=24.

Friedman, Amy. "Harvard Alum Creates 'Hack' Program at Yale," *The Harvard Crimson*, October 12, 2011.

Gerber, Scott. "Why We Should Help Veterans Start Their Own Businesses." *Time.com*. February 7, 2012. http://business.time.com/2012/02/07/why-we-should-help-veterans-start-their-own-businesses/.

Global Youth Entrepreneur Survey 2011. The Prince's Youth Business International, 2011. http://www.youthbusiness.org/pdf/YouthEntrepreneurshipSurvey2011.pdf.

Greenberg, Danna, Kate McKone-Sweet and H. James Wilson. *The New Entrepreneurial Leader: Developing Leaders Who Shape Social and Economic Opportunity*. San Francisco: Berrett Koehler Publishers, Inc., 2011.

Help Veterans Own Franchises Act. H.R. 2888. 112th Congress. 2011.

Heschmeyer, Mark. "NYC Financial Industry Facing Another Round of Huge Layoffs." CoStar Group. October 12, 2011. http://www.costar.com/News/Article/NYC-Financial-Industry-Facing-Another-Round-of-Huge-Layoffs/132767.

Ho, Erica. "Survey: 85% of New College Grads Move Back in with Mom and Dad." *Time.com*. May 10, 2011. http://newsfeed.time.com/2011/05/10/survey-85-of-new-college-grads-moving-back-in-with-mom-and-dad/.

"Hoover's IPO Scorecard Reveals First Year-Over-Year Triple-Digit Percentage Increase in More Than a Decade." Hoovers.com (press release). January 11, 2010. http://www.hoovers.com/about/press-releases/100003124-1.html.

Horrell, Michael and Robert Litan. *After Inception: How Enduring is Job Creation by Startups?* Kauffman Foundation, July 2010. http://www.kauffman.org/uploadedFiles/firm-formation-inception-8-2-10.pdf.

The Importance of Startups in Job Creation and Destruction. Kauffman Foundation, July 2010. http://www.kauffman.org/uploadedfiles/firm_formation_importance_of_startups.pdf.

"Income-Based Repayment Plan." Federal Student Aid. U.S. Department of Education. Last modified December 7, 2011. http://studentaid.ed.gov/PORTALSWebApp/students/english/IBRPlan.jsp.

JA Worldwide. *The Entrepreneurial Workforce*. 2009. http://www.ja.org/files/polls/The_Entrepreneurial_Workforce.pdf.

Junior Achievement USA and the National Chamber Foundation. *The Free Enterprise National Survey: Viewpoints from U.S. High School Juniors*. 2011. http://www.ja.org/files/polls/2011-Free-Enterprise-Survey-Exec-Summary.pdf.

"Job Growth in U.S. Driven Entirely by Startups, According to Kauffman Foundation Study." Kauffman Foundation. July 7, 2010. http://www.kauffman.org/newsroom/u-s-job-growth-driven-entirely-by-startups.aspx.

"Late Payments to Small Businesses on the Rise." National Federation of Independent Businesses. 2011. http://www.nfib.com/video?video=1054527906001.

Learn to Earn Act of 2011. H.R. 3445. 112th Congress. 2011.

Lewin, Tamar. "Burden of College Loans on Graduates Grows." *NYTimes.com*. April 11, 2011. http://www.nytimes.com/2011/04/12/education/12college.html.

"A Lifelong Learning Process." http://www.entre-ed.org/Standards_Toolkit/nurturing.htm.

"Local Area Unemployment Statistics." Unemployment Rates for the 50 Largest Cities. Bureau of Labor Statistics, U.S. Department of Labor, last modified February 29, 2012, http://www.bls.gov/lau/lacilg09.htm.

Ludden, Jennifer. "Helicopter Parents Hover In The Workplace." *NPR*. February 6, 2012. http://www.npr.org/2012/02/06/146464665/helicopter-parents-hover-in-the-workplace.

Marlar, Jenny. "Worldwide, Young Adults Twice as Likely to Be Unemployed." Gallup. April 27, 2011. http://www.gallup.com/poll/147281/worldwide-young-adults-twice-likely-unemployed.aspx.

"The Millennials: Confident. Connected. Open to Change." Pew Research Center. February 24, 2010. http://pewresearch.org/pubs/1501/millennials-new-survey-generational-personality-upbeat-open-new-ideas-technology-bound.

Morales, Lymari. "More U.S. Workers Unhappy With Health Benefits, Promotions." Gallup. September 5, 2011. http://www.gallup.com/poll/149324/workers-unhappy-health-benefits-promotions.aspx.

Morrison, David. "Kiva New Orleans, ASI FCU Team Up to Rebuild a Ravaged City." *Credit Union Times*. September 7, 2011. http://www.cutimes.com/2011/09/07/kiva-new-orleans-asi-fcu-team-up-to-rebuild-a-rava.

"MultiFunding's Second Quarterly: Small Businesses Aren't Applying for Loans." Multifunding. August 11, 2011. http://www.multifunding.com/uncategorized/multifunding%E2%80%99s-second-quarterly-small-small-businesses-arent-applying-for-loans/.

NACE Salary Survey: Starting Salaries for New College Graduates January 2012 Executive Summary. Bethlehem, PA: National Association of Colleges and Employers, January 2012. http://www.naceweb.org/uploadedFiles/NACEWeb/Research/Salary_Survey/Reports/SS_January_exsummary_4web.pdf.

National Content Standards for Entrepreneurship Education. Consortium for Entrepreneurship Education. 2004. http://www.entre-ed.org/Standards_Toolkit/.

"National Education Technology Plan 2010." U.S. Department of Education. Accessed February 25, 2012. http://www.ed.gov/technology/netp-2010.

National Standards of Practice for Entrepreneurship Education, (Columbus, OH: Consortium for Entrepreneurship Education, 2006), http://www.entre-ed.org/_what/stds-prac-brochure.pdf.

"Next Steps for Harvard Seniors: 2011." Harvard University Office of Career Services. May 2011. http://www.ocs.fas.harvard.edu/students/jobs/seniorsurvey.htm.

Partnership for 21st Century Skills. *Framework for 21st Century Learning.* Washington, DC. http://www.p21.org/storage/documents/1.__p21_framework_2-pager.pdf.

Pélissié du Rausas, Matthieu, et al., "Internet matters: The Net's sweeping impact on growth, jobs, and prosperity," McKinsey Global Institute, May 2011, http://www.mckinsey.com/Insights/MGI/Research/Technology_and_Innovation/Internet_matters.

President's Council of Advisors on Science and Technology. *Designing a Digital Future: Federally Funded Research and Development in Networking and Information Technology.* Executive Office of the President Report to the President and Congress. December 2010. http://www.whitehouse.gov/sites/default/files/microsites/ostp/pcast-nitrd-report-2010.pdf.

PricewaterhouseCoopers and National Venture Capital Association. *MoneyTree*™ *Report.* 2011. https://www.pwcmoneytree.com/MTPublic/ns/index.jsp.

Reedy, E.J. and Robert E. Litan. *Starting Smaller, Staying Smaller: America's Slow Leak in Job Creation.* Kauffman Foundation, July 2011. http://www.kauffman.org/uploadedFiles/job_leaks_starting_smaller_study.pdf.

Report to the President: Empowering Veterans Through Entrepreneurship. U.S. Small Business Administration. Interagency Task Force on Veterans Small Business Development, November 1,2011. http://www.sba.gov/sites/default/files/FY2012-Final%20Veterans%20TF%20Report%20to%20President.pdf.

Sarasvathy, Saras D. *Effectuation: Elements of Entrepreneurial Expertise.* Northampton, MA: Edward Elgar Publishing, Inc., 2008.

"Self-Employment Needs Role in Jobs Programs: View." *Bloomberg View.* August 23, 2011. http://www.bloomberg.com/news/2011-08-24/self-employment-should-play-a-bigger-role-in-jobs-programs-view.html.

Shapero, Albert and Lisa Sokol. "The social dimensions of entrepreneurship," in *Encyclopedia of Entrepreneurship.* Eds. Calvin A. Kent, Donald L. Sexton, and Karl H. Vesper. Englewood Cliffs, NJ: Prentice-Hall, 1982.

Sherman, Arloc and Chad Stone. "Income Gaps Between Very Rich and Everyone Else More Than Tripled in Last Three Decades, New Data Show." Center on Budget and Policy Priorities. June 25, 2012. http://www.cbpp.org/files/6-25-10inc.pdf.

"The Situation of Youth Employment: Trends and Young People's Views." In *United Nations World Youth Report*. United Nations. December 29, 2011. http://unworldyouthreport.org.

Small Business Economy Report. U.S. Small Business Administration. 2010. http://www.sba.gov/sites/default/files/sb_econ2010.pdf.

Staley, Oliver and Henry Goldman. "Cornell and Technion Chosen by NYC for Engineering Campus." *BloombergBusinessweek*. December 20, 2011. http://www.businessweek.com/news/2011-12-20/cornell-and-technion-chosen-by-nyc-for-engineering-campus.html.

Startup Technical Assistance for Reemployment Training and Unemployment Prevention Act. S.1826. 112th Congress. 2011. "State by State Data." The Project on Student Loan Debt. 2010. http://projectonstudentdebt.org/state_by_state-data.php.

"Statistics." Kiva. Accessed March 17, 2011. http://www.kiva.org/about/stats.

"Student Startup Plan." U.S. Small Business Administration. Accessed February 12, 2012. http://www.sba.gov/startupamerica/student-startup-plan.

"Survey of Business Owners – Veteran-Owned Firms: 2007." U.S. Census Bureau. Last modified June 7; 2011. http://www.census.gov/econ/sbo/get07sof.html?17.

"Table 2-7. Undergraduate Institutions Supplying 100 or More White Applicants to U.S. Medical Schools, 2011." AAMC, 2011. https://www.aamc.org/download/161116/data/table2-7.pdf.

Taylor, Paul, et al. *Young, Underemployed and Optimistic: Coming of Age, Slowly, in a Tough Economy*. Pew Research Center. Pew Social & Demographic Trends, February 9, 2012. http://www.pewsocialtrends.org/files/2012/02/SDT-Youth-and-Economy.pdf.

"Teach For America Announces the Schools Contributing the Most Graduates to its 2011 Teaching Corps." Teach For America (press release). August 2, 2011. http://www.teachforamerica.org/press-room/press-releases/2011/teach-america-announces-schools-contributing-most-graduates-its-201-0.

Top 240 ABA Applicant Feeder Schools for: Fall Applicants. 2005-10. http://www.lsac.org/LSACResources/Data/PDFs/top-240-feeder-schools.pdf.

Tozzi, John. "Small Business's Shrinking GDP Contribution." *Bloomberg Businessweek.* February 16, 2012. http://www.businessweek.com/articles/2012-02-17/small-businesss-shrinking-gdp-contribution.

Tracy, Brian. *Be a Sales Superstar: 21 Great Ways to Sell More, Faster, Easier in Tough Markets.* San Francisco: Berrett-Koehler Publishers, Inc., 2003. Google e-book.

Tucker, Allen et al. *A Model Curriculum for K-12 Computer Science: Final Report of the ACM K-12 Task Force Curriculum Committee.* Computer Science Teachers Association, October 2003. http://www.acm.org/education/education/curric_vols/k12final1022.pdf.

2012 Franchise Business Economic Outlook. Prepared by IHS Global Insight for the International Franchise Association. January 2012. http://emarket.franchise.org/EconOutlookFactSheetfinal.pdf.

Veterans Entrepreneurial Transition Act of 2011. H.R. 3167. 112th Congress. 2011.

Walstad, William B. and Marilyn L. Kendall. *Seeds of Success, Entrepreneurship and Youth.* Dubuque, IA: Kendall/Hunt Publishing Company, 1999.

Wandner, Stephen. *Solving the Reemployment Puzzle.* W.E. Upjohn Institute for Employment Research. Kalamazoo, MI: 2010.

Wilson, Cameron, et al. *Running on Empty: The Failure to Teach K-12 Computer Science in the Digital Age.* The Association for Computing Machinery and The Computer Science Teachers Association, 2010. http://www.acm.org/runningonempty/fullreport.pdf.

Young People Want to Be Their Own Boss to Realize Their Ideas. Kauffman Foundation, 2007. http://www.kauffman.org/uploadedfiles/KF_Harris_Poll_Fact%20Sheet.pdf.

Young Invincibles Policy Brief: New Poll Finds More Than Half of Millennials Want to Start Businesses. Kauffman Foundation, 2011. http://www.kauffman.org/uploadedfiles/millennials_study.pdf.

The power to do more

dell.com/eir

QUESTION:

Which online company
was named #2 in Forbes'
*The 10 Best Digital Tools
for Entrepreneurs?*[1]

ANSWER:

legalzoom®

Create your LLC or corporation
online in 3 easy steps.
Go to www.legalzoom.com
and enter "FYA" for special savings
at checkout.

How can you use this book?

MOTIVATE

EDUCATE

THANK

INSPIRE

PROMOTE

CONNECT

Why have a custom version of *Fix Young America*?

- Build personal bonds with customers, prospects, employees, donors, and key constituencies

- Develop a long-lasting reminder of your event, milestone, or celebration

- Provide a keepsake that inspires change in behavior and change in lives

- Deliver the ultimate "thank you" gift that remains on coffee tables and bookshelves

- Generate the "wow" factor

Books are thoughtful gifts that provide a genuine sentiment that other promotional items cannot express. They promote employee discussions and interaction, reinforce an event's meaning or location, and they make a lasting impression. Use your book to say "Thank You" and show people that you care.

Fix Young America is available in bulk quantities and in customized versions at special discounts for corporate, institutional, and educational purposes. To learn more please contact our Special Sales team at:

1.866.775.1696 • sales@advantageww.com • www.AdvantageSpecialSales.com

Printed in the USA
CPSIA information can be obtained
at www.ICGtesting.com
JSHW012021140824
68134JS00033B/2806